Colonial Georgia

By Trevor Richard Reese

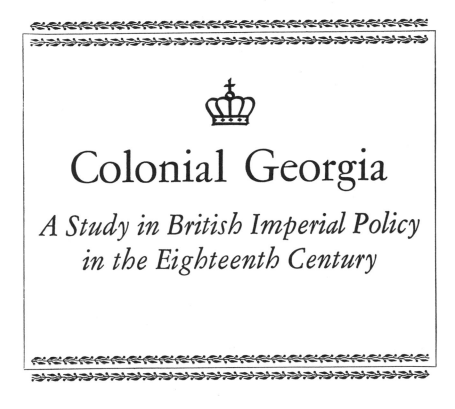

Colonial Georgia

A Study in British Imperial Policy
in the Eighteenth Century

UNIVERSITY OF GEORGIA PRESS • *Athens*

Contents

Preface

THIS STUDY represents an attempt to relate the history of colonial Georgia in the light of British imperial policy in the eighteenth century. With this objective in view the sources and evidence have been re-examined from the vantage-point of the mother-country, in whose interests colonial policy was devised, to whom the colonies owed their allegiance, and of whom they were legally a part. Internal affairs have received the attention required to keep the narrative rightly proportioned, but always the general imperial setting has been kept in mind.

This approach lends itself more satisfactorily to some aspects than to others, and in a few instances produces results that largely confirm the work of American scholars, finding differences only on an occasional point of detail or the validity of an opinion. Consequently, certain matters are dealt with relatively briefly, while others are given more lengthy consideration; but so far as exemplifying British policy is concerned, as reasonable a balance as possible has been maintained. Religion and education are omitted entirely, not because they are unimportant subjects in Georgia's history, but because they were found to be of little value for the purposes of this study. It may be noticed, also, that this account seldom goes beyond 1765. This was not an arbitrary choice as the date to close the story; it seemed essential to keep the subject clear of the embroilments that formed the preliminaries of the American Revolution, which properly are, and have been made, the matter for another book. Wherever necessary, however, there has been no hesitation in venturing beyond 1765, especially in the final chapter, but any mention of the Revolutionary troubles themselves has been carefully avoided.

Some explanation is necessary regarding quotations and dates in the text. Except in a few cases where use of the original forms has seemed preferable, quotations from documents have been changed in spelling, punctuation, and capitalization so as to conform to modern English usage. As to dates, writers on this period are always faced with a difficulty. Before 1752 two calendars were in use in England; the Julian or Old Style was the legal calendar and was eleven days behind the Gregorian or New Style which was used in all other European countries except Russia. Moreover, the year in England began on March 25 and not on January 1 as in other countries. In the present text all dates mentioned prior to January 1, 1752, are given in the Old Style, but the year is taken as commencing on January 1. In the footnotes, however, the actual dating of the document is cited, and will often be found to be in both styles; for example, January 14/25, 1732/3. This no longer applies after January 1, 1752. A Bill to regulate the commencing of the year and correct the calendar had passed Parliament in the spring of 1751. The correction of the calendar was made by calling the day after September 2, 1752, the 14th, thus omitting the discrepant eleven days.

Finally, acknowledgment must be given to all those persons who, in one way or another, have assisted and encouraged this study, to Professor G. S. Graham of King's College, London, for his helpful criticism and advice, and to the editors of the *Georgia Historical Quarterly* and the *William and Mary Quarterly* for permission to use material published in their journals.

T. R. R.

Introduction

IN THE EIGHTEENTH CENTURY, colonial affairs were subsidiary issues in English political life; Sir John Seeley's dictum that the British people founded an empire in a fit of absence of mind is true in the sense that imperial expansion seldom commanded public attention. Although there were always a few critics in the country who expressed anti-imperialist sentiments and feared that the empire would ultimately escape from the control of the mother-country, they represented only a small minority. Generally, when people thought about the colonies, which was not often, they regarded them with mild approval, and believed in the advantages of an empire even though they knew little about it.

It was a universally accepted principle that the purpose of a colony was to be of service and value to the state under whose aegis and authority it was established. Whether that service be economic in its contribution to the trade of the nation, strategic in its promotion of the military position of the imperial Power against foreign competitors, or social in its removal of unfortunate persons who embarrassed the community, the principle was the same: a colony was designed to serve the best interests of the mother-country, who was not altruistically concerned with the benefits accruing to those who were to inhabit it.

If the three components of this principle are applied to Britain's empire of the eighteenth century, it can be said that three corresponding strands then ran through the pattern of British colonial policy. Firstly, there was the commercial instinct of a trading people which sought expansion in the direction of imperial self-sufficiency. Secondly, there was the accession of power in the face of that foreign rivalry which the commercial objective was bound to provoke, for the nations of western Europe neglected no opportunity of seeking positions of advantage over their rivals. And thirdly, there was the element of useful social and economic relief which overseas possessions might bring; whether it was to provide work for unemployed, better opportunities for the poor, new hope for the persecuted, or a convenient outlet for the undesirable, the social benefit to England was always an operative factor in the minds of those who conceived the plans for settlement abroad.

If the function of a colony was to serve the mother-country, it necessarily followed that the colony's development must be regulated and directed towards that end. Accordingly, a restrictive system was devised with the object of ensuring that the overseas territories progressed in a manner that suited the requirements of England. This concept was not altogether fallacious or discreditable; indeed, there was much sound sense in it. The error lay not so much in the system itself as in the criteria upon which policy was based. Too often the governing bodies in London were unable to fully appreciate conditions in settlements three thousand miles away across the Atlantic and acted in the light of the situation as it appeared to them by hearsay and report. Because a particular commodity was in demand, it was convenient to assume that it could be easily produced in the plantations, and consequently, instead of permitting the settlers to exploit the natural proclivities of the soil, attempts were made to determine precisely what should be produced, and very often persistent encouragement was given to articles which were inappropriate. The narrow, if well-intentioned, policy towards early Georgia, for instance, demonstrably helped to impede that development of the colony most befitting its natural resources, eventually gave rise to local discontent, and ultimately brought about its modification to harmonize more happily with the prevailing geographical, climatic, and economic circumstances.

As the last of the original thirteen American colonies to be established, Georgia is of special significance in the explanation of British colonial policy in the eighteenth century. The motives behind its foundation illustrate the outlook upon overseas possessions held by the mother-country; the factors influencing its administrative development reflect the code of colonial government devised by the Ministry in London in the light of long experience of American settlements; and the pressures shaping its history exemplify the objects, the methods, and the failings of the old colonial system of empire.

The foundations of Georgia were laid in a royal charter of 1732.[1] The new colony was to comprise "all those lands, countries and territories situate, lying and being in that part of South Carolina in America which lies from the most northern part of a stream or river there, commonly called the Savannah, all along the sea coast to the southward unto the most southern stream of a certain other great water or river called the Altamaha, and westerly from the heads of the said rivers respectively in direct lines to the South Seas; and all that share, circuit and precinct of land within the said boundaries, with the islands on the sea lying opposite to the eastern coast of the said lands, within twenty leagues of the same, which are not inhabited already or settled by any authority derived from the Crown of Great Britain."

The magnitude of these boundaries would not have appeared improper to the British Government, which regarded the Carolinas as stretching along the eastern coastline of America from latitude $36\frac{1}{2}°$ to latitude $29°$, and into the interior without any limit at all; so far as Britain was concerned Georgia would be merely a part of the territory that King Charles II had granted to the Carolina proprietors in 1663. To the Spaniards, however, the new colony represented a trespass upon their empire in Florida and a formidable obstacle to any move against South Carolina; while to the French it could have appeared as the inauguration of a westward movement of English expansion round the southern verge of the Appalachian Mountains aimed at reaching the Mississippi and severing communications between Louisiana and Canada. For a generation after 1732 the history of the southern colonies was to be dominated by the hostility between the English and the French and Spaniards.

In order to put the new settlement plan into effect a corporation was constituted under the name of the Trustees for Establishing the Colony of Georgia in America and with the authority to legislate for its government over a period of twenty-one years, after which the grant was to revert to the Crown. Since the whole body of Trustees in England could not be expected to convene as often as business would require, a Common Council was established, to consist at first of fifteen members, and empowered to transact business on behalf of the Corporation when not in session. The first president of the Corporation was to be Lord Percival, and on July 7, 1732, he took the oath before the Baron of the Exchequer; on the 20th the Trustees held their first regular meeting and ordered a Common Seal to be made.[2] On November 17, a two-hundred-ton frigate carrying 114 pioneer settlers carefully selected by the Trustees left the English shores and sailed for a land of which the most extravagant hopes were entertained.[3]

The leadership of this first emigration was entrusted by the Trustees to one of their own number, James Edward Oglethorpe, a man of thirty-six, in the middle of an active, vigorous life.[4] He came from a family with strong Jacobite sympathies and of high military and Parliamentary traditions. After a respectable education at Eton and Oxford and reputable military service in eastern Europe under Prince Eugene of Savoy, he had been elected in 1722 the Tory Member of Parliament for the borough and market town of Haslemere in Surrey, and it was in this capacity that he had acquired his interest in the scheme for the colonization of Georgia.

Oglethorpe's had been the principal inspiration from the start, and although he was now to be in America more than in London, his influence on the shaping of policy towards the colony was always to be extensive and often decisive. The unwillingness on the part of the majority of the Trustees to oppose Oglethorpe's views was one of the reasons for Thomas Coram's resignation from the Corporation in 1735.[5] Since there was no governor in Georgia nominated as such, Oglethorpe, as the personal representative of the Trustees, naturally assumed the supreme authority. In the main, his rule was just and sensible and his concern for the public welfare undoubted. His work was commended both in Georgia and in England, and there is ample evidence of the respect with which the settlers regarded him. On the other hand, he was, by nature, a man of earnestness and conviction, with a keen sense of personal dignity that easily slipped into a dictatorial manner which alienated some people in Georgia, while the confidence he possessed in his own judgment led him into increasing independence in the management of affairs and aroused apprehension among the Trustees in London.

Oglethorpe left Georgia finally in 1743, and in September of that year acquired financial security and a home at Cranham Hall in Essex by his marriage to the heiress, Elizabeth Wright. For many years thenceforward he occupied a prominent position in the social life of the capital, passing his time in the literary circle of Samuel Johnson and James Boswell, of Goldsmith, Burke, and

Hannah More, until his death at Cranham in 1785. His interest in Georgia seems to have diminished after his marriage; his attendance at meetings of the Trustees became spasmodic and he attended none after March 1749. Nevertheless, he was the most important figure in the early history of Georgia, and his was the principal influence in the shaping of policy.

Oglethorpe and the first shipload of emigrants reached America in January 1733. After travelling some fifteen miles up the Savannah, they found a suitable place for a settlement on a sandy, pine-crowned bluff, and there was built the town of Savannah, the administrative centre and chief port of early Georgia. Other villages and towns grew up from this beginning. Protestant exiles from Salzburg established the village of Ebenezer farther up the river from Savannah; some Scottish Highland families erected Darien on the northern bank of the Altamaha; French families settled at Highgate, about five miles southwest of Savannah; Swiss colonists established Purysburgh, and German-Swiss settled at Vernonburg.

These early settlements were necessarily small, primitive, and precarious, and their position was, indeed, an unenviable one: "Located in the depths of a primeval forest, the tangled brakes and solemn shadows of which proclaimed loneliness and isolation; the vast Atlantic rolling its waters between it and the mother-country; the Carolina settlements at best few in numbers and contending in a stern life-struggle for their own existence; Spaniards in Florida jealous of this disputed domain, and ready at any moment to frustrate by stealthy approaches and with force of arms all efforts of the English to extend their plantations along the southern coast; and, above all, Indian tribes in the occupancy of the country attached to their grand old woods and gently flowing streams, watchful of the graves of their ancestors, imposed upon by Spanish lies, disquieted by French emissaries, cheated by Carolina traders, and naturally inclined to resist all encroachments by the whites upon their hunting grounds, it did indeed appear that the preservation and development of this province were well-nigh impossible."[6]

Despite the difficulties, however, the settlement was soon firmly established. By 1737 five towns and several villages had been erected in Georgia. Savannah consisted of about 140 houses and was growing; Augusta, 125 miles upstream from Savannah, was prospering on the Indian trade; Frederica, on St. Simon's Island, and Darien, on the Altamaha, had just been founded; Ebenezer

was being built by the Salzburgers, and forts had been constructed
to protect the southern frontier. Several ships had been loaded in
Georgia during 1736 and there seemed to be prospects of a flour-
ishing commerce.[7] Peaceful relations had been established with
most of the neighbouring Indians and trade with them was
expanding. South Carolina was benefiting from its improved
security, and land on its southern border which had previously
lain waste and desolate was now cultivated and the price of
it enhanced.[8]

Unfortunately, the people of Georgia were not allowed to
devote themselves wholeheartedly to the improvement of their
little settlements, for the Spaniards in Florida to the south were
turning their eyes towards the newcomers on their northern border, and what they saw they did not like. The question of who
should control the Georgia area was a cause of Anglo-Spanish
diplomatic controversy that culminated in war after 1739.

Spanish hostility was not the only difficulty with which the
colony had to contend. The well-intentioned but restrictive policy
pursued by the Trustees gave rise to local discontent which
revealed a melancholy picture of the province's deficiencies. Merchants in Charleston, fearing competition in their trade, disseminated grotesque descriptions of Georgia.[9] There was certainly
much distress and real need, and there was common talk of
returning to the mother-country.[10]

Relentless pressure from the settlers eventually obliged the
Trustees to modify their policy, and by 1751, when the period
of their authority was drawing to a close, their regulations on
land, labour, and liquor had been mitigated and many of their
cherished schemes left by the wayside. In a memorial to the Privy
Council in 1751 the Trustees adumbrated what they had achieved
during their charter period of government; with the assistance of
Parliamentary grants totalling £130,000, large numbers of British
and foreign Protestants had been sent over and Georgia was now
an expanding province with over 1,700 white men and about four
hundred Negroes; courts of judicature had been established, forts
and other public works constructed, and a civil government maintained.[11] In May 1752, Georgia duly became a royal province,[12]
and its government assumed a character similar to that obtaining
in the other Crown colonies.

Georgia undoubtedly benefited by the transference of control
from the Trustees to the Crown. According to Chief Justice
Stokes, "Georgia continued under the King's Government to be

one of the most free and happy countries in the world; justice was regularly and impartially administered, oppression was unknown, the taxes levied on the subject were trifling, and every man that had industry became opulent."[13] Before 1752 the colony had lacked the strong direction that a royal governor and a Legislative Assembly were able to give it. Georgia gained under the Crown from a more stable administration which entrusted more influence to the inhabitants, and thenceforward it developed more rapidly towards parity with the other colonies.

It was, as yet, an exceedingly small province. It is impossible to quote exact figures, but of the one and a half million people in the American colonies in 1760 fewer than ten thousand lived in Georgia, and even this tiny number included about 3,600 Negroes, while the white inhabitants were a heterogeneous collection lacking homogeneity both in nationality and background.[14] Still relatively small in population, therefore, still comparatively poor in resources, and still largely dependent on assistance from the mother-country, Georgia, nonetheless, was growing rapidly into a partner not unworthy to accompany the older colonies on the road to independence. But in its short life as a British colony, in a span of less than fifty years, Georgia illustrated practically every facet of British colonial policy.

I

＊＊＊＊＊＊＊

Origins

＊＊＊＊＊＊＊

AN ACT OF POLICY seldom has a single origin. It is more likely to have been occasioned by several motives, of which one would be of primary significance in the sense that without it the others would have been ineffective, but the others, for their part, may have produced the environment or attitude of mind required for the primary motive to lead to definite action. Thus the conception of Georgia was due to the philanthropy of private individuals in London who originally had in view the plight of insolvent and unemployed debtors. Its support by the Government, however, was due to the strategic and commercial benefits that Britain was expected to derive. In this way, the three principal strands in the pattern of British policy were represented in the foundation of Georgia; firstly, in the social relief envisaged by the Trustees, secondly in its strategic value as a barrier against French and Spanish expansionist tendencies in America, and thirdly in its commercial potentiality as a contributor to the imperial economy, a useful subsidiary in the attempt to establish a well-regulated, interdependent family of territories with the United Kingdom as the business centre.

Founding a colony for the purpose of getting rid of an inconvenient or burdensome element in society was not a novel idea. The use of colonies as a dumping ground for the surplus or idle population of the mother-country had been suggested in Queen Elizabeth's time, and variations on the theme had been composed throughout the seventeenth century. No authority except Parliament could send an English subject out of the land against his will; "no, not even a criminal," according to Blackstone: "For exile and transportation are punishments at present unknown to the common law; and, whenever the latter is now inflicted, it is

8

either by the choice of the criminal himself to escape a capital punishment, or else by the express direction of some modern Act of Parliament."[1] The prevalence of the practice during the seventeenth century under an Act of 1597[2] can be deduced only from hints in State papers and occasional mention in private correspondence, but we know that judges and town councils adopted transportation as a remedy for dire conditions at home. In 1621 the Virginia Company unsuccessfully sought Parliamentary legislation requiring city corporations to send their poor to Virginia; and in a petition to Parliament in 1624, the Company gave as one of its objectives the removal of destitute persons, thereby leaving improved opportunities for those who remained.[3]

The theory predominated during most of the seventeenth century, and although benevolence perhaps played some part in it, the principal motive was clearly one of convenience in enabling the mother-country to rid herself of persons she did not want. An Act of 1717[4] ordered the transportation of "wicked and evil-disposed" criminals, and, by virtue of this Act and another two years later,[5] several hundred convicts were removed annually to Virginia, where it was hoped they would be able to re-start their lives after their misfortunes in England.[6] From the earliest days of the empire there had been this conception of lands abroad as lands of hope for those who had been unfortunate at home.

The inspiration behind colonization of this character was the social problem of dealing satisfactorily with undesirable persons without debasing and endangering the society which had either misused or condemned them. It was in one aspect of this problem that the foundation of Georgia was germinated. In 1729 an Act for the relief of insolvent debtors[7] liberated large numbers of prisoners who could not find employment and were left to wander, beg, and starve in the streets of London. By itself, therefore, the Act was what Oglethorpe called an "imperfect charity" because so many derived no other advantage from it "but the privilege of starving at large."[8]

The problem turned attention towards the possibility of forming these poor people into a new colony in America. There is some doubt as to who first proposed the idea. Thomas Coram attributed it to Dr. Thomas Bray, an Anglican clergyman and founder of a charitable group known as Dr. Bray's Associates, which for several years had been interested in missionary work in the plantations;[9] Lord Percival, on the other hand, intimated that James Oglethorpe "gave the first hint" of the project.[10] In any event, Bray died in February 1730 and thereafter Oglethorpe became the leader of the movement to found a new colony, although the organized support which he needed came from the Bray Associates. Their meeting on March 5, 1730, approved a scheme for procuring territory in America and populating it with English unemployed, and at the end of July it was agreed to petition the King for land to the southwest of the Carolinas.[11] After some delay in Government circles, a royal charter was granted and the Georgia Trustees were constituted.

In advertising the project it was argued that "as every wise government, like the bees, should not suffer any drones in the state," so these unfortunate people should be transferred to places where they might be an asset to the nation instead of a burden on the community.[12] "There are many poor unfortunate persons in this country," it was alleged, "who would willingly labour for their bread if they could get bread for the labouring for; such persons may now be provided for by being sent to a country where there are vast tracts of fertile land lying uninhabited and uncultivated."[13] Since these persons were obliged at present to live on others, their exodus would be no loss to society.[14]

The Georgia Trustees were careful to emphasize that they would not deprive the country of anyone who might be useful at home, for there had long been apprehension lest emigration from England endanger the domestic economy. It was thought by many people that Britain could not afford to lose workers, and since 1718 the emigration of skilled artisans had been discouraged.[15] It was argued in a Parliamentary debate in May 1732 that labour was urgently required in England, and that it would be doing the public a disservice to send too many to America.[16] Opinion in the Commons on the subject was still divided when, a year later, the Georgia Trustees petitioned for money. Opposition speakers did not question the good intentions of the Trustees, but were opposed to sending Englishmen abroad because the country was already short of inhabitants; they recommended, instead, that the English poor should be found useful employment within their native country.[17] This anxiety over the possible effects on the country's population was common in England in the eighteenth century and was often expressed in Parliament. Few economic writers of the period approved of emigration, and it was, in fact, a capital offence to inveigle artificers and mechanics to leave the Kingdom.[18]

As a consequence of the fear that free emigration would lead to depopulation of the mother-country, there was a tendency throughout the eighteenth century to look outside English society proper for emigration material, whether it be convicts, unemployed, or persecuted Protestants from the Continent. Peopling America with foreign Protestants was generally regarded as a prudent way of expanding the empire, and the Government had long preferred the colonies to be used as an asylum for European refugees. When Charles II sent two shiploads of Huguenots to Carolina in 1679 he set on foot a movement which continued down to the time of the Seven Years' War.[19] In 1705 one of the Carolina proprietors made arrangements for a settlement in the province by what was called the High German Company of Thuringia. Three years later English colonial proprietors distributed throughout the Rhine Valley and in the Palatinate books and papers extolling the life and climate in the New World and urging people to come to England where means would be found to enable them to go to the colonies.[20] In 1710 the Government defrayed the expenses of transplanting several thousand poverty-stricken refugees from the Palatinate to New York and North Carolina.[21] The Georgia advocates alleged that by sending over persecuted German Protestants, Britain would be both performing a religious duty and strengthening her empire with industrious subjects, and it was announced that the Society for the Propagation of the Gospel had resolved to supply the Trustees with money to organize the emigration of seven hundred Protestants from Salzburg, where the Roman Catholic archbishop was pursuing a repressive religious policy. "Subjects thus acquired," it was said, "by the impolitic persecutions, by the superstitious barbarities of the neighbouring princes, are a noble addition to the capital stock of the British Empire."[22]

This encouragement of foreigners to settle in the colonies as a method of increasing the population and strengthening the defences of the empire remained a feature of British policy until the end of the century. When the Board of Trade made a report on imperial expansion in 1763 it emphasized that the manpower for any new settlements was to be drawn not from Britain but from continental Europe or the other colonies.[23] The principal concern was to preserve Britain's working skill and manpower; therefore, the only elements within the population which could be sent overseas were those which embarrassed the community, and they should be supplemented with additions from the Continent.

Georgia, then, was intended initially to relieve the mother-country of a small, unwanted section of her population; it was to

be a social service to the British public. A viable settlement could
clearly not be founded upon this basis alone, however, and as the
economic thinking of the time would not permit extensive free
emigration, new colonists had to be sought elsewhere and the best
source was among the persecuted religious minorities on the Continent. In assisting European Protestants to settle in Georgia, the
Trustees and the Government believed they were strengthening
the British Empire with the least disturbance to the domestic
economy. Georgia could not easily have existed without this reinforcement from outside but the foreign element would not have
been so acceptable if the British Government had not been conscious of the strategic and commercial advantages that might ultimately be acquired.

In sanctioning the Georgia project the British Government was
not motivated by any such charitable intentions as inspired the
Trustees. The Ministry was not much interested in the plight of
insolvent and unemployed debtors, but it was very concerned
about the defence of the empire. The French in New France and
Louisiana, the Spaniards in Florida and Cuba, and the Indian
nations along the back of the English settlements were a constant
source of danger to the security of British territory in America.
Of vital importance was the southern frontier, which the Government realized must be defended.[24] Ever since the foundation of
Carolina, England and Spain had contested the ownership of the
land between Charleston and St. Augustine on account of its strategic value, potential wealth, and importance in the fur trade with
the Indians; if South Carolina was lost the fur traffic and growing
rice trade would be endangered and the French and Spaniards
brought so close to Virginia as to imperil the tobacco trade.

The boundaries of the southern colonies had never been satisfactorily defined and alarms and frontier incidents were common.
The colonists were ever fearful of attack by the Spaniards in
Florida, and by the eighteenth century the British Government
recognized the need for defensive precautions.

In 1720 the Board of Trade discussed the safety of South Carolina with its new governor, Sir Francis Nicholson, and its agents,
Colonel John Barnwell and Joseph Boone. It was alleged that the
French were encroaching on the colony, having recently seized an
English settlement, and were being rapidly reinforced with men
from France. In order to guard against further encroachments and
preserve the trade with the Indians, it was suggested that forts
should be built on the frontiers, and the mouth of the Altamaha

possessed immediately, as the French were pretending a right to it. The Board endorsed these suggestions a week later and the construction of a fort on the Altamaha was enjoined on Governor Nicholson.[25] The fort was named after King George and built near the mouth of the Altamaha.

In 1721 the Board of Trade prepared an account of the state of the plantations which noted that South Carolina was open to French, Spanish, and Indian incursions and might be lost if reinforcements were not sent; its boundaries should be clearly defined and forts built, particular care being taken to secure the navigation of all rivers. The urgency of these precautions was emphasized by the fact that the French were experiencing difficulty in navigating the Mississippi and it was possible that, having but recently restored Pensacola to the Spaniards, they would attempt to open another communication from their settlement at Mobile down the Altamaha to the ocean. Such a move would jeopardize British interests in the whole South Atlantic region and, with the Spaniards in Florida adopting an unpredictable attitude, it was essential for adequate precautions to be taken against foreign encroachments. For this purpose, both the northern and southern extremities of the British colonies would have to be fortified, the friendship of the Indian tribes assiduously sought and carefully maintained, and government in the several plantations strengthened and improved.[26]

Britain could not allow the Altamaha to fall under foreign control. Fort King George had been designed to this end, but unfortunately had a chequered history and eventually had to be abandoned. The Spanish agent in London complained about the fort throughout 1725 and, no doubt, was delighted when, in January 1726, it was burnt down, possibly with the connivance of its turbulent garrison, who were dissatisfied with living conditions and twelve of whom seized the opportunity to desert to the Spaniards at St. Augustine.[27] The Governor of South Carolina had it rebuilt, but in the autumn of 1727 its garrison, a company of invalids, "old, infirm, inactive and morose," and so lazy and mutinous that they could not be prevailed upon to fetch themselves wholesome water, were finally withdrawn.[28]

The significance, however, of this and other fortifications was that they were clearly intended to become the nuclei of frontier settlement; in this sense, Fort King George pointed the way to the ultimate establishment of the barrier colony of Georgia.[29] In the years following the abandonment of the fort, various proposals were considered for erecting buffer townships on the frontier to

cushion South Carolina against hostile incursions, and a definite
plan was formulated in the instructions to the governor in 1730
which included provision for the immediate repair and garrison-
ing of the fort on the Altamaha.[30]

All this indicates that there was considerable anxiety over the
frontiers in America. Relations with Spain and France were in a
parlous state generally, and the British Government could not be
indifferent to hostile moves by either of them, whether in the New
World or in the Old. When the House of Commons debated the
nation's position at home and abroad early in 1730, Sir William
Wyndham pointed to the danger of French encroachments at the
back of the American plantations and doubted whether English
acquisitions either there or in Europe were safe.[31] The Government was certainly conscious of the insecurity of the frontiers in
America, and when a petition was received for lands on which to
plant a new colony in the south, the possibility of its functioning
as a defensive barrier must have been a strong argument in its
favour.

The social and strategic motives behind the foundation of
Georgia were closely associated with a third, that of commercial
development and enterprise. Under the mercantilist concept of a
self-sufficing empire, the true function of a colony was to produce
commodities that would remove the need for the mother-country
to buy in foreign markets, and at the same time to serve as an
outlet for her manufactured goods. Englishmen had romantic im-
pressions of all uninhabited territories in America and believed
that almost any tropical product could be raised there. Valuing
colonies as sources of raw materials, they liked to imagine that
overseas settlements would supply the homeland with the luxury
goods that so often had to be sought from foreign lands. This
conception was based largely on arguments of geographical latitude. Silk, for instance, could be expected from the southern colonies because their latitudes and proximity to the sea were similar
to those of the coastal provinces of China, India, Persia, Turkey,
Italy, Provence, and Languedoc.[32] One writer claimed that it had
been proved that no place could grow silk better or easier than
the Carolinas, where mulberry trees grew in vast quantities at a
prodigious speed.[33] When Sir Robert Montgomery proposed to
establish a new colony in the south in 1717, he hoped its fertile
soil would eventually render the mother-country independent of
foreign markets in an immense variety of commodities, including
coffee, tea, silk, wine, and cochineal: "Its gentle hills are full of

mines, lead, copper, iron and even some silver," he wrote; " 'tis beautiful with odoriferous plants, green all the year."[34] In 1721 Jean Pierre Purry sought permission from the British Government to found a new settlement in South Carolina and claimed that by reason of the latitude the area could be as productive of the richest plants as anywhere on "the terraneous globe," and, like Montgomery, dilated fondly on the valuable commodities such as silk, cotton, and indigo that might be produced.[35]

No doubt these fanciful predictions were embroidered for the benefit of potential investors, but no Government could overlook all the economic and commercial advantages which writers, ever since Tudor times, had described as likely to accrue to the mother-country from colonial possessions. Colonies, it was thought, might help to tip the balance of trade heavily in Britain's favour if such commodities as silk, wine, and sub-tropical fruits were produced. The possibility of cultivating olives, grapes, and silkworms had been the motive behind sending Huguenots to Carolina in Charles II's time. Silk was always regarded with particular favour, and there was nothing remarkable in the hopes entertained by the founders of Georgia that it would become the staple of their settlement. Earlier attempts to raise it in the southern colonies had had disappointing results, but the idea remained implanted in the minds both of Government ministers and of those interested in colonial development. In emphasizing the possibility of cultivating silk the Trustees were applying an old and widely advertised notion to ingratiate their project with the Government. Among other articles which the United Kingdom would value from her colonies were naval stores, for which she was almost entirely dependent on the countries of the Baltic. Timber, deal boards, spars, and iron came from Norway; tallow, hemp for cordage, and flax for sail-cloth came from Russia, who, realizing England's dependence on her, monopolized the trade and demanded what prices she chose.[36]

This state of affairs had long been attracting increased attention from the Board of Trade, which, in 1694, had been ordered to set a time for hearing all proposals for bringing naval stores from the plantations and to encourage all who would undertake it, and during the succeeding ten years several attempts were made to form chartered companies for that purpose. At the beginning of the eighteenth century the problem had been further accentuated by the formation of the Stockholm Tar Company, which aimed to monopolize the trade in tar and pitch.[37] In October 1703, the

Board of Trade was directed to consider the possibility of obtaining supplies from the plantations, and recommended the subsidizing of colonial naval stores and the removal of the existing duties on importation.[38] By 1705 Parliament had enumerated naval stores and granted premiums on their importation,[39] thus laying the foundations for a gradual accumulation, during the early part of the eighteenth century, of an elaborate system of bounties on masts, hemp, bowsprits and spars, resin, pitch, tar, and turpentine.

One of the staunchest advocates of colonial production of those commodities, especially naval stores, for which Britain depended on foreign countries, was Joshua Gee, who in 1729 first published his treatise on British trade. He pointed out the disadvantage the Kingdom was under in depending so heavily on the Baltic countries for naval stores, and how convenient it would be if they could be produced in America, estimating that with proper encouragement the colonies, with their many navigable rivers ensuring easy communication to the sea, could supply enough naval stores to meet all the requirements of the mother-country. Of equal importance, according to Gee, was silk, large quantities of which still had to be imported from Italy, with whom the balance of trade was now unfavourable. He maintained that articles such as hemp, flax, silk, potash, and indigo which were essential to English manufactures were easily producible in the plantations. And where were these commodities most likely to succeed? In the south, asserted Gee, and particularly in "that noble colony of Carolina," with its excellent climate and fertile soil, to which large numbers of settlers might be attracted and the frontiers secured against hostile encroachments.[40]

It is not surprising, therefore, that the founders of Georgia should have looked forward to their province's sending home many valuable products in abundance. Informed opinion in the country was on their side, and the contribution their enterprise might make towards the realization of the commercial principles of the old colonial system must have been an important recommendation to the Government.

Hence it is clear that Georgia originated not only in social problems but also in strategic and economic policy. The philanthropists looked mainly to its charitable benefits; the Government looked more to its defensive and commercial advantages. All these motives were embodied in the preamble to the charter. This declared that many poor and unemployed persons, if given the means would gladly go to America and there obtain a living for themselves, strengthen the colonies, and increase the commerce and wealth of the whole empire. It mentioned the exposed state of the southern frontier and the great distress brought on the people of South Carolina by the ravages of the Indians, and concluded that the best protection would be afforded by the establishment of a permanent settlement in the southern territories of the province.

The project was well advertised, the wonders of Georgia were listed and adorned for public consumption, and all classes of the community invited to subscribe. Government departments helped the emigrants in various ways; at Lord Percival's request the Admiralty instructed all warships on the Atlantic and American stations to render assistance, and gave Oglethorpe a general requisition on any ships from which he might require aid;[41] and all governors in America were asked to lend support to the new colony.[42] Thus in 1732 the colony of Georgia was born in a public climate of goodwill and high hopes, but with an irregular and difficult history ahead.

II

⚜⚜⚜⚜⚜⚜

Government and Justice

⚜⚜⚜⚜⚜⚜

IT WAS SAID in the eighteenth century that there was scarcely any known form of government which could not be found in the British plantations,[1] and Georgia certainly added to the variety. The British Government had learned by experience that colonial proprietors and local assemblies tended to acquire excessive powers, and therefore was reluctant to erect private or charter provinces. The danger of these lay in the scope they provided for the construction of independent authorities, and this was contradictory to the whole principle of colonization. A petition from the Earl of Doncaster and Dalkeith for a proprietary grant to the south of Carolina was rejected by the Board of Trade in 1782 because of the inadvisability of the King's granting away powers that might lessen the dependence of the plantations upon him.[2] "Charters from the King," wrote a pamphleteer in 1774, "are a branch of his prerogative, within the constitution. To raise any superstructure upon them, subversive of legislation, would be attempting to build a house sideways."[3] Consequently, the early charters to individuals or corporations had been largely revoked or surrendered in the course of time, and private ownership replaced by royal control.

The Georgia charter in 1732 did not involve any deviation from this line of policy. Georgia was not made into a proprietary province; it was made into a trust colony, with the Trustees enjoying only a limited independence. The charter set forth that "for and during the term of twenty-one years, to commence from the date of these our letters patent, the said corporation assembled for that purpose shall and may form and prepare laws, statutes and ordinances fit and necessary for and concerning the government of the said colony, and not repugnant to the laws and statutes of England,

and the same shall and may present under their common seal to us, our heirs and successors in our or their Privy Council for our or their approbation or disallowance; and the said laws, statutes and ordinances, being approved of by us, our heirs and successors in our or their Privy Council, shall from thenceforth be in full force and virtue within our said province of Georgia." Not only were the laws drafted by the Corporation subject to approval by the Crown, but accounts of the colony's progress were to be submitted to the Government periodically and details of all receipts and expenditure presented annually. Furthermore, it was laid down that after a term of twenty-one years the grant should revert to the Crown, the only instance of such a limitation in point of time in the history of the old colonial empire.

The Common Council of the Trustees could appoint the governors, judges, magistrates, ministers, and military as well as civil officers, but every governor had to undertake to observe the Navigation Acts and obey all the instructions sent him by the King. No governor was ever appointed by the Trustees. The reason for this has been attributed to the provision that every governor was to be answerable to the Crown; the Trustees were always jealous of their powers, and there may be some truth in the assumption that they were unwilling to permit their authority to be reduced in this way.[4] It is not the whole explanation, however. In a letter to Bishop Berkeley in May 1731, Oglethorpe stated that those concerned in the Georgia project "will use their utmost endeavours to prevent luxury and oppression in the officers, and idleness and vice in the people. They intend to send no governor to prevent the pride that name might instil."[5] The validity of this reasoning and the amount of influence it had on the Trustees' policy are open to question, but it is to be remembered that they were men of high ideals and sincerely concerned for the settlers' welfare. There is, at least, some justification for doubting whether unwillingness to allow their authority to be reduced in favour of the Crown was the sole reason for their failure to appoint a governor.

By the terms of the charter all legislative power was vested in the hands of the small group of men in London, and on the grounds that the colonists were inexperienced in the art of ruling, powers of local self-government were withheld, so that for eighteen years all regulations were made at meetings of the Trustees or their Common Council. Throughout nearly all its trusteeship period Georgia was without its own provincial assembly; there was no representative system, and no regular elections to any of

the local or general administrative offices, with the result that
Georgia's development was a mechanical one imposed from without. At first the colonists complained little against this, possibly
because the need for an assembly was not urgent where there was
no taxation and expenses were met by Parliamentary grants, but
in time the deficiencies of the trusteeship system and the advantages of putting their government on a better foundation were to
be widely recognized and freely canvassed in the province, notwithstanding the inflexibility of the Trustees.

It was the pressing need of the Trustees to be kept fully acquainted with the true state of all parts of the colony that ultimately brought a resolution in March 1750 for an annual meeting
of representatives in Georgia. The Assembly was to meet in Savannah for no longer than one month every year, "at the most leisure
time," and debate and propose what it considered would benefit
the province as a whole. It had no legislative power, that remaining with the Corporation as set forth in the charter. It was to be
composed of four deputies from Savannah, two each from Augusta, Ebenezer, and every other town or village with over thirty
families, and one deputy from each town or village with ten families. No suffrage requirements were laid down, but the qualifications for membership were the most absurd in all America.[6] A man
could not be elected unless on every fifty acres of land he owned
he had one hundred mulberry trees planted and fenced and producing fifteen pounds of silk a year, while at least one female in
his family had to be instructed in the art of reeling silk.[7] This silk
mania, however, must not obscure the important fact that in 1750
Georgia was at last graced with its own Assembly. Admittedly its
powers were restricted, but the seed of local self-government had
been sown nonetheless, and the settlers were now enabled to give
public expression to their grievances and wishes instead of having
to cabal or make disjointed complaints.

It has been argued that if the Trustees "had taken the inhabitants of Georgia into their confidence at the beginning, and if
they had established there an assembly like that of 1750, it is
probable that the colonists might have aided in the solution of
their own problems; but the Trustees waited until it was too late
to be of service to them to establish the colonial assembly."[8] This,
surely, over-simplifies the issue. It is agreeable to imagine local
democracy functioning in an infant settlement, but it is difficult
to believe it would have done so successfully in early Georgia. The
population was small, the settlements scattered; the people were

diverse in nationality and background, many were uneducated, some were irresponsible, and few could have possessed any real sense of public obligation. An Assembly might well have been established sooner than it was, when a community spirit had grown, but for one to have been established at the beginning would have been to invite its breakdown and perhaps, thereby, to have further retarded the development of local responsibility.

The special system of government associated with the Trustees ended upon the surrender of their charter in 1752. The transition to a royal province, however, was neither sudden nor immediate; difficulties had to be overcome, the departments of Government were not inclined to hurry, and it was not until 1754 that a royal system of government was erected in Georgia.

The first problem was to keep civil administration operating in the colony during the transference from Trusteeship to Crown control, and to answer this the Privy Council issued a proclamation directing that all persons who held offices in Georgia under the Trustees were to continue the performance of their duties until the King's pleasure was known.[9] It then remained to put the administration on a permanent footing, and in April 1753 the Board of Trade was ordered to prepare a plan for establishing a civil government in Georgia.[10] The plan put forward in the following June and approved by the Privy Council in March 1754 recommended a constitution similar to those obtaining in the other colonies more immediately subject to the authority of the Crown.[11]

A governor was to be appointed by commission under the Great Seal with power to call an assembly, pass laws, erect courts of judicature, grant lands, and discharge all other functions necessary for the proper administration of the colony. A council was to be nominated consisting of twelve persons and possessing the same powers and privileges as other colonial councils. The governor was to be the vice-admiral and, in association with other officers, to constitute an admiralty court for the regulation of matters subject to admiralty jurisdiction. Other appointments were to include customs officers for collecting duties and regulating matters subject to the Treasury and Customs Commissioners; a register and receiver of quit-rents; a surveyor of lands; an attorney-general to assist the governor and council on legal issues; a provost-marshal to perform the duties of a sheriff; and a secretary to register deeds, keep public records, and act as clerk of the council. On August 6, 1754, the various offices were filled in accordance with this plan, and John Reynolds became the first Governor of Georgia.[12]

Coincident with the appointment of Reynolds a draft of his instructions was prepared, containing all the general articles usually given to governors in the colonies, with the addition of such particular points as befitted Georgia individually.[13] The instructions were precise on the composition of the legislature. As soon as possible the colony was to be partitioned into counties, each of which would then send two representatives to the Assembly. Membership qualifications debarred Roman Catholics and anyone not owning a freehold estate of at least five hundred acres, while suffrage franchise was limited to freeholders who were not Roman Catholic and who possessed fifty acres of land.[14] If this was not democracy as the term is understood today, it was, nevertheless, in full accord with liberal opinion on both sides of the Atlantic in the eighteenth century. As the authority on royal government in America has pointed out, the principle of universal manhood suffrage "seemed as undesirable to the great majority of colonial politicians as it did to the authorities in Great Britain. Nearly everyone agreed that the right to vote or sit in the assembly ought to be limited to freeholders, those who had a tangible stake in the community."[15] It was therefore in keeping with the tenets of the time for a government of property-holders to be established in Georgia.

The legislative powers and privileges of the Assembly were similar to those in the other colonies. It could pass no law inconsistent with the law of England; the Governor could veto any Bill or reserve it for royal consideration, and even if he agreed to a Bill the British Government might veto it. The Assembly elected its own speaker and chose its own doorkeeper and messengers, but the Governor appointed the clerks and could adjourn, prorogue, and dissolve it at pleasure, except that from Saturday to Monday it might adjourn itself. The first General Assembly met conformably with the instructions on January 7, 1755, and was soon complaining against the system that had been established.

A remonstrance dated February 21, 1755, objected to the requirement for representatives to have five hundred acres, because it excluded many residents in towns who possessed property worth more than the specified land qualification; similarly, the suffrage franchise disqualified freeholders of town lots, although their one or two acres might exceed in value the fifty acres which enabled others to vote. For these reasons the Assembly asked to be allowed to settle the qualifications by laws more conducive to Georgia's interest and welfare.[16] Another objection to the system of government was that the power of the Governor and Council to settle the fees of public officers without the concurrence of the Assembly might operate to the detriment of the inhabitants, whose representatives were unable to procure them any redress if they should complain on this head; it was suggested, therefore, that these fees should be fixed by the Assembly, as was customary in other colonies.[17] The response of the Board of Trade was to reaffirm the Crown's ultimate authority in these matters and warn against any violation of the royal prerogative by provincial laws, pointing out that any Bills passed by the provincial legislature for the purpose of altering the system would have to be sent to the King for his approval or else a suspensory clause inserted until his pleasure was known.[18] The home government clearly had no intention of permitting too much power to pass to the Georgia Assembly.

This sort of policy was the undoing of British authority in the eighteenth century. The Government always asserted that fundamentally the privileges and powers of the Lower House depended on the royal prerogative, by virtue of which it was created and through which its functions should be regulated. As early as 1718 the Governor of Jamaica had been told that the right of the Lower House to meet and debate was solely on account of a clause in the royal commission.[19] On this basis each advance of the Assembly was necessarily regarded as an encroachment on the prerogative, and since the Assembly had been created by the grace and favour of the King its legislative powers were only such as he chose to confer on it. This fundamental principle with the home officials was being increasingly disputed by the colonists, who insisted that their rights as Englishmen were as great as those living in the mother-country and claimed that their Assemblies had been created in the image of Parliament and with comparable legislative functions. The basic attitude of the British Government was inflexible, however, and even though circumstances might call for liberal change there always remained the long-standing jealousy for the royal prerogative and the apparently irremovable assumption that colonies by their very nature must be subordinate.

The Council in Georgia was designed to perform legislative functions similar to those of the House of Lords in England, namely, to serve as the Upper House of the legislature, to temper the actions of the Lower House and to act as a court of appeals. Its members were appointed under royal commissions, selection being made by the Board of Trade and approved by the King, with the Governor having the right to make recommendations. Thus the Council was neither an hereditary, nor an elective, nor a representative body, but it was not necessarily out of sympathy with the populace as a consequence, for its members were colonials and were directly affected by the measures of the provincial government. When membership of the Council fell below seven the Governor could nominate new members up to that number until the Crown made the necessary appointments. Three members made a quorum, although by his instructions the Governor was discouraged from acting with less than five except in emergencies. Councillors were appointed during good behaviour and could be suspended by the Governor if there was just cause. They were expected to advise the Governor and furnish him with the benefit of their intimate knowledge of conditions in the colony.[20]

This intended partnership between Governor and Council was soon broken. Governor Reynolds quickly earned the hostility of all the Councillors by his impatience with their rights and privileges. He objected to many on personal grounds,[21] he omitted to consult them on important administrative matters, he did not seek their advice on the distribution of presents intended for the Indians, and he concealed from them that section of the royal instructions by which he was obliged to seek their opinion and obtain their consent to his actions.[22] He was recalled in August 1756, to answer for his behaviour, and it is significant that the charges against him were regarded in a serious light by the Government and that he was punished in spite of his friendship with Lord Hardwicke.[23] The refusal of the British Government to countenance the conduct of Governor Reynolds towards his subordinates in Georgia illustrates the mother-country's evident intention that the executive authority in the colonies should be exercised by the Governor in Council and not by the Governor individually.[24] Reynolds's successor, Henry Ellis, dealt more tactfully with his Council, consulted it on all matters of public interest, and, by creating a harmonious relationship, came close to making the Council a partner of the Governor in colonial politics and a foundation upon which his political power might have been erected.[25] Unfortunately, ill health overtook him, and in 1760 he was replaced by James Wright, a man of ability and fortitude; but from this time forward until the Revolution the Council became more provincial in outlook and its connection with the Governor was gradually relaxed.

All Acts passed in Georgia had to be approved by the King before they could become law. Private Bills and those affecting revenue or the trade of Great Britain were required to include a "suspending clause" deferring their operation until the royal assent had been secured. This suspensory clause made the King in a sense a direct participant in the actual legislative process instead of a mere external reviewing authority with an executive prerogative.[26] Although the Crown's legal right to the suspensory device was indisputable, the colonies objected to it strenuously and accepted its use reluctantly.

The royal power to disallow an Act was absolute and need not be exercised immediately or, indeed, within any time limit, so that laws might be disallowed several years after they had passed the colonial legislature. Furthermore, in disallowing an Act no discrimination was made between the clauses that were objectionable and those that were not; the whole Act would come under the disapproval, thus requiring the re-enactment of those clauses against which nothing was held.[27]

Between 1696 and 1765 nearly four hundred laws from the American colonies were disallowed by the King in Council, and the subjects of disallowance, as indicated in the Governors' instructions, grew noticeably in perplexity.[28] Any law affecting the material interests of the Crown or encroaching on the royal prerogative to the extent of lessening its authority over the local government was sure to be disallowed. Cancellation of measures was not always due merely to the wish to emphasize royal authority and provincial dependency, however; there was often good reason for abrogating colonial legislation, especially laws that were partisan, technically poor, or detrimental to the interests of the empire in general. The Act passed in Georgia in 1757, for example, declaring that all persons who, during the ensuing three years, immigrated from one of the other colonies were to be protected for seven years from arrest and action for debts contracted by them before their settlement in Georgia, was rejected for the very good reason that it established an asylum for debtors against their lawful creditors, and as such was manifestly both unjust and prejudicial to the other colonies.[29] In the eighteenth century the power of disallowance helped to protect the colonists from unwise laws, prevented exploitation of the unrepresented classes, and safeguarded general imperial interests from the consequences of indiscreet colonial legislation, and its usefulness in this respect was recognized well on into the nineteenth century.

The most significant disallowance of a statute in Georgia occurred in July 1761, when the British Government repealed a
colonial Act of November 1759, designated to confirm the inhabitants in the titles to their lands and tenements. It was repealed,
firstly, because it had been passed without a suspensory clause,
and, secondly, because, it was alleged, "the determining upon a
question of this nature by a partial Act of Legislature without any
hearing of parties or any of those regulations and exceptions which
justice and policy has prescribed in all general laws for quieting
possessions, is arbitrary, irregular and unjust, and subversive of
those established principles of the constitution by which disputes
and questions in all matters of private property and private claims
are referred to the decision of the courts of law."[30] This censure
of legislative interference in matters not properly cognizable by
an Assembly was in line with the policy pursued in England since
the end of the seventeenth century. The status of colonial judici-
aries was regarded in the light of English constitutional notions,
so that statutes which implied the assumption of appellate jurisdiction by the assemblies were disallowed by the Crown. The
repeal of Georgia's Act of 1759 was an outstanding example of
Britain's policy of preventing interference by colonial assemblies
with the courts of justice.[31]

By one of the articles of his instructions Governor Reynolds had
been required to erect courts of justice and judicature within the
colony, taking care that powers vested in them were no greater
than those of English courts and the procedure as near as possible
to that followed in England. Accordingly, in December 1754 the
Governor issued letters patent under the Great Seal of Georgia
constituting a court of record under the name of the General
Court, to be held before two or more judges appointed by him
with the advice and consent of his Council. It was to sit in Savannah every three months and have jurisdiction over all actions,
real, personal, and mixed, exceeding the value of forty shillings,
except where the title to a freehold was in question, and over all
criminal matters, with the same power and authority in Georgia
as the Courts of King's Bench, Common Pleas, and Exchequer
exercised in England.

In November 1755 letters patent were issued for erecting a
Court of Session of Oyer and Terminer and General Gaol Delivery, to be held twice a year, where, in order to prevent long
imprisonments, all offenders committed after the sitting of the
General Court were to be tried by two members of the Council

or judges of the General Court commissioned by the Governor for that purpose. If required, a Court of Chancery under the presidency of the Governor sat after each General Court to hear and determine all matters of equity.[32] By an Act of April 1760, Courts of Conscience were designed to avoid the heavy expense incurred in the ordinary method of suing for and recovering small debts in the General Court. Every settlement had its own justices of the peace commissioned by the Governor to determine in these courts all actions of debt and damage, except those concerning titles to land, in which the amount involved did not exceed £8 sterling.[33]

During the Trusteeship period there had been no admiralty court in Georgia, but one was established in January 1755, and consisted of four members, the Governor granting commissions to a judge, an advocate-general, a marshal, and a registrar of the court. It tried breaches of the Acts of Trade, had jurisdiction over cases concerning salvages, mariners' wages, piracy, enemy ships taken as prizes, and over other maritime affairs, and "proceeded according to the course of the civil law and the established method of determination used in Great Britain and other maritime nations."[34]

As in the other colonies the Governor of Georgia had, from his commission, the authority to pardon all criminal offenders excepting those convicted of treason or wilful murder, when he could only reprieve until the King's pleasure was known. He could also remit fines and forfeitures imposed in the provincial courts excepting those above the sum of £10, when he could only suspend payment and refer the question of remission to the royal authority. This prerogative of mercy was exercised without the advice of the Council, so that the Governor was the sole local agent with the power to check the execution of justice.[35]

At a time when the knowledge and impartiality of colonial judges were often suspect, the right of appeal to the Crown seemed essential and was never seriously questioned, whatever form a colony's constitution might take. In the early days of the Trusteeship in Georgia, for instance, the judicial system had inevitably left much to be desired, there had been no lawyers in the province, most of the magistrates had been untrained and inexperienced, and some of the bailiffs could neither read nor write. There had been no provision in the Georgia charter concerning appeals to the King in Council, but the same principle applied as had been enunciated by an Order in Council of March 9, 1698, when the

Governor and Company of Connecticut had been informed that it was "the inherent right of His Majesty to receive and determine appeals from all His Majesty's colonies in America." This principle had been further expounded in 1701 by Attorney-General Trevor and Solicitor-General Hawles, who said that although the Connecticut charter did not mention appeals to the King in Council, the right of such appeals was inherent in the Crown.[36] The first precise statement on the conditions of appeal had been in 1679 in the commission for New Hampshire where the right of appeal was granted in real and personal actions of a value exceeding £50, and in 1746 the rules were finally codified, when the minimum was set at £500, the appeal having to be brought within fourteen days and security given by the appellant.[37]

The Governor had the authority to grant commissions to judges, justices of the peace, and all other officers necessary for the administration of justice, such commissions to be granted "during pleasure only." Britain had always refused to allow judges to hold office during good behaviour ostensibly on the grounds that to grant a more permanent tenure would "lessen that just dependence which the colonies ought to have upon the Government of the mother-country."[38] The revised instructions foreshadowed in those to the Governor of Georgia in 1754 provoked the colonial assemblies, who claimed the same power that Parliament had exercised in 1701 of protecting judges against dismissal at executive pleasure, and passed laws providing that judges hold office during good behaviour and be removable only on an address from the assembly. The British Government stood firm and the general instructions to American governors of December 1761 absolutely forbade assent to any Bill regulating judicial tenure or the grant of commissions except *durante bene placitia*.

British policy was evidently not open to modification, and it is a pathetic commentary on its progress that even after the American Revolution and well on into the nineteenth century British colonists elsewhere were obliged to seek rectification of grievances that had existed in the American provinces a hundred years before.

III

❧❧❧❧❧❧❧

Finance

❧❧❧❧❧❧❧

ALMOST FROM its very beginning Georgia was dependent upon the financial support of the home Government. Before the end of 1733 it was apparent that the private contributions sought by the Trustees would never provide adequate funds. They campaigned energetically in an attempt to stimulate people's generosity, making emotional appeals for support and ridding possible apprehension over the disposal of the money with guarantees that it would be deposited in the Bank of England, each contribution registered in a book kept for that purpose, and printed copies of the accounts distributed to every important subscriber.[1] The directors of the Bank of England subscribed £300, the directors of the East India Company £600, and the trustees of the Earl of Thanet's legacies £300, and by October 1732 a total of £2,000 had been received.[2] Nearly all towns of any size, with the notable exception of Bristol, had collections in aid of Georgia;[3] the town corporation of Liverpool promised to give £50 out of its corporate stock but became reluctant to part with it;[4] several ladies at Bath promoted a collection in 1737 and George Whitefield preached a special sermon for the purpose.[5] The Earl of Abercorn was particularly generous, and Thomas Penn of Pennsylvania was quick to offer his assistance.[6] Gifts of money and articles such as books were always coming in but were insufficient to meet the needs of the Trustees, who by the beginning of 1733 were already hoping for Parliamentary assistance.[7]

The prospects for a grant were good. Many of the trustees were themselves Members of Parliament, and the circulation in both Houses of a book advertising their scheme helped to create a favourable attitude. With an uncommon amount of vagrancy in London at this time weighing heavily on the parishes of the city,

the Ministry and most of the prominent figures in the Commons
seem to have been favourable towards the project, and there was
no disposition to oppose a motion for financial assistance.[8] In
1733 the Trustees were voted £10,000 out of a fund arising from
the sale of lands in St. Christopher's Island that had originally
been part of an endowment voted to Bishop Berkeley in 1726 for
a college in the Bermudas. Payment to Berkeley had been so delayed that he had wearied of the idea, and now £80,000 of the
money was appropriated to the dowry of the Princess Royal on her
marriage to the Prince of Orange, and the remainder given the
Trustees "to be applied towards defraying the charges of carrying
over and settling foreign and other Protestants in the said colony."[9]
Government favour went even further, for the money was paid
out of the Exchequer without any deductions, the Treasury and
Exchequer officers waiving their customary fees and perquisites
as it was for a charitable use and the national benefit.[10]

One grant, however, could not permanently relieve the Trustees
of their financial difficulties. Money came in in small quantities
and went out in large and increasing expenses. There was the cost
of subsidizing the transportation and settlement of emigrants, of
providing for public works, and of fortifying the frontier. In 1736
the Trustees informed the Secretary of State they could no longer
finance emigration to Georgia from their own cash resources.[11]
The urgency of their needs grew, and they were obliged to grasp
pathetically at any possible source of income. In 1738 they entertained hopes that the Master of the Rolls had remembered Georgia in his will.[12] An even cruder commentary on their penury was
provided by their vain expectancy of financial profit from a Parliamentary investigation into the misappropriation of charitable
collections by a certain Henry Walker, an aged, bedridden Staf-
fordshire gentleman with his reason impaired by attacks of palsy.[13]

Constant need of money made the Trustees permanently dependent on Parliament, without whose support their colony could
not have been maintained. Georgia was voted £26,000 in 1735,
£10,000 in 1736, £20,000 in 1737, £8,000 in 1738, £20,000 in
1739, and varying annual sums so on until the end of the charter
period, by which time a total of £136,000 had been granted. In
the same period less than £16,000 was collected by the Trustees
from other sources.[14] Such Governmental benevolence towards a
colony had no precedent in British imperial history. One of the
fundamental tenets of imperial thinking at this period was that,
except perhaps for naval and military protection, each colony

should maintain itself. Georgia, however, was regarded as a special case by virtue of its immaturity and its situation as a barrier province. Nevertheless, the Trustees were obliged to petition the House of Commons nearly every year for their grant, and this tiresome process tended to demoralize them, especially as opposition increased and criticism became more pungent. The necessity of living from one Parliamentary grant to the next had a staccato effect on the policy of the Trustees, for a fluctuating annual income meant that no long-term decisions could be made with assurance.

The disadvantage of this yearly recourse to Parliament gave rise to a movement among the Trustees to get their financial requirements included in the general estimate laid before Parliament by the Crown. In April and June 1737 they begged Sir Robert Walpole for an annual sum of £7,000 supplied by way of the estimate, saying it was impossible for them to petition Parliament every year and reminding him of their constant expenditure on civil government, maintaining new arrivals, keeping Indian friendships, and improving cultivation.[15] Oglethorpe, who had temporarily returned to England, personally presented the letter to the Minister, who received it amiably and, a week later, promised that Georgia should receive £7,000 a year in the estimate; but after thinking it over for another week he began to harbour doubts and asked Oglethorpe the reason for the application. Oglethorpe's argument that it was essential to have a fixed revenue apparently satisfied him, for by September the Minister was assuring Oglethorpe of £8,000 a year for Georgia by way of the estimate. But the wind did not blow favourably for long and by the following February Walpole had changed his mind and withdrew the promise.[16] Consequently, in 1738, after Walpole had led them round in a circle, the Trustees had to repeat the hazardous procedure of petitioning the Commons for financial assistance.

They continued to ask for their grant to be included in the estimate, but without success, and were obliged to petition Parliament annually until the expiration of their charter rule. Much of the instability in early Georgia's administration can be attributed to the fact that voluntary subscriptions were never sufficient to meet the needs of the Trustees, who from the very beginning had to rely on uncertain and variable grants from a frequently critical Parliament.

Criticism of the province and its Trustees increased noticeably in the troublous years after 1739. Malicious rumours were diffused; Georgia was described as a chimera and the Trustees were accused of sharing out the Parliamentary grants among themselves. The critics began to find their ammunition in allegations sedulously publicized by malcontents in the colony itself, and though much of it misfired, sufficient hit the target to cause damage and distress. After Parliament's voting of the grant in February 1740 Lord Egmont "came away with a heavy heart to see so great an affair as the settlement of our colony treated so ludicrously, and so little regarded by the majority and the minority."[17]

Most prominent of the Members of Parliament taking up the disaffected cause was Lord Gage, an inveterate opponent of the whole Georgia project. In the Commons debate of January 1740, Gage said he wanted to know what Georgia really was before he would vote money towards it. Later, he accused the Trustees of pursuing a policy that would bring ruin on the whole province, and to prove it cited a representation from malcontents in Georgia in 1738: "I have my pocket full of papers that show it cannot subsist in the manner it is, and that the people have almost deserted it." In his view the settlement was obviously not worth public assistance, and he deprecated the way Parliament was prone to "give away the nation's money blindfold." He even moved that all communications between the colony and the Corporation in London over the last two years should be laid before the House, but withdrew the motion when Lord Baltimore banteringly remarked that "there might be some ladies in Georgia who had a correspondence with the Trustees." Horace Walpole sardonically observed that the only way to reconcile Lord Gage was to make him a Georgia Trustee and then all would be well.[18]

Another critic was Sir John Barnard, M.P. for the City of London and an authority on financial and commercial matters, who argued that the prohibition on the admission of Negroes into Georgia prevented competition on equal terms with South Carolina, which would always be able to undersell Georgia. John Mordaunt, M.P. for Whitchurch, and a constant enemy of Georgia, pointed out that seven years had gone by without the inhabitants' producing any silk or wine: "he therefore believed they would not have silk enough to clothe themselves, and as to wine, he believed it would be well to give it to the inhabitants for their own drinking, and wished them good luck with it, for it would be all would ever be seen of their wine, and if the people of the place drank no other they would be the soberest subjects in the world. That the colony had cost the nation a vast sum and it was time to put an end to it, and this sum would probably be the last granted, for he could venture to foretell that if the Trustees came next year for more there would not be a farthing."[19]

Nevertheless, the Trustees did come for more the next year, and a majority of 115 against 75 was for giving £10,000. At the same time they came in for more censure, not only from the inevitable Lord Gage but also from the ill-natured Sir John Hind Cotton, who opposed granting any more to Georgia, because it was of no benefit to Britain, nor likely to be, and he was for transferring the inhabitants to South Carolina. Samuel Sandys, known as the "motion maker" on account of his persistent attacks on the Walpole Ministry and who was soon to become Chancellor of the Exchequer, said he did not know what to think of Georgia, but thought there should be an inquiry into the propriety of supporting or not supporting the colony, and criticized the Trustees for sending there so many idle people who would not labour here at home and assuredly would not labour anywhere.[20]

The main source of information for the Parliamentary critics was Thomas Stephens, the wayward son of William Stephens, the Trustees' faithful secretary in Georgia. In October 1739 he arrived in England determined to bring the state of the colony to public notice, and, except for a few months at the end of 1741 when he returned to America, disseminated for three years accounts of deplorable conditions prevailing in the province as a result of its government and laws.[21] On April 1, 1742, a petition from him in this vein came before the Privy Council,[22] and at the end of the month it was debated in the House of Commons.

The petition alleged that the failure and impracticability of their schemes in Georgia had been "properly represented from time to time to the Trustees" and the necessary alterations recommended and requested of them for nearly seven years: "and through a refusal of these alterations, and misapplication of the public money, great delay in discharging the debts due from the Trustees to the people, and many abuses in the civil power, the colony is greatly reduced, both in the number and condition of its inhabitants, as to be incapable of fulfilling His Majesty's most gracious designs in establishing it, unless such present redress be found for the injured people, and such means procured for their encouragement as may concur with the natural fertility of the soil, the commodious situation of the province, and its excellent harbours for trade, to answer the generous purposes of an effectual establishment."[23] In June a committee of the House resolved that Stephens's petition contained "false, scandalous and malicious charges tending to asperse the characters of the Trustees," and that the preservation and support of Georgia were necessary and advantageous to the mother-country. Accordingly, the culprit was brought to the bar of the House, where, on his knees, he was severely reprimanded by the Speaker before being discharged upon payment of his fees.[24]

These resolutions were, no doubt, gratifying to the Trustees, but the fact could no longer be disguised that the Georgia project was falling into disrepute. Neither the Ministry nor the Opposition was much concerned for the colony as such, and the Trustees were regarded with disfavour by both sides. Walpole himself was never particularly zealous for the enterprise, his wife was known to be an opponent of it, and he distrusted the independence of the Crown which the Trustees had acquired under their charter. A large section of the Court party held the Board of Trustees in great distaste and resented the tendency of some of them to vote against Ministerial measures in Parliament. "They had rather see the Board dissolved and the colony in the sea," wrote Lord Egmont, "than that an election should be lost by our means."[25] Those Trustees who spoke and voted against the motion in February 1736 for a Parliamentary grant to continue repairs to Henry VII's chapel aroused considerable Ministerial antagonism which bade fair to negative the Trustees' petition for money, Walpole observing that "it was indiscreet in gentlemen who were themselves to apply for money to refuse it to others." It was the Ministry's coolness towards Georgia that helped to induce Lord Egmont and others to eventually resign their membership on the Common Council.[26]

It would be wrong, however, to attribute to the Trustees as much influence or significance in Parliament as Lord Egmont was inclined to do. They were never an effective group in Parliamentary affairs because their interest in Georgia was seldom so keen as to affect their political loyalties, and their prestige was due more to the early popularity of Georgia itself than to any united action on their own part. It is true that of the twenty-one Trustees mentioned in the charter, eleven sat in the House of Commons, and that of the seventy elected to the Board between 1732 and 1752, forty-four sat in the Commons and five in the Lords. On the other hand, there were never more than twenty-five of them in the Commons at any one time, and none could accurately be described as a prominent member of the House.[27] Again, although it was at first in Walpole's interest to patronize the Trustees in order to avoid alienating his supporters among them, and perhaps incidentally to win some Opposition votes, it gradually became apparent that the Trustees were more dependent upon him than he was upon them. Most of them were "Walpole's men" in any event, and by 1739, when the criticism of Georgia was increasing in Parliament, some were clearly more interested in supporting the Ministry than in helping Georgia, and after 1740 few of the Trustees in Parliament were prepared to speak out boldly on behalf of the colony or to risk offending Walpole.[28]

The Government was not entirely indifferent to Georgia's affairs, however. Whatever Walpole may have said in private conversation, and whatever some of his colleagues may have thought of the Trustees, the fact remains that Parliament continued to make grants for the support of the province. The animadversions from Gage and others represented a small minority, and the emotion aroused was generally out of all proportion to the numbers involved. It was natural for the Trustees to feel themselves unjustly treated when the Ministry belittled their project and condemned their Parliamentary activities, but in doing so they were making the worst of a reasonably good job, for, when seen in its proper perspective, the Government's attitude towards Georgia appears in a relatively favourable light.

The financial worries of the Trustees in London were matched by the monetary difficulties of the settlers in Georgia. During the first few months of the colony, when there had been no external commerce and trade with the Indians was by barter, the weekly issue of provisions from the public store had made possession of money unnecessary. But as population increased, some sort of currency became essential and was provided in the form of sola bills, which were promises of payment by the Trustees, distributed by them to their agents in Georgia; they could be passed on from hand to hand and so function as a normal currency.[29] This system could not entirely answer the needs of the colony, especially as external commerce expanded, and a demand for hard money soon arose.

The Trustees were aware of the problem and occasionally sent over English coin, but it never stayed in the province long, being soon remitted either to the mother-country or to the other colonies in exchange for essential goods. Sola bills, therefore, remained the principal circulating medium under the Trusteeship, but unfor-

tunately they did not circulate well in other colonies, nor were
there always sufficient to meet requirements within Georgia
itself.[30] The shortage remained until the surrender of the Trustees'
charter in 1752, when only £1,149 issued as sola bills had not been
returned to England for payment, and the holders of these outstanding bills were required to secure their payment before the
end of 1755.[31]

The extreme shortage of money in Georgia led the Board of
Trade in 1756 to relax its principles to the extent of sending over
part of the annual Parliamentary grant in copper coin and milled
dollars,[32] but this was not sufficient to ease the situation permanently, and the continued scarcity of bullion made a paper currency imperative. Neither public nor private business could be
carried on without it, for there was no commerce that brought
specie into Georgia, and even if there had been it would not have
stayed there long because of the adverse balance of trade and the
payments made to creditors in South Carolina.[33] The mother-
country could not welcome the issue of paper currency in the
colonies on account of its likely inconvenience to international
trade, but there was no effective means of preventing it. By the
time the Board of Trade had decided to disallow an Act creating
paper money, the bills would already be in the possession of third
parties and disallowance would be inexpedient, inopportune, and
ineffectual. As far back as 1690 the Massachusetts legislature had
issued promissory notes as a medium of exchange in anticipation
of tax collections, and by 1755 bills of credit had been issued by
New York, New Jersey, the whole of New England, the Carolinas,
Pennsylvania, Maryland, and Virginia.

In February 1755 the Georgia General Assembly passed an Act
for circulating £7,000 in paper money to remedy the serious inconveniences to the inhabitants of their lack of gold and silver and
inability to raise the money to pay any tax that might be levied.
The bills were declared a legal tender in liquidation of all debts
and dues, and provision was made for securing their effectual
payment by the parties to whom they were issued.[34] The Act was
not to be enforced until the King's pleasure was known, but while
it was being shelved in England by the doubts of the Board of
Trade, not only were some of the bills issued in Georgia but
another Act was passed in 1757 for emitting £638. 7s. 1¼d. in
paper bills to discharge the public debt.[35] The British Government
regarded these measures as contrary not only to the Parliamentary
resolution of April 1740, that bills of credit issued in the colonies

were illegal by virtue of an Act of Queen Anne's reign, but contrary also to the Act of 1751 forbidding the issue of paper money
in the four New England governments except for certain specified
objects. The measures in Georgia, therefore, were a violation of
the constitution, and as such the Government would not approve
them.[36] Of particular significance was the manner in which the
bills had been issued in spite of the suspensory clause for awaiting
the royal pleasure. The suspensory clause had never been very
effective in colonial legislation, and Massachusetts and Pennsylvania especially were consistent offenders;[37] but in the case of
Georgia its non-observance may be taken as an indication of the
urgency of the currency problem and of the unwillingness to allow
the situation to deteriorate while the Government vacillated in
London.

Notwithstanding the attitude of the home Government, an Act
was passed at the beginning of 1759 to print nearly £800 in bills
of credit in order to defray the expenses of various public works
in the province and to make good a deficiency in the last public
tax.[38] This was followed by the important Act of May 1760, for
issuing and applying £7,410 in paper money, which was confirmed
by the Government in July 1761.[39] "Upon the whole," opined the
Board of Trade, "although we are sensible of the mischiefs which
may arise in Your Majesty's plantations by the increase of paper
currencies, and are therefore desirous of checking and discourag-
ing the growth of them in general," in this particular instance it
would seem to be so much for the benefit of Georgia that the Act
might safely be allowed.[40] Thus the Government ultimately ac-
knowledged the inevitable and reluctantly countenanced the issuing of a paper currency. It had disallowed all the Acts passed for
the same purpose between 1755 and 1759, and the discourage-
ment of measures of this nature in America remained a principle
in the mother-country's policy. Only three years after confirming
Georgia's Act of 1760 the issue of legal tender paper money in the
colonies was forbidden by Parliament.[41]

The Crown was necessarily obliged to continue to bear the
charges of government in Georgia after the Trustees had surrendered their charter, but it was expected that as soon as circumstances permitted, the Assembly would pass a law providing for
the salaries of the Governor and officials and for the costs of fortifications and other public works.[42] The British Government naturally looked forward to Georgia paying its own way, for the support of its administration was a considerable burden on the Treas-

ury. The cost from June 1754 to June 1755, for example, was
£2,957, only a small part of which remained for spending on
public works after the salaries of officials and bounties on silk
cocoons had been paid.[43] By the beginning of 1756 lack of money
was hampering much important work in Savannah, particularly
the building of a gaol, repairing the light-house, court-house, and
church, and clearing the river of old wrecks and trees that were
obstructing navigation.[44]

The likelihood of the inhabitants' being able to support themselves tended to recede rather than improve, for expenses increased steadily. Georgia's civil establishment cost Britain £3,557
in the year 1757-58, and by 1759-60 the amount had risen to
£4,057.[45] There was some advantage to the mother-country in this
arrangement. With the Crown bearing the charges of government
in Georgia neither the Governor nor officials were at the mercy of
the Assembly, as was the case in other colonies, where the Governor's dependence was "a constant source of pressure on him to
neglect his obligations to the Crown."[46] The need for a fixed civil
list in each colony had been illustrated during the wars of 1691
to 1709 when the powers of the Assemblies to control the consequent unusual expenditures enabled encroachments to be made
on the authority of the Governor and Council, especially in New
York. In 1703 the Governors had been instructed to secure permanent appropriations for salaries of all executive officers in order
to prevent the abuse of temporary grants which made them dependent on the Assemblies,[47] but although some progress was made
in Maryland, Virginia, and Jamaica, the Board of Trade had little
success in this respect. Georgia, therefore, was on a somewhat different footing from the other provinces, being more directly responsible to, and dependent upon, the home Government, but
there is no evidence to support the theory that the arrangement
was the result of deliberate, conscious policy on the part of the
Board of Trade.[48] In the general sense British policy on this matter
was unequivocal, and the persistent ideal of an independent revenue finally bore fruit in Townshend's legislation of 1767 with
disastrous consequences to the old colonial system.

The dependence of Georgia on the continual assistance of the
United Kingdom was some justification for regarding it more as
British property than as an individual entity within itself. There
was never any idea of the colony's being other than subordinate and
contributory to the welfare of its mother-country. At the end of
their charter rule the Trustees declared that they had "applied

their principal attention to make the province of Georgia sub-
servient to the interest and trade of Great Britain."[49] Under the
royal government the Board of Trade, through its inability to
place the Governor and other officers at the mercy of the Assembly
for their salaries and through its consequent obligation to keep
the administration of the province strictly responsible to the home
Government, was, perforce, conforming to the imperial theories
of the time.

IV

❧❧❧❧❧❧❧

Land, Labour, and Liquor

❧❧❧❧❧❧❧

"GEORGIA," wrote an inhabitant in 1735, "which was seemingly intended to be the asylum of the distressed, unless things are greatly altered, is likely to be itself a mere scene of distress."[1] "In our present circumstances," wrote another in 1737, "there seems to be a dark cloud over us, and most of our people are cast down at the thoughts of what they expect to be."[2] By 1739 the province was in such a poor condition that it became quite fashionable to ridicule it.[3] In whichever direction the colonists turned there were restrictions, benevolently imposed by the Trustees but irritating to the people who had to suffer them, and soon dissatisfaction was spread wide among the population.

The main grievances related to land, labour, and liquor. By 1738 several persons had declared their intention to leave Georgia unless alteration was made in the existing system of land tenure, and the Trustees' secretary did not doubt that many others were "caught with such opinions."[4] Many inhabitants deemed slave labour essential if the colony was to compete at all with South Carolina. In the words of one eighteenth century writer, possibly Edmund Burke: "It is the nature of man not to submit to extraordinary hardships in one spot, when they see their neighbours on another, without any difference in the circumstance of things, in a much more easy condition."[5] South Carolina possessed slaves, Georgia did not. The demand for a restricted admission of Negroes arose early in the history of Georgia and grew steadily in volume, and the refusal to permit it remained for many years a prominent cause of discontent. Another grievance was the prohibition on rum, a law it was impossible to enforce, and by 1738 "private rum shops were become as common among the people, in proportion, as gin-shops formerly at London."[6] The Trustees, however, were convinced that the prohibition was in the best interests of the settlers, for whatever febrifugal advantages rum may have had, the Trustees considered only its pernicious effects.

In founding their colony the Trustees had built up a system of rules they judged most fit and necessary for its welfare; the reasons for their policy had been lucidly and logically put on record, elaborated and advertised to the public, giving their administration an aura of righteousness. Yet, within a decade of the experiment's inauguration, censure of their policy was coming from all quarters. A policy intended for the common weal was the cause of common woe; what was to have been the ideal had proved to be far from that. Evidence that the Trustees were travelling the wrong road accumulated with the years, but they were loath to change direction, and it was only with extreme reluctance and under heavy pressure from the settlers that the regulations on land, labour, and liquor were eventually modified.

The policy of the Trustees towards land ownership in Georgia was motivated primarily by concern for defence and the need to fit each person not only as a settler but also as a soldier. The maximum grant for someone emigrating at the expense of the Corporation was laid down as fifty acres, while a man going out at his own charge with at least four and not more than ten men-servants was entitled to five hundred acres; each servant, on the expiry of his period of indenture, was to be allowed twenty acres.[7]

Everyone receiving land was expected to clear, fence, and cultivate it, and plant a thousand mulberry trees to every hundred acres within ten years, failing which the land was to revert to the Corporation. All land was held in tail-male, so that in the event of there being no male heir it reverted to the Trust and was not inherited by the female issue, and alienation by landholders was forbidden without the Trustees' permission. These restrictions were not intended to be enforced rigidly and were modified whenever circumstances demanded.[8]

The Trustees had good arguments to support their policy. It did not seem advisable to allow absolute possession of property to persons who had in many cases been sent to Georgia on account of mismanagement in England. Moreover, the restriction on the amount of land which any one person could possess was in tune with the ideas of the Government, which insisted on laws to break up exorbitant land grants in New York and refused consent to laws in other colonies that would encourage large individual land-holdings, because they hindered rapid growth in population.[9] In

its report to the Privy Council at the end of 1731, the Board of
Trade expressed its opinion that the proprietors of Georgia should
be restrained from granting more than five hundred acres to any
one person.[10] The Trustees' decision that fifty acres be the maximum for a person emigrating at their expense was based mainly
on military considerations. Since each planter was regarded as a
soldier, it was necessary for the number to be maintained at a high
level so that the province would have a respectable militia, and
fifty acres was judged to be generally adequate to support one
planter and his family.

The other restrictions were all justified by this theme of defence
requirements. Female inheritance was forbidden on the grounds
that otherwise the strength of each township would be reduced,
inasmuch as an unmarried woman might hold an allotment to the
exclusion of a man who would have been a member of the garrison. Other inconveniences were likely to arise; women were un-
suited to duties like watchings and wardings and serving on juries,
and therefore as the number of males in a township decreased so
would each man's turn for these duties become more frequent and
consequently more burdensome. The principal idea behind the
Trustees' policy was to maintain a number of men equivalent to
the number of allotments for the better defence and improvement
of the colony, and it followed from this that alienation of land
must be prohibited in order to keep the lots entire and undivided
and prevent any individual from engrossing too much land, which
would have meant the diminution of the garrison.

This land policy may have been based on the best of motives,
but as far as the colonists were concerned it was quite unrealistic.
Governor Belcher of Massachusetts told Oglethorpe that the restriction of land tenure in Georgia to tail-male would discourage
settlement there because land could be held on much better terms
elsewhere in America.[11] Thomas Coram realized that a wrong
beginning had been made and at a meeting of the Trustees in
March 1734 declared that under the existing system the inhabitants would desert the province "like leaves from a tree in autumn."[12] Two months later he sought relaxation in the regulations
against female inheritance, but the majority supported the views
of Lord Egmont, who had always been against inheritance by a
woman on the ground that she might marry a man who would
neither live on the land nor attend to its cultivation, thus depriv-
ing the colony of its small freeholders in whom its strength resided.[13]

But whatever justification there may originally have seemed to be for primogeniture and tail-male, by 1734 it was evidently already apparent to some members of the Corporation that the regulations were impolitic. Besides keeping the province militarily strong the Trustees were, no doubt, aiming to prevent monopolization of land and to develop an economy of small farms. Such an aim was bound to be detrimental to a colony in Georgia's situation. Prosperity and progress in America were coming more and more to depend on capitalism, and conditions favoured large enterprise and the concentration of property in a few hands. It followed that Georgia could not prosper as long as the restrictions on landholding remained. They made impossible the establishment of a plantation system, especially after the use of Negro slaves was prohibited in 1735. The Trustees were, in effect, cramping the poor, small farmers of Georgia in their competition with rich, large landowners in South Carolina. This was the upshot of a policy coloured too much by moral and military considerations and too little by the economic and human factors.

As disaffection mounted it became increasingly obvious that some alteration was essential if settlers were to be kept in the province. In March 1738 some members of the Common Council met by private agreement and decided on a compromise by which lands might descend to a female heir on condition she married a man who would reside in the colony and who at the time of marriage possessed no land of his own. By this means the main purpose behind the regulations, namely the retention of inhabitants capable of bearing arms, would still be answered.[14] By March 1739 the Trustees realized they would have to allow unqualified female succession, and in September a resolution embodying the change was ordered to be printed in the newspapers.[15] Other resolutions were passed to the effect that in the event of there being no issue, male or female, an estate need not revert to the Trustees but could devolve upon a person appointed by the landholder.[16] In June 1740 it was agreed that freeholders should be allowed to lease land for rent to tenants for a period of up to seven years, on condition that the tenant resided on the land and improved it.[17] In the following month the maximum amount of land any one person could accumulate by inheritance was raised from five hundred to two thousand acres, and the stipulations as to cultivation and the planting of mulberry trees considerably reduced.[18]

These changes were not sufficient to completely satisfy the colonists. The liability to forfeit lands remained if the stipulated improvements were not made inside the specified period, and with the exigencies of war pressing hard the opportunity to make such improvements was unavoidably curtailed. In March 1741 the Trustees reduced again landholders' obligations as to cultivation, and twelve months later resolved that on the death of a tenant his wife should have the house and the land be divided between her and the eldest son; if there was no son then that half of the property could be devised by will or inherited by the eldest daughter.[19]

In July and August 1742 it was decided that in future a person who took servants to Georgia and settled there at his own expense should be granted land in fee-simple instead of tail-male, but should be forbidden to alienate any of his property until after a period of ten years, by which time he must have cultivated at least an eighth of it. At the same time, in order to prevent inconveniences that might arise by monopolization, accumulation of realty was restricted to two thousand acres, although a person becoming entitled by inheritance to more than that was to be allowed to sell the excess.[20] Finally, in March 1750 the tenure of all lands was enlarged to absolute inheritance.[21] Thus the colonists at last obtained what they had sought for so long, and the way was opened for the creation of larger landholdings and for the gradual development of a landed aristocracy.

Together with the mitigation of conditions of land tenure went a reduction of charges upon it, a measure necessary to stimulate economic development. The early grants were all made on condition of payment, after ten years, of an annual quit-rent of ten shillings per hundred acres, but in 1733 the Trustees increased the quit-rent for those who went out at their own expense to twenty shillings per hundred acres.[22] By this means the Trustees hoped, after paying the Crown the stipulated rate of four shillings, to be left with a surplus for use as a fund to support administration and promote settlement. It was a fallacious and impracticable policy, and naturally gave cause for dissatisfaction among the colonists. The payment of quit-rent was the chief bond between lord and tenant in the colonial form of feudal tenure, but it did not mean a release from onerous services, as in England, but rather was it an additional burden on people who were trying to build themselves a new life and shake off a background of debt. Furthermore, it is difficult to condone a policy which demanded payment in specie, of which there was certain to be a grave shortage in Georgia. Experience showed that quit-rents were a recurring source of popular discontent in the colonies, and for the

Trustees to fix theirs at an exorbitant amount was asking for trouble and making collection virtually impossible. Even after reductions were made in later years, collection of quit-rents proved to be an impracticable proposition.[23]

When the Trustees surrendered their charter, the Crown remitted all arrears of quit-rent due it at that time and reduced the charge in future from four to two shillings per hundred acres, to become payable two years after the date of the grant.[24] Since quit-rents had never hitherto been collected in Georgia, however, there was no machinery ready and operating for the Government to use. The impossibility of obtaining the quit-rents under the existing system made some new provision for their collection essential, and in February 1760 the Upper House of Assembly recommended a bill for that purpose; the Commons House did not pass it until two years had elapsed, and then only in an amended form.[25] Thereafter the Act was bandied about in England, criticized by the Treasury, and never confirmed. Since no other Act for the purpose was passed, the collection of quit-rents in Georgia was never successfully attempted.[26]

The reduction of the quit-rent to two shillings under the royal government was accompanied by instructions to the Governor to confirm the grants of land made by the Trustees on terms similar to those already prevailing, except that in future at least one twentieth of the land must be cleared and cultivated every year. Furthermore, provision was made to prevent persons from accumulating more land than they could properly cultivate.[27] Anomalies and misunderstandings soon arose. The requirement to clear and cultivate a twentieth of his land every year meant the grantee would almost certainly forfeit his property before long because normally at least half the grant was unfit for cultivation. "These terms and conditions, therefore," Governor Reynolds pointed out, "very much alarm the inhabitants, for they say it will at least retard the settlement of the colony for some time, notwithstanding the hopes they have of the terms being altered."[28] In January 1755 the Georgia legislature prepared a remonstrance asking for alterations; it was considered by the Board of Trade in May.[29] It was decided that Reynolds must have misconstrued the intention of his instructions, which was that the requirements about cultivation should extend only to grants made in the future and not to lands already assigned. Nevertheless, the Board prepared new land regulations for Georgia, taken largely from an Act passed in Virginia in 1713 under which the settlement and cultivation of that colony had been greatly extended.[30] The new regulations distinguished between good and bad land and varied the obligations attached to grants accordingly, besides making the terms generally easier and more practicable. It was a fair treatment of a difficult problem.

In the early days of the colony one of the reasons advanced by freeholders for the slow cultivation of lands was the lack of servants. The shortage was due partly to the unattractive conditions of service provided by the Trustees. In most of the colonies a servant, on the expiry of his contract, was not sent empty away but was entitled, either by custom or statute, to receive what was known as freedom dues, which usually included suitable clothing, agricultural tools and seeds, sometimes arms and other provisions, and often a grant of fifty acres. In contrast, a servant in Georgia could expect no more than a mere twenty acres when he had completed his term of service. Such frugality was bound to deter settlement and encourage transfer to other colonies, and it was not long before servants in Georgia were deserting to South Carolina where a ready welcome always awaited them.[31] Even the German servants, so often described as models of industry and fidelity, were, in some instances, disobedient and refractory, and clandestinely quitted their masters.[32] Many masters shortened their terms as an inducement to faithful service, but they could not prevent most of the single men from escaping and "skulking about the out-settlements of South Carolina," whence it was almost impossible to retrieve them. Even when some were recovered no reliance could be placed on them, for they would only remain until another opportunity of escape presented itself.[33]

Gradually, conditions of service for servants in Georgia were necessarily made more generous. In August 1737 it was resolved that all servants of good record who served out their time before Christmas of that year should be granted fifty acres of land together with a sow and a cow.[34] In March 1741 it was ordered that all servants in the colony who completed their period of service and produced certificates of good behaviour from their masters should receive, in addition to a year's maintenance and tools, fifty acres of good land instead of the twenty to which they were at present entitled.[35] Then in March 1743 the Trustees decided that all servants were to receive an allowance for twelve months following the expiration of their contract, thus extending to all servants with a minimum indenture of four years a privilege which those indented to the Trustees had enjoyed since 1741.[36]

Undoubtedly the most pressing labour problem, however, was the persistent demand for Negro slaves. Slave status was unknown to English law and there had been no Act of Parliament formally establishing it in any of the American plantations, but its existence was apparently taken for granted under the municipal law of the colonies. In the south especially, in the tobacco plantations of Virginia and Maryland and in the rice fields of South Carolina, slavery had been proved the most economical and effective form of labour. Hence the Trustees were assuming an independent line when, in 1734, they drew up a law prohibiting the importation and use of slaves in Georgia.[37]

The Trustees had a wealth of arguments and evidence to support them in this measure. South Carolina was living in constant apprehension over its large Negro population, and it was fear of slave rebellion, coupled with the menace of French and Spanish influence among frontier Indian tribes, which in 1740 moved the encouragement of more white immigration.[38] Colonel William Byrd, a Virginia planter, wrote to Lord Egmont in 1736 wishing that a similar prohibition could be enjoined in his province: "They import so many negroes hither that I fear this colony will some time or other be confirmed by the name of New Guinea. I am sensible of many bad consequences of multiplying these Ethiopians amongst us. They blow up the pride and ruin the industry of our white people who, seeing a rank of poor creatures below them, detest work for fear it should make them look like slaves."[39] The Trustees, too, thought a white man owning a black slave would be disinclined to work himself, and they feared that the Spaniards in Florida would be continually inciting insurrections among the slaves or enticing them away. There was always the danger that slaves might become the allies of hostile Indians on the borders. The Trustees believed that slave labour would not be required for the products which they intended to be raised and that to admit Negroes into the population would seriously weaken Georgia as a defensive barrier on the exposed southern frontier.[40]

The arguments advanced by the Trustees to vindicate the prohibition were well-reasoned, supported to a large degree by the experience of other colonies, and in harmony with Georgia's original *raison d'être*. But natural progress would unavoidably be slow under a hypothetical policy contrived by a Corporation practically unacquainted with actual conditions prevailing in America. Immediately he heard of the prohibition Sam Eveleigh, perhaps the most discerning of contemporary observers of Georgia, wrote from South Carolina noting with surprise that the Act had been described in some quarters as necessary and useful: "But do assure you that here, where they ought, at least, to be better acquainted in these affairs than the gentlemen in England, they are of far different sentiments, and they all unanimously agree (at least such as I have talked with) that without negroes Georgia can never be a colony of any great consequence. But since the Trustees have thought fit to pass such a law, I shall say no more, only this one remark. That I observed, whilst at Georgia, great quantities of choice good land for rice, and am positive that that commodity can't (in any great quantities) be produced by white people because the work is too laborious, the heat very intense. . . ."[41]

The reasons for the prohibition seemed logical enough on paper, but when considered in the light of actual conditions they fell apart. Here again is seen the serious disadvantage of government benevolent but remote, well-intentioned but based over much on theory: "It can't be supposed," wrote Eveleigh, "that the Trustees know the circumstance of this country as well as those who have lived several years in it, and we are all here generally of opinion that Georgia can never be a place of any great consequence without negroes."[42] Several years elapsed before the Trustees had to acknowledge the truth of his words. Their opposition to Negro labour was, in fact, contrary not only to contemporary opinion in the colonies but also to that of economic theorists in Britain, and was out of tune with the policy of the Government. The best course for the Trustees to have followed would have been to permit the importation and use of slave labour under certain quantitative restrictions, instead of attempting to impose a complete prohibition which, for fifteen years, remained a cause of warm debate and bitter complaint.

The inevitability of slaves' being ultimately admitted must have become obvious to the Trustees by the 1740s when they were subjected to increasing pressure on the issue. The inhabitants had not been slow to evade the prohibition, one method being to hire Negroes from South Carolina whose owners would reclaim their property whenever an attempt was made to enforce the regulations.[43] In June 1742 a committee of the House of Commons announced its opinion that the employment of slave labour "under proper regulations and restrictions" would be beneficial to Georgia.[44] But it was difficult to move the Trustees on the subject. In July 1742 they relaxed sufficiently to instruct William Stephens to inquire into the advisability and method of admitting Negroes into the province, and appointed five members of the Common Council to consider the matter.[45] No progress was made because the Trustees willingly accepted Stephens's opinion that it would be unwise to admit slaves while Spain remained in Florida and there was a possibility of their being incited to rebel.[46] The Trustees were still adamant in the summer of 1746, and expressed surprise at the continued expectancy in the colony that the prohibition would be removed; once the settlers had slaves, it was argued, "they would soon become such themselves by being debtors to the negro merchants."[47] At the end of 1746 the Trustees learned that the Reverend Thomas Bosomworth had sent to South Carolina for six Negroes to be employed on his plantation, and a sharp letter was despatched to the President and Assistants in the colony deploring their failure to take any step to punish and prevent such violation of the law, having "contented themselves with seeing and complaining of it."[48] At the beginning of 1748 the Trustees were surprised to hear that settlers even in the south were in possession of slaves, and they testily repeated their resolve never to permit such contravention of the law because of the dangers to the security of the frontier settlements: "And as the people who continue to clamour for negroes declare that the colony can never succeed without the use of them, it is evident they don't intend by their own industry to contribute to its success and must therefore rather hinder than promote it; the Trustees therefore require it may be signified to all the inhabitants of the colony that if any one of them persist in declaring they cannot succeed without negroes, it would be of service to the colony as well as themselves for them to retire into any other province, where they will be freely allowed the use of negroes."[49] Nothing could be more unequivocal than that, and yet just over twelve months later the Trustees were compelled to change their minds.

In May 1749 they considered a letter from their officers in Savannah which described the impossibility of effectively preventing slaves from being brought into Georgia and stated that any further attempt to enforce the prohibition would depopulate the province. With control of the situation now unmistakably removed from their hands, the Trustees had no alternative to acknowledging the fact of the matter, and they decided to petition the Crown for the repeal of the Act.[50] The repeal legislation of August 8, 1750, contained provisions intended to safeguard the interests of the colony against the dangers intrinsic in permitting Negro labour. For every four Negroes employed on a plantation there was to be one white manservant capable of bearing arms; an office was created for the registration of all Negroes imported, and provision made for ships carrying slaves to be inspected by health officers before landing their cargoes; intermarriage between black and white was forbidden.[51]

Thus, at the last, the Trustees had to bend before the pressure of the settlers. Their reluctance to yield had been based originally on solid premises, but it is impossible to escape the conclusion that, once the colony had been properly settled, the admission of Negroes was essential to its progress and prosperity. Economic factors made the eventual introduction of slaves inevitable, but it may well be that it was to Georgia's benefit that they were not permitted until the province had been given time to establish itself.

Simultaneous with the law against Negroes had been another important measure, designed to prevent the use of spirituous liquors in Georgia. After June 24, 1735, "no rum or brandies nor any other kind of spirits or strong waters by whatsoever name they are or may be distinguished" were to be allowed in the province. "And the better to prevent profane cursing and swearing, vice and debauchery, too frequently occasioned by tippling houses and disorderly public houses," the sale of any wine, beer, ale, or other liquors without a licence from the authorities was forbidden.[52] Here again the Trustees were acting paternalistically in what they believed was the best interest of the colony. In their opinion all sorts of maladies were attributable to rum, "that pernicious liquor," and they expected the people to abstain from it for their own sakes.[53] The preamble to the Act stated that it had been found by experience that the consumption of rum and brandies in Georgia was the cause of "dangerous maladies and fatal distempers," and should be checked in order to save the colony from ruin.

In spite of impassioned dissent from the settlers, therefore, the restrictions were genuinely regarded by the Trustees as beneficial to the inhabitants, preventing ill-health and laziness and improving material conditions. Morever, the policy was in keeping with English thought in the eighteenth century. Drunkenness had long been common in England among both upper and lower classes of society, at each of the universities, in country as well as town. Porter, salep, and brandy intoxicated the upper classes, while Dorset beer and Oxford ale fuddled the common man. The early Hanoverian period witnessed, too, the spread of the gin-drinking habit, a potent cause of much misery and crime. Intemperance was not a monopoly of the Georgia settlers, nor were the Trustees being narrow or pedantic or exceptional in attempting to suppress it. Businessmen in England deplored the habit because it produced indolence among the work people and wasted labour and time. Colonel Byrd commended Lord Egmont on the Trustees' policy and hoped it would be enforceable: "I entirely agree with Your Lordship," he wrote, "in the detestation you seem to have for that diabolical liquor rum, which does more mischiefs to people's industry than anything except gin and the Pope. And if it were not a little too poetical, I should fancy as the gods of old were said to quaff nectar, so the devils are fobbed off with rum. . . . Thrice happy Georgia if it be in the power of any law to keep out so great an enemy to health, industry and virtue! The new settlers there had much better plant vineyards like Noah and get drunk with their own wine."[54] The attempt to prevent the evils of intemperance in Georgia was not a new departure, therefore, but rather an application of principles acquired from knowledge of excesses in England as well as in America.

In practice the law was not so restrictive as it seemed on paper, and in any event it was impossible to stop the people's obtaining rum illegally, the principal source of supply being South Carolina, whose traders were adept at smuggling it.[55] There was never any possibility of the law's being enforced effectively, and the private sale of rum increased rapidly until most people in Savannah were drinking it in 'defiance of the regulations, very often to excess.[56] By 1742 the Trustees were aware that their prohibition was ineffective, except in causing discontent, and in January an instruction was sent to William Stephens to "wink at the importation of rum and discourage seizures thereof." In July the Corporation's seal was affixed to two Acts, one for amending the existing law so as to permit the importation of rum from any of the other colonies in exchange for lumber and other goods from Georgia, and another for regulating the purchase and sale of the rum imported and "suppressing the odious and loathsome sin of drunkenness."[57]

Repeal of the prohibition was prompted by the resolution of a House of Commons committee that it would be "an advantage to the colony of Georgia to permit the importation of rum into the said colony from any of the other British colonies," and by the opinion expressed in debate in the House that a moderate quantity of rum mixed with water was a necessary tonic for the

settlers and that its importation from other colonies would promote the export of lumber.[58] The Acts were transmitted to the
Privy Council in January 1743 and referred from there to the
Board of Trade, which dallied with them for three years.[59] The
Board had no objection to the general tenor of the Acts but took
exception to some particular points of detail, alterations to which
the Trustees firmly refused to countenance.[60] Consequently, the
amending legislation was never officially approved, and theoret-
ically the original prohibition imposed in 1735 remained in force,
but by this time rum was being sold widely in the colony as if
there were not, nor ever had been, special regulations attached to
it. The liquor law had always been an anomaly, incapable of
enforcement, and the perversities of the Trustees and the Board
of Trade could make no appreciable difference to the situation.

Any discussion of these problems tends inevitably to become an
indictment of the Trustees, but the shortcomings in their policy
must not be allowed to detract from the distinction of their
achievement. By 1752 Georgia had travelled the first part of the
road towards becoming an integral part of the American colonial
scene, and although the journey had not been as easy or successful
as many had anticipated, nor the direction exactly that designed
by the Trustees, nevertheless some distance had been covered
along a difficult route. When all is said, they had succeeded in
founding a barrier province which improved Britain's position in
her rivalry with France and Spain in America. Moreover, they had
done this for genuinely charitable reasons and without financial
reward to themselves. The inception of the project and the government of the colony was not the full-time occupation of any of
the Trustees; it was largely a leisure interest from which they
gained nothing for themselves, and which they pursued solely
because they believed that in doing so they were serving their
country and their fellow men.

V

❧❧❧❧❧❧

Anglo-Spanish Diplomacy (1736-1739)

❧❧❧❧❧❧

DISAGREEMENT over the boundaries of Florida and Georgia was one of the causes of the Anglo-Spanish war which opened in 1739. For several years preceding the conflict there had been controversy over this subject between the two nations, each adapting former treaties and accounts of discovery to suit its respective case. It would be wrong, however, to imply that this question was a prime reason why Britain and Spain went to war in 1739. It was a subsidiary issue in the general pattern of international relations at that time and never figured largely in the argument between the Courts of St. James and of Madrid. Much more important was Spanish vexation at the British privilege of supplying slaves to the Spanish colonies, the *asiento de negros* exacted at the Peace of Utrecht in 1713. Another grievance was the South Sea Company's practice of fraudulently overloading the one ship it was permitted to send every year to trade at Cartagena and Vera Cruz. Spain complained also of English contraband in the West Indies, of illegal logwood-cutting on the Honduras coast, and of the claimed right to collect salt in the Tortugas. For her part, Britain resented the measures taken by Spanish *guarda-costas* to prevent smuggling, particularly their harsh exercise of the right of search. As stories of losses and atrocities at sea multiplied, the advocates of war found a sympathetic audience. Sir Robert Walpole, however, favoured a settlement of differences by negotiation, and so the years before 1739 were full of claims and refutations, notes and memorials between ambassadors and ministers.

Although the Governments were concerned with the boundary of Georgia less than with the other causes of dispute, that problem did have a part in the discussion and it did influence the policy of each side. It was, furthermore, obviously a matter of vital significance both to the pioneers in the little colony itself and also to the philanthropic gentlemen in England to whose initiative its foundation had been due and in whom, as its Trustees, the government of the province had been entrusted by royal charter.

The dispute has been described in detail in a somewhat confusing and repetitive book, based on Spanish as well as English sources.[1] The purpose of this chapter is to elucidate, by a chronological survey, the basic principles upon which the diplomatic controversy was conducted and, by a re-examination of the English sources, to describe the main features of the controversy insofar as they concerned the Government of Great Britain.

Spain rested her case on prior discovery and settlement. In 1512 a royal patent had been granted Juan Ponce de León to discover and occupy the coasts of the Florida region, mentioned in the patent as "the Islands of Beniny," where according to Indian legend was to be found a rejuvenating spring of running water. Exploration was to be made within three years and, if successful, the discoverer was to be appointed life governor of the newly found territory with the title of *adelantado*.[2] The following year Ponce de León explored both the east and west shores, landed near the mouth of the St. Johns River, and commemorated with the name Florida the woodland beauty of the countryside and its discovery during the Season of Flowers. He did not, however, establish a settlement there.[3]

Subsequently, Spanish Jesuits and Franciscans began missionary activity in the Georgia country—a century and a half before the arrival of the English—and their influence extended up the coastline as far as Santa Elena (Port Royal, South Carolina).[4] But Spain valued the South Atlantic littoral principally for its strategic importance and never seriously intended to make it commercially productive. The lower part of the Florida coastline is close to the Antilles, and the eastern shore runs nearly parallel to the Bahama Channel, which was the natural route to Spanish ports in the Caribbean. Consequently, if a rival Power controlled Florida, the sea lanes along which the Spaniards sent home their treasure ships would be unsafe. As a protective step an outpost was established at St. Augustine in 1565, and this, together with the military and naval forces stationed at Havana, should have ensured Spanish command of the vital Bahama Channel.[5]

There is not much evidence to support the English contention that John Cabot was the first European to sail along the coast of the Florida peninsula when he made a voyage in 1497 from Cape

Breton to the latitude of Cuba. The sole foundation for this contention was a passage from the sixth chapter of the third *decade* of Peter Martyr's *De Orbe Novo Decades,* and there is reason to doubt whether Cabot did, in fact, travel farther south than Cape Hatteras in latitude 36°.[6] Of much greater weight to the English argument were the actual settlement of Carolina by the English and the extensive contacts of their traders with the Indians. Whereas England had colonies agriculturally productive and trafficking with the Indians, Spain had little to show except a garrison ensconced behind the walls of St. Augustine. Nevertheless each side wanted control of the country south of the Savannah River, and it was inevitable that clashes should occur.

As early as 1726 merchants petitioned Parliament against the severity of Spanish *guarda-costas* and their failure to discriminate between smugglers and legal traders in the West Indies.[7] Negotiations between Britain and Spain brought about the Treaty of Seville in November 1729 which promised restoration of Anglo-Spanish trade to the position of 1725, full restitution for seizures, and the detailing of other matters to the adjudication of commissaries at Madrid.[8] In April 1730 John Goddard, Benjamin Keene, and Arthur Stert were appointed British commissaries, and although their chief task was to settle particulars of the South Sea Company's claims, they were also instructed to maintain Britain's rights on the South Carolina border.[9] No satisfactory solution of the territorial question came from these discussions, and within a few years Spain's ambassador in London was complaining of incursions into Guale, the region between the Savannah and the Altamaha rivers, which the English had unlawfully appropriated under the title of Georgia.

By 1736, indeed, the Spaniards in Florida had developed a profound antipathy for the settlement in Georgia and were especially suspicious of its leader, James Edward Oglethorpe, in whom wide and ill-defined powers of authority had been confided by his fellow Trustees. In the hope of discovering a way of relaxing tension in the area, the Duke of Newcastle, as Secretary of State, commissioned his own representative, Charles Dempsey, to go to St. Augustine and arrange an agreement between Oglethorpe and the Governor of Florida on the boundary dispute.[10] The Spanish governor, Don Francisco del Moral Sánchez, received Dempsey civilly but expressed concern over the settlement of Englishmen on Spanish territory and complained that three hundred of them, accompanied by some Indians, had moved into the province of the Uchees with the intention of building a fort there.[11]

In April, Oglethorpe wrote personally to Sánchez proclaiming a desire for peace and informing him that he had issued orders for Spanish subjects not to be molested and had posted a boat and guards to prevent anyone from crossing the St. Johns River without permission.[12] At the same time he wrote to Dempsey in a similar conciliatory tone, telling him it was better for Britain that Spain and not another Power should possess Florida: "The Spanish and the English interests are naturally the same. We furnish them with provisions, they us with silver. They have more lands in America than they can use, the King of Great Britain also has more lands than sufficient, therefore he is not desirous of increasing by injustice his dominions, but of cultivating and peopling with regular towns and establishing good laws in those which he already possesses." He had no knowledge of any of his men settling among the Uchees, but in any case, he wrote, that country belonged to Britain.[13]

Having thus struck a propitiatory note in America, Oglethorpe then wrote home to the Secretary of State emphasizing the importance of retaining Georgia, a valuable province in his view—"the land capable of the richest production, the sea full of good ports near which all the large homeward bound ships from the Spanish America must pass." With the continued assistance of Parliament and the support of neighbouring Indians he would, he said, more than be able to hold his own against an enemy attack. He might even perhaps be able to conquer Florida, Cuba, and Mexico.[14] Oglethorpe's desire for peace was obviously not deep, and there was some justification for Spanish mistrust of his motives. The British Government, too, had its doubts about him, and in July instructed him to act cautiously and give no cause for any complaint from the Spaniards.[15]

These orders arrived too late, however. Clashes had already occurred in Georgia, and in September 1736 Spain's ambassador in London, Don Tomás Geraldino, presented Newcastle with a memorial against English activities. It consisted of five postulates. First, that in the previous March some Indians in alliance with the English had attacked a Spanish fort near St. Augustine and decapitated one member of its garrison. Second, that settlers from Georgia had constructed and garrisoned a fort twenty-five leagues north of St. Augustine and inside the boundaries of Florida.

Third, that proof of Spain's title to the land on which the fort was built lay in the fact that a previous English outpost there (Fort King George, on the north bank of the Altamaha) had been demolished at Spain's request in 1724. Fourth, that a fort was being erected among the Uchees and the Indians incited to war against the Spaniards. And lastly, that all Georgia and part of South Carolina was Spanish property by virtue of article seven of the Treaty of Madrid (1670) and article eight of the Treaty of Utrecht.[16]

The Georgia Trustees discussed the memorial with the Board of Trade and an answer to it was prepared.[17] This asserted that the alleged attack in the previous March had been made not by Indians in alliance with the English but by neighbouring tribes in revenge for "a most unheard of and outrageous injury acted by some Spaniards or Spanish Indians, who had killed some Indian women and children and two men, and, after most wickedly abusing another Indian woman, had burnt her alive." Geraldino, declared the Trustees, was misinformed about the rebuilding of a fort formerly demolished: "For that the said fort, having been left by the Independent Company without the consent or knowledge of His Majesty, was ordered to be rebuilt by an instruction from His Majesty to the late Governor Johnson." All forts were being built within British territory and at the desire of the Indians, and were required for the peace and defence of the country; no directions had ever been given for establishing settlements or fortresses beyond the charter limits of Georgia, and if the Uchees lived within the same then they were British, and not Spanish, subjects.

Finally, reports that Georgia colonists were inciting Indians to attack the Spaniards were almost certainly unfounded; the Trustees "have always had it at heart in the making of their several settlements to avoid all occasions of contest with the neighbouring nations in alliance with the Crown of Great Britain, and do not believe that any of their people can have acted so contrary to the design and intention of the Trustees." The apprehensions of the Governor of St. Augustine were more probably caused by the activities of certain traders from Charleston who had gone up among the Indians without the knowledge, and contrary to the orders, of the Trustees, and for whose conduct they who sent them were alone answerable.[18] Newcastle communicated this answer to the Spanish ambassador in November,[19] but by then the issue had been complicated by recent events in America.

Oglethorpe, who in the spring of 1736 had constructed Fort St. George on San Juan Island at the mouth of the St. Johns River, insisted that the frontier lay along the St. Johns, and tried to convince his Government by sending home a map showing a southern mouth of the Altamaha debouching near the St. Marys River.[20] As a counterblast, the Governor of Havana, Guemes y Horcasitas, had in August 1736 sent to Frederica, on St. Simons Island in Georgia, a diplomat and engineer named Antonio de Arredondo with a demand that the English withdraw beyond Port Royal.

War seemed likely, but frequent talks eventually brought agreement, and on October 11, 1736, Oglethorpe made a treaty with Governor Sánchez. Each was to restrain his Indian allies and leave the fixing of boundaries to the home Governments; Oglethorpe promised to evacuate in the meanwhile Fort St. George, provided no Spaniards moved in and the British title to it remained.[21] This put the dispute on a different footing, for it not only placed the onus of defining the frontier entirely on the shoulders of the ministers and diplomats in Europe but also helped to stiffen the attitude of each side. Oglethorpe thought he had struck a good bargain for England in making the treaty. Spain thought so too, and the unfortunate Sánchez, who had consented to it, was recalled and prosecuted, while Dempsey's brother, who was an officer in the Spanish service, was cashiered on account of his brother's part in concluding the treaty.[22]

From this time forward Georgia began to assume more prominence in the wrangling that was going on with Britain. Responsibility for all British interests in Spain rested on Benjamin Keene, a man of considerable parts and agreeable temper, who combined the posts of English ambassador and South Sea Company agent, a double role which caused some anomalies in that he had often to present grievances against Spain on behalf of the Company before being ordered to do so by the Government.[23] Throughout the negotiations from 1736 to 1739, which revolved mainly around commercial questions and depredations, Keene was watchful for signs of a Spanish attempt on the English colonies in America, and tried to keep himself so informed as to be able to anticipate any orders for an attack on Georgia.[24]

He had some wily individuals to deal with in Madrid. In the spring of 1737 he broached the subject of Oglethorpe's treaty before the two principal Spanish ministers, Torrenueva and La

Quadra. The latter, whom Keene found "a little pettish upon this subject," said he had not examined it but had heard it was prejudicial to Spain's interests, and implied that the King, Philip V, disapproved of it. He tried to pass off the colony of Georgia as merely "a private grant to some particulars to form a sort of company of adventurers, and consequently not a thing that could immediately interest the two Courts." This attitude drew a sharp statement to the contrary from Keene, who declared "that it was a public and national concern, encouraged and protected by the whole legislature." Torrenueva took a line similar to Quadra's and, "in a blundering way," denied all knowledge of the treaty.[25]

The Spanish ministers thought they were in a good position. Oglethorpe's activities were causing the British Government some anxiety, and the Spaniards believed the Walpole Ministry disliked the Georgia colony and would disavow it were it not that the support of the Trustees was needed in Parliament for other matters. If the garrison at St. Augustine was strengthened, Geraldino reported, it might be possible to cause a breach between the Trustees and the Government which would lead to the abandonment of Georgia.[26] There may have been some justification for this belief, but it failed to take into account the increasing resentment in England against everything Spanish, and the presence in the Ministry of a group, including Newcastle, which, while desiring peace, was not afraid of risking war.

On receiving intelligence from Lieutenant Governor Broughton of South Carolina concerning Spanish designs against Georgia, Newcastle instructed Keene in March of 1737 to discover if such an attack was being contemplated. He was to make strong representations to Quadra that Oglethorpe's agreement with Sánchez had removed all grievances, and that if Spain began hostilities in those parts then Britain would not fail to defend her subjects there.[27] Six weeks later Newcastle reaffirmed the Government's determination; Keene was to ensure that any intended attack on Georgia was cancelled forthwith and, in talking with the Spanish minister, was "not only [to] use the strongest expostulations upon this subject but make him see the ill consequences that must certainly follow the making any such attempt." Furthermore, "although that country is by His Majesty's grant become the property of some of the King's subjects, it is nevertheless under His Majesty's sovereignty and protection: and you will give them to understand that his Majesty will always consider it in that light."[28]

The Ministry had now discarded its former complaisance and, under Newcastle's guidance, was adopting a more resolute policy. Spain cannot have been unaware of the change, and her apprehension was increased by the appointment in June 1737 of Oglethorpe as commander-in-chief in Georgia and South Carolina. An assurance that he would be under the King's commission and not, as previously, under the Trustees, did not placate the Court of Madrid.[29] The inevitable memorial from the Spanish ambassador was duly presented at the end of July. He protested that the settlement of Georgia was continuing apace in spite of the fact that all territory as far north as latitude 33° 50' (which included Georgia) was part of Florida. He asserted that Britain had been encroaching on Spain's dominion ever since the 1688 Revolution, and demanded the cessation of colonizing in Georgia and the demolition of new forts there. The King of Spain, he said, was resolved to reannex all that had once belonged to him, and unless the English removed themselves peacefully Spanish troops would eject them by force. Finally, he required the cancellation of Oglethorpe's new appointment and threatened war if troops were sent to America and placed under his command.[30]

If the memorial was meant to intimidate, it did not succeed. A correspondent in the *Daily Post* regarded the demand for Oglethorpe's dismissal as proof of Spain's dread of his abilities and decried Spanish hopes of "a James the First upon the throne of Great Britain or a Gondomar now at our Court." Whatever right to Georgia the Spaniards may have had by virtue of an article in the treaty of 1670, he maintained, they had forfeited by the spoliation of English shipping and the infringement of every other article in the treaty. "A very merry way of proceeding indeed! to claim the benefit of one single article of a treaty, and with the utmost insolence and barbarity to break all the rest. This is Spanish logic with a witness." But whatever the attitude of Spain, the correspondent continued, it may be assumed that "our ministers will as soon consent to part with their eyes as to part with Georgia."[31]

The hostility of Geraldino's second memorial, indeed, brought about a general effect contrary to that intended; instead of cowing Britain it made her more concerned for Georgia. Everybody resented it and only Walpole was afraid to make it a *casus belli*. He felt that the nation was in no position to wage a successful war, and in a heated argument with Oglethorpe suggested the general should accept command of a regiment in England instead of in America. Oglethorpe lost his temper at this, "and asked him what man he took him to be, and whether he thought he had no conscience, to be the instrument of carrying over 3,000 souls to Georgia and then abandoning them to be destroyed by the Spaniards, for the consideration of a regiment." If the intention was to surrender Georgia, he said, then it ought to be admitted at once so that the inhabitants could be given time to withdraw safely. All the Trustees, commented Lord Egmont, "think it a melancholy thing to find the low credit the nation is in with foreign Princes on account of our facility in bearing insults, which proceeds from Sir Robert Walpole's natural timidity, and his apprehension of not sitting so firmly in the seat of Chief Minister in case of a war, which he colours with the inability the nation is in to enter into one."

Walpole's attitude, however, was not shared by the rest of the Government, and when Geraldino's memorial was considered in August 1737 by the King in Council there was frank indignation at it, especially on the part of Sir Joseph Jekyll and Lords Wilmington and Islay.[32] Its first reading was followed by a long pause until the Duke of Argyll declared: "The memorial should be answered, but not in the usual way—the reply should be a fleet of line-of-battle ships upon the coast of Spain." This remark broke the silence of the King, who cried out: "Well done, your Grace—your advice is agreeable to mine."[33] Georgia, it was decided, must be protected; a battalion of troops was transferred from Gibraltar to America and ships were sent to guard against attack by sea.[34]

Early in September 1737 Geraldino received his reply from the Duke of Newcastle. The Government, he was told, was surprised at the contents of the memorial, denied the accusation of trespassing in Florida, and repudiated the territorial allegations. Oglethorpe had given no occasion for complaint from the Spaniards, and the King reserved the right to employ whomsoever he wished in his service. Britain had no desire to cause a dispute but was determined to defend her rights and protect her subjects in America, remaining nonetheless willing to refer the frontier question to adjudication by commissaries.[35] The Spanish ministers in Madrid were informed of the measures Britain had taken to defend her dominions, measures at which, they were told, they ought not to be surprised in view of the tone of their recent memorial.[36]

At this the Spaniards became temporarily more cautious and conciliatory. Geraldino tried to palliate the truculence of his original assertions, though he retained hopes of Oglethorpe's being prevented from returning to America,[37] while in Madrid a desire for settlement of differences by negotiation prevailed.[38] But news of the coming departure for America of Oglethorpe and his regiment stirred up Spanish apprehension again. Geraldino tried to obtain definite assurances from both Walpole and Newcastle that no aggression was intended, but neither of them would oblige, denying him any satisfactory answer by each referring him to the other.[39]

In fact, the Government's policy was now being more and more decided for it by the political situation in the country and by events generally. The *guarda-costas* had of late been as ruthless and efficient as ever, and stories about depredations were growing daily. The Parliamentary Opposition seized on popular indignation at the treatment of British shipping and used it as a stick to beat an Administration that was visibly weakening. Walpole's pacifism was isolating him from both Parliament and the people, and it was Newcastle who reflected public opinion. The West Indian merchants complained to the King about Spanish depredations, and in November 1737 Newcastle sent Quadra a long memorandum on the outrages.[40] At the same time Keene was instructed to demand restitution on the basis of existing Anglo-Spanish treaties, and also to point out that the recent answer to Geraldino's memorial contained demonstrative proof of Britain's title to Georgia and that any talk by Spain of settling the issue by negotiation was meaningless, "since the stating the fact is sufficient to show His Majesty's right to that colony."[41]

This was palpably untrue, of course, and merely stating the fact was no argument whatever. Indeed, all the evidence, theoretical and historical, supported Spain's title to the Georgia country, and although there are some subtle and painstaking memorials preserved in the Public Record Office which attempt to build up a British case, no convincing answer was ever made to the Spanish argument.

England's difficulty is best illustrated by consideration of Spain's case as put forward by Antonio de Arredondo, a Spanish officer and engineer from the garrison at St. Augustine, who had made numerous journeys along the South Atlantic coastline and into the interior and who, with information gleaned from the archives of St. Augustine and from Andrés de Barcia's *Ensayo Cronologico, para la historia general de la Florida* (Madrid, 1723), presented proof of Spain's title to Georgia. Arredondo claimed that Spain

was entitled to the coastline as far north as Port Royal in latitude
32° 30'.[42] The treaty of 1670 had stipulated that England should
retain such lands as she then actually possessed, the southernmost
limit of which at that time was Charleston. All territory to the
south was understood to belong to Spain, and therefore England's
settlements there were a violation of her treaty obligations. He
pointed out the inconsistency of Newcastle's allegation that, on
the one hand, neither the treaty of 1670 nor that of 1713 had
defined the limits of Carolina, and, on the other hand, that the
limits of Georgia and South Carolina had been publicly recognized and always agreed to. "Therefore it is easy to see that the
Court of London, being obfuscated and not knowing how to com-
bine at once a negative and an affirmative into one proposition,
asserts in its own favour the very thing it denies, and inadvertently
denies, on the other hand, the very thing it admits, without seeing
that its self-contradiction convicts it of its own lack of logic."[43]

Arredondo's arguments were irrefutable, and as long as the controversy remained on theoretical grounds Britain had no case. But
in international affairs *de facto* is always more important than
de jure. Britain had one argument which far outweighed the historical and ethical evidence Spain could muster—she was in actual
possession of the debated land. She held all the territory north of
the Altamaha and threatened, besides, the Florida settlements.
Spain could do little about it except fight, and that would be
jeopardizing her possession even of Florida for the sake of a possible, and certainly only temporary, conquest of the English southern colonies. Neither Government really wanted war, yet neither
could afford to relinquish its claims.

By the beginning of 1738 the idea of the boundary issue's being
settled by commissaries appointed for that purpose by the two
Courts was acceptable to each side. An obstacle, however, lay in
the Spanish demand that the forts recently built by Oglethorpe
should be evacuated and demolished before the proposed commission opened. Keene, on behalf of the British Government, objected to this condition and asked the reason for it, telling Torrenueva that so far from its being a preliminary it was the most
Spain could expect after the conclusion of the commission if she
had proved her allegations incontestably. Quadra, too, insisted that
the forts be evacuated prior to the opening of any conferences,
and said Oglethorpe's recent activities could be construed only as
a contravention of treaty stipulations. Keene replied that if Britain
chose to erect forts on her own territory, that was her business

and not Spain's, and the assertion that they constituted new encroachments was one that could not be proved until there was
"a candid and impartial examination of facts by commissaries
named on both sides."[44] At the same time Geraldino in London
reiterated that Spain would agree to such a conference provided
it lasted no longer than six months, that neither side occupied the
disputed territory during that time, and, particularly, that the
forts erected by Oglethorpe were demolished beforehand.[45]

A few months earlier the British Government might conceiv-
ably have compromised on this matter. But when the Spanish
ambassador presented his conditions in March 1738 any conciliatory gesture was impossible. On the seventeenth of that month
Parliament had met in an angry mood, and Captain Jenkins re-
cited his wrongs and displayed his notorious ear at the bar of the
Commons. Pulteney and Pitt voiced the indignation of the House,
watched from the gallery by a sympathetic Prince of Wales. In-
censed at Spanish depredations and the patrolling of the seas by
guarda-costas, Parliament was not disposed to yield to Spain on
any point, not excluding that of the colonial frontier. Walpole
remained anxious for peace at almost any price, but Newcastle,
more susceptible to popular clamour, realized the Government
could not surrender Georgia.[46] A resolution was passed by the
Commons that measures should be taken to enforce the right of
British ships to sail in all the seas around America, and at the end
of March the English naval commander in the Mediterranean
was ordered to station his squadron at Minorca.

And so, when Newcastle answered the Spanish note in April
1738, he had no alternative to affirming his original stand. England
had no objection to the suggested time limit of six months but
would not comply with a prerequisite to evacuate territories and
demolish forts. She would consent to refer the boundary question
to commissaries only so long as everything in the disputed area
remained on its present footing.[47] This show of determination had
some effect, for at the end of May the Spanish ambassador, while
still declaring that the forts ought to be destroyed, laid more stress
on his sovereign's desire for an amicable settlement and willing-
ness for England to send two delegates to Madrid to discuss Georgia's boundary with two appointed by himself.[48] The British Government responded to Spain's overtures and made arrangements
accordingly; but it was also resolved to negotiate from strength,
and in June a reinforcement was sent under Admiral Nicholas
Haddock to cruise in the Mediterranean, while Keeene was di-

rected to warn British merchants in Spain to withdraw their property from the country at once.[49]

Meantime in London the Council met to consider Geraldino's recent statement and decided that preparations for the Madrid conference should go ahead immediately.[50] Geraldino was then informed, first by Walpole and then by Newcastle, that the King would nominate his commissaries without delay.[51] In acquiescing in these arrangements Spain mitigated her original terms as gracefully as possible. She accepted the principle laid down by Newcastle in April, namely, that circumstances in the debatable lands should remain in their existing state and neither side increase its fortifications or occupy new positions there.[52]

Prospects now seemed good for a peaceful solution. Although the public was suspicious of this sudden friendliness between the Courts, the British Government undoubtedly hoped the way was open for a permanent settlement of all differences and perhaps even for an Anglo-Spanish alliance. When, in August, Keene was advised to familiarize himself with the points at issue in preparation for the proposed commission, he was also told: "It is the King's view and desire to live upon a foot of the utmost friendship with Their Catholic Majesties; and therefore His Majesty wishes to remove all future causes of complaint or dispute. Such an alliance would not only be for the mutual advantage of both Kingdoms but might also greatly tend to the security of the balance of power in Europe."[53]

The advice to acquaint himself thoroughly with the matters likely to be raised was indeed urgent, for Keene confessed he had only a hazy notion of what the dispute in Florida was about and begged for clear instructions.[54] He and Abraham Castres, the other British delegate, wrote to Newcastle that the two chief questions to be resolved by the negotiations would be the limits of Georgia and freedom of navigation in America, but that on the former they had nothing to offer, "having had little or no information hitherto of the real state of our dispute with this Court upon this important subject."[55] The need for precise knowledge on this matter was demonstrated by the objection of the Spanish Court raised in October against the first draft of a convention. Exception was taken to an expression in the second article, to wit: "Les frontières de la Caroline meridionale, dans laquelle on entend être comprise la colonie de la Georgie." Spain held, with some justice, that her ambassador in London had been outwitted, for this parenthesis incorporating Georgia in South Carolina would support the British title to all that region, and although Spain might have no claim to South Carolina she had a good one to all, or at least the greater part, of Georgia.[56]

Such equivocation was typical of the proceedings which delayed the signing of a convention until the beginning of 1739. Discussions continued throughout the autumn of 1738 and obstacles were gradually overcome or removed. The principal impediment was haggling over the discharge of debts between the two nations. Britain owed Spain £180,000 but claimed that Spain owed her £343,277 for damages to her shipping. A bargain was eventually struck whereby Spain was to pay £95,000, representing the balance of her depredations over those committed by England. All outstanding obstructions were seemingly overcome by Christmas, and in January 1739 the convention was signed at the palace of El Pardo.

Article 1 of the Convention of El Pardo stipulated that each country should send plenipotentiaries to Madrid to arrange a settlement of commercial differences and of the Florida and Carolina boundaries. Article 2 stated: "The regulation of the limits of Florida and Carolina, which according to what has been lately agreed was to be decided by commissaries on each side, shall likewise be committed to the said plenipotentiaries to procure a more solid and effectual agreement; and during the time that the discussion of that affair shall last, things shall remain in the aforesaid territories of Florida and Carolina in the situation they are in at present, without increasing the fortifications there or taking any new posts; and for this purpose His Britannic Majesty and His Catholic Majesty shall cause the necessary orders to be despatched immediately after the signing of this convention." By a separate article Benjamin Keene and Abraham Castres were named as the British plenipotentiaries, and Don Joseph de la Quintana and Don Stephen Joseph de Abaria as the Spanish.

That this represented a genuine desire of both Governments to eliminate differences is attested by Spain's beginning to disarm her fleet and by Newcastle's hankering after an alliance. But there were some serious weaknesses in the convention. In the first place, the right of search was not abandoned. Secondly, the claims of the South Sea Company had been left for separate arrangement, and the Company's determination to drive a hard bargain angered the Spaniards and marred the negotiations.[57] And thirdly, the question of colonial boundaries was not settled but only referred to the further consideration of the commissaries. The history of the previous three years indicated that agreement on this head would not be easy. Spain wanted the frontier problem to be decided first, whereas Britain was more interested in depredations.

Whatever hopes of peace the British Government may have harboured were rudely shaken by the reception of the convention in England. The Georgia Trustees were very suspicious of Walpole's intentions, fearing he was not averse to relinquishing the colony in order to pacify Spain, but there is nothing to indicate the surrender of Georgia was ever seriously considered by the Government. Walpole's desire to pacify Spain was a reasoned outcome of his recognition of the value of maintaining the lucrative West Indian trade, which was bound to be precarious without Spanish goodwill.[58] He recognized the fact that the Spaniards were justified in searching ships and attempting to prevent illicit traffic, and wanted little beyond an arrangement checking excesses in the exercise of this right. He undoubtedly desired peace and might privately have contemplated using Georgia as a bargaining counter in the negotiations, but he must have realized that the strength of public feeling rendered such a manoeuvre impracticable if his waning authority was not to disappear altogether.

It was popular clamour which provoked Walpole to announce emphatically at the beginning of February 1739 that English ships ought not to be searched at sea by Spaniards, and that the colony of Georgia would not be relinquished. When, on February 16, Henry Archer, who was sitting by him in the House of Commons, warned him that unless the Trustees were convinced Georgia was to be retained they would vote against the convention, Walpole immediately asked Colonel Martin Bladen if he would undertake to demonstrate Britain's title to the province. Bladen said he would. "Then . . . by G—," said Walpole, "the Spaniards shall not have it."[59] Criticized by the Opposition, reproached by the public, and caricatured in the press, the minister was compelled to hearken to the national demand for Britain to stand firm by her alleged rights and not yield in any way.

The Ministry was to receive some rough treatment in Parliament and must have known it. Public feeling had been inflamed by a factious Opposition whose aim seems to have been to make a settlement impossible and a war inevitable, and by this means to procure Walpole's removal from power.[60] Sir William Wyndham, leader of the Opposition, denounced the convention as the most dishonourable treaty ever made by his country, contending that both Georgia and South Carolina were endangered by it and some, if not all, of the inhabitants faced with the prospect of losing their possessions, for, he said, "if we happen to be infected with the same complaisant humour when we conclude the definitive treaty, with which we seem to have been infected when we concluded the preliminary articles, I do not know but the whole, or a great part of South Carolina may be made a present for keeping the Spaniards in good humour. At least, some of the southern parts of Georgia must be given up; for it would have been ridiculous in us to refer the limits between the Spaniards and us in Florida to be settled by plenipotentiaries, if at the same time we had been resolved not to part with an inch of what we then pretended to."[61] This was the standpoint adopted by the Opposition throughout the debates in February and March. The convention, so the argument ran, was ignominious because it failed to prohibit the right of search and included an article casting doubt on Britain's right to Georgia.

Many celebrated figures joined in the attack on the Government—Carteret, Chesterfield, Argyll, and Bathurst in the Lords; Wyndham, Lord Gage, and William Pitt in the Commons. To Carteret, national honour was involved in the preservation of Georgia, for the title to it was manifest and it would be unjust to forsake those people who had emigrated thither trusting in the protection of the United Kingdom. "The nation," he said, "has been at immense charges in settling and supporting that colony; and should we now give it up, or even suffer our possession of it to be called in question, all Europe must look upon us, either as the most unjust, or most weak people under the sun." Although not definitely implying that it was the Government's fixed intention to surrender the colony, he went on, "it is ignominious to this nation, to suffer so much as her right of possession to be questioned. It is a prostitution of the public faith."[62] Chesterfield harped on the ingloriousness of the convention, while Bathurst likened it to a *carte blanche* offered to Quadra to write down whatever he pleased. The second article, said Bathurst, "was the same as if we had sat down to hazard, and had staked North Carolina, South Carolina, and Georgia, against the insignificant Spanish fort called Fort Augustine; for that is the only fort or settlement the Spaniards have in Florida."[63]

All the critics dwelt on the clause suspending defensive precautions in the disputed area, arguing that it benefited the Spaniards more than the English and left Georgia defenceless against attack from Havana or St. Augustine.[64] The only reason Lord Gage could see for this clause was that the Government, finding Spain disliked Georgia and not daring to give it to her by treaty, expected to be able to whisper to the Spanish ministers: "we are sorry we do not dare give it you up, but we will agree it shall be left defenceless, and then you may easily take it, and we not called to an account for it." This, he said, was not at all improbable considering the industry with which the Government had sought to retain Spanish goodwill.[65] Pitt described the convention as odious and fallacious: "nothing but a stipulation for national ignominy; an illustory expedient to baffle the resentment of the nation; a truce without a suspension of hostilities on the part of Spain; on the part of England, a suspension, as to Georgia, of the first law of nature, self-preservation and self-defence."[66] Much of the Opposition's argument was sophistic and unconvincing, but the vehemence of its delivery and the clamour in the country helped to make it effective.

The Government took a more responsible view of the situation, seeing the disputes about Georgia and the right of search in their wider contexts. The Family Compact of 1733 meant that a war with Spain might entail war also with France, who then appeared to be the most formidable Power in Europe.[67] In the Government's opinion the great virtue of the convention was that it held the door open for a peaceful settlement at a time when war might have brought disaster. This was the point made by Henry Pelham in the February debate on the Trustees' petition, when he rejected the charge that Spain's title to Georgia had been admitted: "we have agreed to hear what they have to say, for no other end but to convince them that there is not the least foundation for the claims they have lately set up; and this we have done out of charity to them, as well as out of regard to our own interest, in order to prevent an open rupture between two nations, whose mutual interest it is to live in mutual friendship."[68]

This point was amplified by Lord Hervey in the House of Lords at the beginning of March. He thought Britain had done well out of the convention. There was no question, he said, of discussing our right to Georgia; the dispute was only about its boundaries. The Spaniards, he admitted, "may perhaps pretend, that we have extended our settlements in Georgia too much towards the southward, and, by that means, have encroached upon their territories in Florida; . . . and if they should, our plenipotentiaries may refuse to treat with them upon such terms; for by this article they are laid under no obligation to do so."[69] Taking the debates as a whole, there would appear to have been less passion and more reason in the Government's than in the Opposition's cause, and in favouring at least an attempt at settlement by negotiation on the basis of the convention the Government was undoubtedly right and the Opposition certainly wrong.

The decisive debate took place in the Commons on Thursday, March 8. The importance attached to the subject is shown by the unusually large attendance, 497 members being present out of a total of 558.[70] Horace Walpole commenced on behalf of the Government at 11:30 in the morning and spoke for over two hours, giving a full explanation of the convention. The debate ended half an hour after midnight with a Government majority of twenty-eight. The following day brought more inflammatory speeches from members of the Opposition, some of whom, led by Pulteney and Wyndham, seceded from the House to mark their disapproval of ministerial policy. The division again gave the ministry a majority, 244 to 214, with the vote of old William Sloper, who had fallen asleep, being counted with the minority.[71]

A favourable Parliamentary vote, however, was not sufficient to allow the Ministry to follow its own line. The nation was exasperated with Spain, especially over the right of search. It was impossible for Walpole and Newcastle to disregard the unmistakable feeling of the country. Ministers were caricatured, Parliament was inundated with petitions against the terms of the convention, and the Prince of Wales led the shouting in the streets for revenge. Pamphleteers fulminated against the Government's failure to challenge the right of search, to exact redress for the severance of Captain Jenkins' ear, or to obtain Spain's disavowal of her claim to Georgia.[72] The agreement to refer these matters to plenipotentiaries was described as indefensible. The British title to Georgia, it was said, was based "in near an hundred years uninterrupted possession" and was better than any right founded on a thousand treaties. The stipulation for neither side to increase its fortifications was criticized on the score that it benefited the Spaniards who were planning to attack Georgia, whereas the English gained nothing because there was no intention of invading Florida.[73]

Although the Ministry had gradually to bow before this storm, it tried hard nevertheless to reach a settlement in the negotiations. Oglethorpe was instructed to observe the conditions laid down in the convention and not give Spain any reason for accusing Britain of bad faith.[74] At the same time extensive research was begun in order to compile a substantial rebuttal of Spanish claims. All the information collected in this way was not intended for use until absolutely necessary, as Britain was in actual possession of the disputed territory and the onus of establishing a title to it lay first on Spain: "For not only by the laws of England but by the general law of nations, it is incumbent upon him who is desirous to recover to show an undeniable right against all the world before the party in possession is obliged to produce his; for which reason, the calling for any papers in either House of Parliament relative to the title of Great Britain to the lands in question would be giving the adversary an advantage to which he is not entitled by any law, and which we ought carefully to avoid."[75] Consequently, Britain entered the negotiations in May 1739 on the defensive as regards the question of the boundaries and ownership of Georgia.

The prospects for a settlement at Madrid were not good.[76] The Spanish Government vacillated so much in its attitude towards Georgia that its unfortunate ambassador exasperated everyone in London, having to "talk backward and forward" as the tone of his instructions changed.[77] In Madrid the plenipotentiaries became more and more estranged. The South Sea Company would not yield to Spain and refused to pay the £68,000 it owed her. Quadra, in May, demanded the withdrawal of Haddock's squadron, which had recently received orders to remain at Gibraltar and not return to England as previously instructed. Walpole explained this to Geraldino as an essential precaution in face of the public hostility towards the Ministry stirred up by the Opposition.[78] In addition, the Spanish minister reasserted the right of search, revoked the *asiento,* and announced the intention to confiscate the South Sea Company's effects as indemnification for the £68,000 it owed.

War was now inevitable, but attempts at negotiation continued. Differences arose over the agenda. The English wanted to discuss navigation first, whereas the Spaniards said it would be impossible to reach any arrangement on that until "their favourite point" of Georgia's frontier had been decided. Keene and Castres were resolved not to give way, saying they would prefer to suspend the conferences "than to incur the reproach of having made our appearance there for no other purpose than to give the Spaniards an opportunity of trying whether Georgia is to be theirs or ours."[79] By the end of June the Spanish plenipotentiaries had become more audacious and were laying claim even to New Providence and all the Bahamas, thus transgressing the articles of the convention.[80]

Spain's refusal to pay the £95,000 stipulated in the convention provided a technical *casus belli,* if one had been needed. The reasons alleged for this noncompliance were the continuance of Haddock's squadron in the Mediterranean and the tardiness of the British Government in sending orders to Georgia to stop extending fortifications. The Spaniards complained, too, that "three men-of-war were sent upon frivolous pretexts to reinforce the squadron at Jamaica, and troops and ammunition were put on board several ships."[81] It was clear that Spain had no intention of paying, and not surprisingly, for she was short of money and war seemed imminent anyway. The deadlock was complete. Newcastle believed Spain had made an alliance with France, and so he could not afford to leave Gibraltar and Minorca defenceless by recalling Haddock's squadron. On the other hand, the Spaniards declared they could not guarantee peace so long as the squadron remained off their coast.[82]

The last chance of peaceful settlement had now disappeared. In June, Newcastle authorized colonial governors to grant letters of marque and reprisal to qualified applicants and ordered the British commissaries in Madrid to cease negotiating.[83] Events in the New World were moving as fast as in the Old. There was reason to believe that the Spaniards were seeking to incite the Indians in Georgia against the English.[84] Then, in September, the South Carolinians were provoked by Spanish policy. The Governor of St. Augustine had published a proclamation that all Negro slaves who escaped to him from the British plantations would be granted their freedom and given his protection. Several slaves from South Carolina had already availed themselves of this offer and the planters were beginning to fear they might lose most of their labour. Their resentment at Spanish policy flared up when, on September 9, 1739, some Negroes at Stono, less than twenty miles from Charleston, started a revolt that cost the lives of twenty-one white men and forty-four black, an insurrection which the South Carolinians attributed to Spanish intrigue and which they were determined should not go unavenged.[85]

With elements both in the colonies and in the mother-country agitating for war, and with diplomatic negotiations broken off, formal declaration of hostilities was merely a matter of time. Already, in July, Vice-Admiral Vernon had been despatched to attack Spanish settlements in the West Indies, and Keene was recalled from Madrid in August. Oglethorpe was ordered "to annoy" the Spaniards in Florida and put Georgia in a state of defence.[86] Finally, on October 19, the King's heralds at Temple Bar proclaimed that war had been declared. Three years of negotiation had failed to solve the differences between the two nations; the problems, not only of the Georgia boundaries but also of the *asiento,* right of search, and log-wood-cutting, were to be settled by force.

VI

‍❈❈❈❈❈❈

War with Spain (1739-1748)

‍❈❈❈❈❈❈

AT NOON ON WEDNESDAY, October 3, 1739, the magistrates and militia assembled at the court-house in Savannah to hear General James Oglethorpe announce that war had been declared between the mother-country and Spain. He assured them that effective measures had been taken to defend Georgia's frontiers and that the Government had promised to reinforce the frigates which were already cruising along the coast. Thereupon, "five cannon were fired and the militia gave three handsome vollies with their small-arms, as it were in defiance, without the appearance of any dread of the Spaniards."[1]

Hostilities between the rival settlements in Georgia and Florida were inevitable. It was, perhaps, inevitable also that the British Government should regard hostilities there as no more than a sideshow, of secondary importance to operations in Europe and especially to the prospects of plunder in the Caribbean, where the *guarda-costas* had committed their offences and where Englishmen, on the principle of making the punishment fit the crime, wished the war to be fought and won.

Georgia was a new colony, little understood, and remote from the real centres of conflict. The southern frontier, it is true, had received a fair proportion of the military expenditure wrung from a grudging Ministry during the recent years, mainly because of persistent appeals from South Carolina, Oglethorpe, and the Trustees, backed by frequent alarms of impending attack. In 1734 the annual cost of His Majesty's military establishment in South Carolina was £3,071 for one company of 115 men, out of a total expenditure of £38,837 on the American plantations as a whole.[2]

The foundation of Georgia drew more attention to defence requirements in its vicinity, especially as Spain's known antagonism towards Englishmen settling near Florida gave rise to easily-credited rumours and reports of imminent retaliation. Bands of Spaniards and Indians were often reported seen on the frontiers and in the woods, and as early as 1733 intelligence was received of a Spanish plan to descend on Georgia from Havana.[3] The need for protection became manifest, and in July 1735 the Trustees drew up a petition to the Crown for a quick delivery of ordnance stores in order that a new settlement they were about to make should be well fortified. This was referred by the Privy Council to the Board of Trade, which was disinclined to act and allowed it to languish for over twelve months, in spite of appeals from the Trustees.[4] Eventually, in December 1736, the Trustees were told that the long delay in answering the petition was due to the fact that they "had gone by bow and not by string" in applying direct to the King and not first to the Board. In any case, the Board's opinion was that ordnance should not be a separate charge but should be defrayed out of the money periodically granted by Parliament for the support of Georgia.[5]

The Government's neglect of the colony's defence in these years upset the Trustees, and they attributed it to the general assurance of peace then prevalent in Europe, which seemed to render any immediate attack on the southern provinces by French or Spaniards a very remote possibility.[6] The Trustees themselves, nevertheless, pressed ahead with security measures as best they could. In November 1735 they asked the Duke of Newcastle to recommend, "in the strongest terms," the Governor and Council of South Carolina to supply a number of Negroes for the construction of a fort on St. Simons Island in the mouth of the Altamaha.[7] Oglethorpe was sedulously preparing defences as efficiently as his means would permit, but direct Government assistance was patently necessary if the inhabitants were to feel safe. The year 1737 witnessed the real beginning of this assistance.

Early in February 1737 Walpole broached the subject of Georgia's security with Oglethorpe, who said that it would be difficult to form a regular militia in America: "that he could form about 300 men capable of bearing arms in Georgia, that South Carolina had money but no men, that North Carolina had men but no money; that Pennsylvania had both, and Virginia only money. That New England had men but no money, and New York had money and few men." In view of this he maintained that it would be cheaper and safer to establish a battalion of five hundred regulars in each province, to be paid for by the colonies themselves.[8] It was at this meeting that the proposal was made for Oglethorpe to take a military command in America, and in the June following he was formally commissioned General and Commander-in-Chief of all His Majesty's forces in South Carolina and Georgia.[9] Soon afterwards a regiment of six hundred men was ordered for the defence of Georgia, and was created by consigning to Oglethorpe all the effective privates of the Twenty-Fifth Foot.[10]

The first detachment sailed in January 1738 in three transports convoyed by the *Phoenix* under Captain Fanshawe.[11] Another detachment embarked at Portsmouth in June in five transports convoyed by the *Hector,* Captain Sir Yelverton Peyton, and the *Blandford,* and landed at the southern end of St. Simons Island on September 19, the *Hector* having parted company on approaching the Georgia coast and sailed for Virginia. These ships were under orders to remain and reinforce the squadron on the colonial coasts, the *Hector* at Virginia, the *Phoenix* at South Carolina, and the *Blandford* at Georgia.[12]

In May 1738 Oglethorpe was directed to discover what military preparations were being made at Havana and St. Augustine, to investigate enemy movements on the frontier, and to position his forces to give security to the settlers without giving umbrage to the Spaniards. He was also given some latitude for personal initiative in that if the Spaniards commenced hostilities he was to act in whatever manner he thought would best serve Britain's interests.[13] His situation was not a comfortable one in 1738. There was a strong suspicion that Spain had made an alliance with France for a joint invasion of the colonies in the event of a rupture with Britain, and the defences of Georgia were in a very poor condition, a circumstance which, in November, Oglethorpe bemoaned in a letter to Alderman Heathcote: "I am here in one of the most delightful situations as any man could wish to be. A great number of debts, empty magazines, no money to supply them, numbers of people to be fed, mutinous soldiers to command, a Spanish claim and a large body of their troops not far from us."[14]

The position at sea was rather better. Ships on the American station were allocated to protect a particular locality, but in the event of any one colony's being threatened they were to act together for its defence, a necessary principle of policy because to leave one or two ships scattered along the coast would be inviting their destruction at the hands of a superior enemy. Thus, on May 9,

1738, Captain Peyton of the *Hector* was instructed that, if he should learn of any design by the Spaniards to attack Georgia, the Bahamas "or any other of His Majesty's colonies thereabouts, you are to do your utmost to defend and protect the same, and to call to your assistance the *Sea Hope* from Virginia or any other of His Majesty's ships stationed in those parts, who are to act in conjunction with you for the preservation and security of the said places." All the other captains on the coast had similar instructions.[15]

In January 1738 a force of five ships under Commodore Charles Brown had been ordered for service on the Jamaica station with instructions not only to protect the trade in that area and observe French and Spanish movements but also to assist the other ships stationed on the American coast in defence of Georgia if that colony should be in danger of attack.[16] Soon after his arrival in the West Indies, Brown detached the *Torrington*, Captain Knight, to Havana in order to obtain intelligence of a suspended Spanish expedition against Georgia and of the condition and strength of the Spanish squadron. Knight learned that, although the expedition had been countermanded by an order from Madrid, three thousand men had been prepared for it and were to have been carried in flat-bottomed boats, "ridiculous things which could all be destroyed at sea by one ship of forty guns and one of twenty," and which were now being kept ready for another occasion.[17]

Oglethorpe himself deplored having to rely on ships stationed at Charleston, which lay at a considerably greater distance from the Florida-Georgia boundary than did St. Augustine. For this reason he made a request in September for the man-o'-war which had conveyed him over from England to be kept at Georgia. Captain Burrish, its commander, had already proved his worth "by standing directly to the southward up to very noses of the Spaniards, whilst all the others went into Charleston, where they generally stay." Oglethorpe reckoned that, in conjunction with Captain Gascoigne's ship already in the region, Burrish would be able to guard the province by sea and keep communications open.[18]

Nearly a year later the strength of Georgia's sea defences was given a fillip when, on June 11, 1739, the Admiralty issued orders to the commanders of the *Phoenix* (S. C.), the *Hector* (Va.), the *Flamborough* (N. Y.), the *Squirrel* (New England), the *Tartar* and the *Spence* sloop (Bahamas) that, in the event of an attack on Georgia, they were to endeavour "to protect the said settlements from any attempts that may be made on them, either by taking, sinking, burning or otherwise destroying the ships, vessels or boats which the Spaniards may employ thereon."[19] These orders were confirmed and emphasized in July, when the commanders of British ships stationed in American waters were directed to go to the assistance of South Carolina and Georgia "upon the least suspicion" of a Spanish attack. When Vice-Admiral Vernon was despatched to the West Indies to destroy enemy settlements and distress their shipping, his instructions included the shielding of the southern provinces should an attack be expected and the sending of "such ships as you shall think proper for the defence of those our possessions, and for taking and intercepting the Spanish ships, sloops or boats that may be sent from the Havana for that purpose."[20]

This, then, was the scene when, in October 1739, the Government instructed Oglethorpe to attack St. Augustine if he thought it practicable. Additional ordnance stores were sent him, and naval commanders on the American station were directed to assist him in the enterprise and prevent supplies from reaching St. Augustine from Havana.[21] The conquest of this outpost would clearly be of considerable value in the security of the southern colonies; the First Lord of the Admiralty believed that "if St. Augustine could be taken, it would be very great service to that part of the continent of America."[22] Nevertheless, in order to create an effective force Oglethorpe would be obliged to rely mainly on the resources locally available, for the British Government could not regard the capture of St. Augustine as anything more than a minor affair compared to the promise of plunder in the West Indies.

So it was that Oglethorpe wrote to Lieutenant-Governor Bull for support from South Carolina, and in March 1740 paid a fortnight's visit to Charleston to plead his case in person before a somewhat skeptical and none too generous legislature.[23] In England Oglethorpe's requirements were kept before the Government's notice by William Horton, one of his lieutenants from Georgia, but any additional naval protection for the colony was out of the question at this time, requests from Barbados, the Leeward Islands, and other parts having to be rejected by the Admiralty on account of the great need for small ships in home waters.[24] As regards land forces, however, it was decided in June to supplement Oglethorpe's regiment with a company of grenadiers and double the number of its subalterns.[25]

These reinforcements were promised too late to be of assistance in the attack on St. Augustine, for Oglethorpe had already begun to move forward into Florida. At the beginning of December 1739 a preliminary incursion was made to within a few miles of St. Augustine, primarily to test enemy strength and learn something about his preparations. Oglethorpe lacked, as yet, either the resources or the manpower to strike direct at St. Augustine, and was merely playing for time: "I am going to make another inroad," he told the Trustees, "and trust in God it will daunt them so that we shall have full time to fortify."[26]

This second incursion began in January 1740, and at daybreak on the 7th his Indian allies burnt the little wooden fort of Picolata which the Spaniards had abandoned; before sunset he reduced Fort St. Francis de Pupa on the opposite bank of the St. Johns River.[27] On May 10 Fort Diego, on the plains halfway between St. Augustine and the St. Johns, was captured and a garrison under Captain Dunbar placed in it to safeguard the line of retreat and preserve a communication with Georgia.[28] Oglethorpe then returned to the mouth of the river where he was joined by a South Carolina regiment under Colonel Vanderdussen and a Highland company under Captain McIntosh.

Meanwhile, the naval squadron at South Carolina was preparing to support the land forces. The *Squirrel*, Captain Peter Warren, was sent to St. Augustine in April, to be joined by the *Wolf*, Commander William Dandridge, at the end of the month, and in May by the *Hector*, Captain Peyton, and the *Spence*, Captain William Laws; and on June 1 the *Flamborough*, Captain Vincent Pearce, which had been lying in the St. Johns River cooperating with the advancing troops, joined the remainder of the squadron off the bar at St. Augustine.[29] On the mainland Oglethorpe now began the march into Florida in earnest, and on the night of June 4 his army arrived before the Spanish principal entrenchments on the western side of St. Augustine.

The ensuing demonstration against the Spanish stronghold has often been recounted by historians of Georgia, always using the same sources. There is little documentary material on the subject among the official records, and the almost complete absence of detailed reports from the War Office, Colonial Office, and Admiralty papers may be taken as an indication of the unconcern in that field of operations then evinced by the home authorities. Such documentary material as there is does not controvert the existing narratives or other original sources, and it would be idle here, therefore, to relate the action at length.[30]

By July 5, the besieging forces had become weary and disheartened in the intense heat of the summer sun, supplies were short, and with the hurricane season approaching the fleet could not risk remaining on that coast any longer; all hope of forcing the town to surrender had completely disappeared, and the siege was abandoned.

The failure can be attributed to insufficient support from the mother-country, but this must be qualified by surveying the campaign in its world setting. To Oglethorpe and the people of Georgia the capture of St. Augustine necessarily seemed of vital importance, but it would hardly have appeared so to the British Government in the summer of 1740. Admiral Vernon had to be supported, and the despatch of an auxiliary fleet under Rear-Admiral Sir Chaloner Ogle to join him in Jamaica sapped national resources considerably. Spain's empire in the Caribbean was an easy, glitteringly attractive prey, but it was essential to be selective and St. Augustine did not appear high on the list. A more lucrative prize was Cuba, the Pearl of the Antilles, or the port of Cartagena, the strongest place in Spanish America and the destruction of which would deal a crippling blow to the enemy's whole position in the New World.

Moreover, expenses were heavy, and it was only with difficulty that Anson's small squadron was fitted out in September 1740 for its expedition to the Pacific. The siege of a lonely Spanish outpost on the distant South Atlantic littoral was bound to receive scant attention in London, therefore, especially when its garrison had been described by the English local commander as weak, its inhabitants as mutinous, and its capture as a task comfortably within his competence.[31]

It was a tired, disappointed man, sick with fever, who drew his army back from before the walls of St. Augustine, but if Oglethorpe had failed in his primary objective he had at least succeeded in delaying Spanish preparations to attack Georgia. His policy now was obviously to strengthen Georgia's defences against a Spanish counter-attack, and for assistance in this he turned again to the mother-country.

On October 7, 1740, soon after the news of Oglethorpe's retreat reached London, the Admiralty ordered the officers in the American service "to be particularly attentive to the security of the province of South Carolina and the colony of Georgia, and at all times to give all the assistance in your power to the people of that province and colony against their enemies and particularly against the Spaniards at St. Augustine."[32] In April 1741 the Secretary at War agreed to the augmentation of Oglethorpe's regiment with a company of grenadiers.[33] This was encouraging, but something more definite was required if Georgia was to feel safe. In the spring of 1741 Oglethorpe told Walpole that the security of all the southern colonies depended on the preservation of Georgia, and asked the Duke of Newcastle for military supplies and some men-o'-war to guard the river and sea approaches.[34] The colony did not possess the resources to ensure its own protection, nor could it depend on its neighbours; it had to seek its support from the mother-country.

On October 5, 1741, a detailed paper containing proposals by Oglethorpe on the war in Florida and Georgia was presented to the Board of Trade by Harman Verelst, the Trustees' treasurer. In order to wage offensive and defensive campaigns, Oglethorpe demanded a battalion of land forces and a small train of artillery manned by gunners from Europe, money for winning alliances with the Indians and raising two troops of rangers and a Highland company, and ships for opposing the Spanish half-galleys and blocking the sea-entrances to St. Augustine.[35] These proposals were referred to a special committee for consideration, but in the meantime British ships stationed at South Carolina were to be ordered to cruise along the coast and prevent provisions reaching St. Augustine by sea.[36]

When the proposals were considered at the beginning of November they were found to be "couched in such general and uncertain terms as required much explanation," and although Verelst and officers recently arrived from Georgia were called upon to amplify them they were unable to add much in the way of precise detail, and the final report stated that this lack of full information made it difficult to recommend large reinforcements for Oglethorpe.[37] The Government had more important things to think about, and the Duke of Montagu admitted that to press the matter further would be of no more use than "speaking to the wind."[38] Oglethorpe was left in uncertainty, even having to write to Walpole personally for definite instructions on whether to maintain or reduce his forces: "For till I receive such orders I am in the greatest uncertainty," he lamented, "not daring to reduce them without orders since I know the consequence may be fatal to this part of His Majesty's dominions, and in continuing them being apprehensive that you would think the expense great and that there might be some misunderstanding which may be of very ill consequence to my own affairs."[39]

By June 1742 the Spanish attack on Georgia was imminent and still Oglethorpe was being left to his own initiative. The defences were unsound, he said bitterly, but it was now too late to ask again for reinforcements; before they arrived the issue would be decided: "I hope I shall behave as well as one with so few men and so little artillery can."[40]

It was natural that Oglethorpe and the inhabitants of Georgia should feel they were being cursorily treated by the home Government. The Spanish menace was very real to them. On the other hand, the campaign in the southern provinces was only one small part of the wider conflict which the Ministry had to consider. Maria Theresa was calling for British troops to protect the Austrian Netherlands against France. It was becoming obvious that the war could not be confined indefinitely to Spain and England but must eventually include the other European powers. Vernon's expeditions against Cartagena, Santiago de Cuba, and Panama had all failed or been abandoned, and the Government's interest in the American theatre of operations waned as the conflict with Spain merged into the War of the Austrian Succession.

The repulse of the Spanish invasion of Georgia in July 1742 was largely a personal triumph for Oglethorpe.[41] His success, however, did not lead him to underestimate the danger of renewed aggression by the Spaniards, perhaps in collusion with the French, and in February 1743 he sent Captain Dunbar to London in order to obtain assistance, "which if we have not, we must certainly perish."[42] "In the present situation I am in," he wrote, "I shall do the best I can, but have reason to apprehend the worst of consequences from the great numbers of the enemy if I have not timely support."[43] The Government was not convinced and would not accede to Oglethorpe's requests. The Privy Council, indeed, observed that large sums of money had already been issued to answer bills drawn by him, and that the expenses were "constantly going on, and justified by nothing but the evident danger of the colony." Oglethorpe was ordered, therefore, to reduce expenditure as much as possible as soon as that danger had been lessened or removed.[44] He continued to apply for supplies and reinforcements nonetheless, but without effect, until, his patience exhausted, he disclaimed any responsibility for what might happen as a result of the Ministry's attitude.[45]

But the Government was fully justified in its policy. It could not afford to waste money or troops on what was undeniably a minor aspect of the war. Oglethorpe said there was danger not only from Spaniards in Florida but also from the French moving in from the Mississippi. This may have been true; but it was true also (and Oglethorpe would not know this) that the danger in Europe was now from France no less than Spain. In October 1743 the Franco-Spanish alliance was tightened by the professedly imperishable Family Compact of Fontainebleau. The war now took on a new complexion, and the tremendous range over which hostilities were now to be conducted, and the important commitments Britain had all over the globe, made it inevitable that the plight of Georgia and South Carolina should have scant attention paid to it. The Government had to dispose its forces with some care. It had obligations in Hanover; it was bound to give support to Austria and Savoy;[46] it had to provide for a struggle with France that would stretch from the sunny waters of the Indian Ocean to the rugged backwoods of North America; and it had to beware lest Gibraltar, Minorca, and the Mediterranean fall under Bourbon domination. It is not surprising, therefore, that Georgia received niggardly treatment by the mother-country during the remainder of the conflict.[47]

By the autumn of 1743, when war with France was expected and plans had to be modified accordingly, the security of the colonies was considered and some recommendations made by the Privy Council,[48] but the constant question of expense limited whatever good intentions the Government had for American defence. There was a growing sense, in the Cabinet as well as in the country, that England was spending a disproportionate amount of men and money, so that it was a critical Government that contemplated the cost of protecting Georgia. Between 1738 and 1743 a total of £91,705 had been spent on the colony,[49] and since regular and exact returns of the men and supplies in the province could not be ascertained, the Government was sensibly reluctant to continue expenditure there. In 1747 Henry Fox, the Secretary at War, wrote firmly to Newcastle, the Secretary of State: "I am not, nor cannot be, answerable for the safety of Georgia, but I must beg leave still to be firmly of opinion that it would be extremely wrong to continue so great an expense for troops, boats, etc., on account of their supposed utility, without knowing whether or no there are such troops, boats, etc., employed."[50]

Fox was quite right, of course. Britain could not afford to waste money on defences of questionable utility. The country had experienced the Jacobite Rebellion and the disasters of 1745, a year of gloom relieved only by the capture of Louisbourg, the capital and port of Cape Breton. At that time it had seemed to the Earl of Chesterfield, Secretary of State and an advocate of peace, that "to carry on the war another year is evidently impossible, from our exhausted condition as to finances, from the universal disposition of the whole nation, and from the dangers to which we are exposed."[51]

Moreover, by 1745 movements for peace were beginning, and although peace did not come for over two years more, preparation and talk of it were afoot. The Dutch were anxious for a cessation of hostilities, and the Pensionary and the English ambassador at the Hague exchanged ideas on the subject.[52] The death of Philip V in 1746 shattered the ambitious power of Elizabeth Farnese in Spain, and his son and successor, Ferdinand VI, began almost at once to seek negotiation with Britain by way of Lisbon. In August 1746 Benjamin Keene was given full power to cross over from Portugal into Spain as soon as possible in order to negotiate on all matters that might conduce to restoring peace and renewing Anglo-Spanish friendship.[53] In the diplomatic exchanges of the ensuing eighteen months the problem of the Georgia-Florida frontier was practically ignored by the statesmen, for there is only very occasional mention of it in the correspondence of the period.[54] Consequently, there was no sign whatever of a proper solution to the problem when, in March 1748, a congress of the Powers was opened at Aix-la-Chapelle to arrange a peace settlement.

Nevertheless, the fact remained that the boundary of Georgia might be discussed at the Congress, and the Trustees were careful to bring the details of the situation before the Government in a thesis attempting to substantiate Britain's title to the Altamaha.[55] The Trustees need have had no fear. After several months of negotiation a treaty was signed in October which did little more than leave the real causes of dispute as they had been before the war.[56] Nothing was said about the boundaries of Georgia and Florida, and nothing about *guarda-costas* searching British ships suspected of smuggling. The *asiento* was renewed for four years in favour of British subjects, but in 1750 was finally abandoned for a money indemnity. The principle of reciprocal restoration of all conquests meant that Louisbourg was handed back to the French, and New England rendered insecure again. Indeed, so far as North America was concerned, the war had decided nothing. But it had revealed one very important fact; that, so far as Georgia was concerned, France was now the greater enemy. The main danger henceforward lay not from the Spaniards in Florida but from the Frenchmen and their Indian allies moving in from the region of the Mississippi.

VII

The French

THE MAP OF NORTH AMERICA in 1754 showed a long but narrow fringe of English colonies hugging the Atlantic coast from the Penobscot to the Altamaha. Westward English settlement died away as it reached the wooded ridges of the Appalachian Mountains, but further on the Frenchman was in Canada, in Louisiana, and along the Mississippi as far as the Illinois country, threatening to control the vast hinterland strip between Montreal in the north and New Orleans in the south. No recognized boundary existed between the French and English settlements, neither Power having ever defined its territorial claims. The charter of some of the English colonies, including that of Georgia, stated or inferred that their westward limit was the Pacific Ocean. On the other hand, France regarded as hers all the interior between the Appalachians and the Rocky Mountains, except the parts already occupied by Spain.

As each nation expanded its area of occupation, clashes inevitably occurred. As early as 1720 the danger of French possession of the Mississippi region had been broached by colonists, and Georgia and South Carolina were particularly concerned about the growth of Louisiana. In 1734 Sam Eveleigh wrote from Charleston: "I beg leave to give my opinion that His Majesty's settlements on this continent, particularly this province and the province of Georgia, ought at this time to be encouraged, because I am informed that the French increase very fast at New Orleans and are extending their limits by building forts; so that His Majesty's British empire in America is more than one half surrounded by the French from the mouth of the River Mississippi to the mouth of that of St. Lawrence."[1] In the same year the South Carolina Assembly alluded to the increase of French strength and traffic at New Orleans and their erection of forts up both sides of the Mississippi, some less than three hundred miles from the English settlements.[2]

These fears were mutual; the foundation of Georgia appeared to the French as the beginning of a westward English thrust in the south which might reach as far as the Mississippi and cut communication between Canada and Louisiana. From the French point of view there was the added consternation that the English population on the continent far exceeded their own, one and a quarter million massed along the coastline against only eighty thousand scattered over the vast stretch of territory from Canada to Louisiana.

The French had remained neutral during the early years of the Anglo-Spanish war after 1739, but when Britain and France became openly involved on opposite sides in the dynastic struggle in Europe, the conflict had unavoidably spread to the colonies. The main scene of Franco-British hostilities in America had been in the north, and the most signal event the fall of Louisbourg. Otherwise, apart from spasmodic raids and counter-raids with the help of the Indians, the war in America had been of little interest and of no lasting influence. Louisiana and Georgia were concerned hardly at all in the conflict, although Oglethorpe in London urged the Government to augment the forces in the southern colonies and assist allied Indians to attack the French on the Mississippi.[3] The Peace of Aix-la-Chapelle which formally ended the war in 1748 was generally regarded as no more than a truce, and during the succeeding seven years both Britain and France prepared for a renewal of the struggle.

France delayed her evacuation from the West Indies and kept control of St. Lucia, Dominica, Tobago, and St. Vincent in violation of an agreement made shortly after the treaty. The Nova Scotian boundary remained in dispute, no definitive limits were drawn for the southwest, and the French continued to erect a series of forts connecting Louisiana with Canada. In the summer of 1753 they erected two forts to the south of Lake Erie and threatened to occupy the valley of the Ohio. Having failed to expel them by a show of force, the Governor of Virginia built Fort Necessity at a place called Great Meadows on the western slopes of the Appalachians, only for it to be captured by an enemy force in July 1754. In the summer of 1755 an expedition under General Braddock set out against Fort Duquesne, the principal new French encroachment on the Ohio, but met defeat in a ravine eight miles from the objective. By the end of the year the French and Indian War in North America had begun in earnest.

The story of this war revolves primarily around the operations in Canada and the West Indies. The southern colonies were not prominent and have been generally omitted almost entirely from the standard accounts, for there were no large or arresting engagements in the south between the French and the English. The danger was always there nonetheless, together with the perilous possibility of Spain's renewing the Family Compact and, remotely perhaps, combining with the French to invade the southern provinces from Florida and the Mississippi.

Being the southernmost of the English continental colonies, Georgia was bound to feel exposed and very susceptible to attack. While admitting that Georgia had not produced benefits commensurate with the expense of its establishment, a writer in the *Gentleman's Magazine* in 1756 declared that the colony was still "thought of some consequence to the British interest, not so much for the value of what it may produce, as because it may serve as a southern frontier against any enterprise that may be formed by the French or Spaniards, if they should fortify themselves in Louisiana, as it is apparently their interest to do."[4]

Malachy Postlethwayt, a contemporary writer on economic affairs, attached great importance to Georgia as a barrier province and criticized the Government for not assisting it more: "When I have considered the colony of Georgia not only in the light of an important commercial one, but as a barrier against both France and Spain in this part of America, where our interests are so essentially concerned, I have frequently lamented that it has not been more zealously supported by Parliament. For what has been done, has been only by piecemeal and with great lukewarmness. . . . Before I leave this point, it will not be improper to observe, at this time of day, that as the colony of Georgia may and ought to be rendered a powerful barrier against both the French and Spaniards in Florida; does it not become the wisdom of the nation to support the settlement on this side no less than Nova Scotia and New York on the other? Is it not an indignation to the nation that it has been so meanly upheld and supported?"[5] This criticism, sound in principle, was too simple to be purely true, for large expenditure on colonial defence could not easily be incorporated into British policy at that time. Nevertheless, from the beginning of the war until the end a stream of jeremiads concerning its defencelessness flowed from the Governors of Georgia.

In 1755 Governor John Reynolds toured the southernmost areas and found Frederica, for long regarded as the main safeguard against Spanish invasion, with its twenty cannon spoilt by neglect and the town "in ruins, the fortifications entirely decayed and the houses falling down."[6] Not that the British Government had overlooked Georgia since the Peace of Aix-la-Chapelle. Three of the seven companies in Oglethorpe's regiment of Foot had been retained after the end of the war and stationed in South Carolina, and those members of the disbanded companies who were willing to stay in the colony were offered five pounds to do so and allowed to keep their arms in case they were needed.[7]

In a letter dated October 26, 1754, Sir Thomas Robinson, Secretary of State, acquainted Governor Reynolds that two regiments of Foot were to be sent to Virginia and another two were to be raised in the colonies themselves for their own defence, the cost of which was to be defrayed by the inhabitants. In reply the Georgia legislature maintained that if their abilities had been equal to their inclination they would not have been found wanting on this occasion, but, they said, "our present circumstances are unhappily such that we can contribute little or nothing either as to men or money, on the contrary, we should be ourselves in a most deplorable situation if this colony should be attacked by French or Indian enemies, unless His Majesty would be graciously pleased to afford us some troops for our relief and support."[8]

This argument was followed up by Reynolds at the close of the year when he asked the Board of Trade for a company of 150 regulars, since in his opinion the province was practically defenceless against neighbouring Indians, whom the French were inciting to attack it.[9] No answer was given until the following August, when Reynolds was told that the Crown could offer nothing on a general representation of the colony's vulnerability, but required precise details of what was necessary and the cost of every item.[10]

By this time Georgia's General Assembly had begun to make some provision for defence. In January 1755 it enacted that all males between the ages of sixteen and sixty who had been in the colony three months were to be enlisted, and regiments formed in every district; they could be mustered at any time, but not more than six times a year, and no one was obliged to go more than twelve miles from his home at ordinary musters.[11] This was considered as no more than an essential minimum, and did not mean that Georgia was prepared to do more than it need towards colonial defence. It could, in truth, have given very little, and in fact gave nothing. When, for example, the King asked for a contribution of men from the province in 1755 to help augment the regiments in North America to one thousand men each, the Governor and Council decided that none could be spared.[12] This was true. None could be spared, and in adopting this attitude Georgia was not being exceptional or selfish, for none of the southern colonies gave much support to Braddock's forces.

Georgia was militarily weak and its so-called forts or defensive works were of an order that would have moved a Vauban of two generations before to laughter. Had it not been for the presence of detachments from the South Carolinian Independent Companies in the forts among the Indians at the back of the province, Georgia's defence would have been negligible, for no reliance could be placed on the local militia. In December 1760 Governor James Wright estimated that only a quarter of the colony's military could be depended upon in a crisis, for the others "would run away into the next province out of danger."[13]

The constant theme of Georgia's relationship with the British Government throughout the war was the colony's defencelessness.[14] Both the outgoing Governor Reynolds and the incoming Lieutenant-Governor Henry Ellis warned the Government in 1756 of the deplorable condition of the fortifications. The only troops in Georgia were detachments of the Independent Company from South Carolina; stores and equipment were short, there was no artillery fit for service, the forts along the frontier were either dismantled or in ruins and the only one remaining was at Augusta, and even that was so rotten that a great part of it was "propped up to prevent its falling"; the eight small guns within the feeble embrasures of the fort were honeycombed with rust and mounted on carriages that were decayed, while in the ruins of Frederica twenty old cannon lay dismounted and without ammunition. The tiny population was scattered, only about 750 were capable of bearing arms, and these were enrolled in eight badly equipped and inefficiently trained companies of militia.[15]

In October 1756 Ellis discussed the matter with the Board of Trade and asked for a ship of war to protect the Georgia coast and for five hundred stands of arms with a proportionate quantity of powder and ball to be sent out immediately.[16] An order to this effect was made the following month, together with one for send-

ing to Georgia small-arms and ammunition worth £1,277, which
the Governor was to ensure would be kept in good order, preserved in a special storehouse so that none would be embezzled,
delivered to the inhabitants when needed, and returned to the
storehouse again immediately afterwards.[17] This was a sign that
the Government did not regard Georgia's defence as unimportant, at the beginning of the war at least, although the warship
requested was never sent and the arms sent out were not so valuable as they might have been, for they were heavy, clumsy, and
difficult to handle, and Ellis reckoned the danger would have to
be very great before the people would use them.[18]

The people, indeed, were far from satisfied with the colony's
condition. Something for defence was being done but to them it
did not seem very much. An Assembly committee investigated the
situation and in February 1757 reported that, apart from a small
battery recently erected at Savannah, there were but few guns
mounted in the province. Fortifications were in ruins, and the
wooden fort at Augusta whose decrepitude had appalled Reynolds
the year before was now so wretched that upon public occasions
the guns had to be removed before firing, "lest the shock should
bring down the whole fort."[19] In July 1757 the Assembly told the
Governor of its alarm at the colony's predicament, "without any
forts that are not utterly in ruins, or artillery but what are in a
manner unfit for service. Without magazines or funds to erect
them, without any troops stationed here save twenty odd rangers
(raised in the hurry of an alarm) yet unestablished, unpaid and
undisciplined, without any vessel of war for the protection of our
coast; with but few inhabitants, and those poor and widely dis-
persed over the province; open on the one side to every incursion
of Indians, and on the other exposed to every possible insult from
the most inconsiderable of the enemy's vessels."[20]

This alarm was accentuated by the appearance off the coast of
French privateers, for there was nothing to prevent the enemy from
landing and plundering the plantations along the rivers.[21] Royal
cruisers operating from Charleston had instructions to protect the
coasts of Georgia, but they did so only spasmodically and very
inefficiently, and French privateers sailed along the coasts with
impunity and captured nearly every vessel they met. Two such
privateers were able to cruise along the Georgia coast for ten
weeks unmolested, notwithstanding the presence at Charleston
throughout the time of three of the King's ships: "a strange cir-

cumstance," remarked Ellis bitterly. Indeed, he felt constrained
to fit out a ship himself in the summer of 1758 which, manned by
a crew of ninety and mounting a battery of fourteen carriage and
an equal number of swivel guns, was placed under the command
of experienced officers and kept cruising along the coast for six
weeks.[22] The general concern at the exposed situation of the
coastal settlements was stated in an address in June 1757 from the
Assembly to the Governor, asking him to station "alarm-men or
look-outs" on the sea coast, the expense of which the House would
defray as soon as possible.[23]

What justification was there for this feeling, a natural one,
that the colony was being left open to attack from the sea? Certainly the occasional patrol of cruisers from South Carolina could
not hope to prevent or discourage enemy raids or piracy, but to
have tried to do so would have required a degree of naval protection that was impossible to provide. The Admiralty could not
keep squadrons everywhere. The tendency of the English Government in the eighteenth century was to devote more naval strength
to the West Indies, where it was well situated both for raiding
and convoying. It is true that Georgia might well have been better
secured by detaching one, or perhaps two men-o'-war to protect
its coast, but it is difficult to admit that such a step would have
been justified by the degree of protection thus given. The squadron at Jamaica gave both Georgia and South Carolina more valuable assistance than this by cruising between Jamaica and Cuba
and in the channel between the west end of Cuba and Cape
Catoche, thus blockading the French at the mouth of the Mississippi and, by preventing the arrival there of troopships and
storeships, mitigating to some extent the danger of French and
Indian attack on the southern colonies. The menace from the sea
was no doubt very real to the inhabitants of Georgia, but it was
not so dangerous as they believed and was, in any case, one of the
inconveniences a border province has to accept in time of war.[24]

Since naval protection was neglected the inhabitants felt it more
essential than ever to have adequate land forces to assure them
their safety was being attended to. Rangers were the most suitable,
for in the event of Indian disturbances they were able to shoot
on horseback and ride at full speed in pursuit through the woods.[25]
In December 1756 Governor Reynolds had begun to raise some
rangers who were maintained for a time by means of negotiable
certificates which acquired credit from the notion that the Crown

would redeem them. In 1757 the Earl of Loudoun, then commanding the British forces in Canada, gave Ellis a credit for £850 drawn on the deputy-paymaster at New York in order to maintain the rangers until further orders. This credit was spent before the end of the year but Ellis had received no new orders,[26] and throughout 1758 the rangers subsisted on the private credit of the Governor, who naturally grew annoyed at what he could only interpret as indifference towards Georgia both by the commander-in-chief and by the British Government. He wrote several times during 1758 to General Abercromby, who succeeded Loudoun as commander-in-chief, but received no answer. By May he had been obliged to disband half the rangers, and he warned the Board of Trade that unless assistance was received soon he would have to disband the rest.[27]

This apparent neglect by the mother-country tended to bring the provincial government into contempt, and Ellis complained of having to "wink at many enormities" and being reduced to various shifts and expedients. "This sort of management may do for a season," he wrote, "but mankind are too penetrating to be long imposed upon even by the most refined policy."[28] Eventually the matter was brought to the notice of Pitt, who, in March 1759, instructed Amherst, then commanding the British troops in Canada, to make arrangements for the establishment of the Georgia rangers on a proper footing if he thought they were "materially conducive" to the colony's security.[29] Amherst thought they were, and at long last, in June 1759, Ellis was empowered to maintain his rangers and draw on the deputy-paymaster for their pay.[30] The Government's reluctance to give prompt attention to the case was inevitable under the circumstances. The principal fields of conflict were elsewhere and the situation in the south seemed quiet enough. In fact it is evidence of the Government's broad conception of the conflict that Georgia's needs were attended to as much as they were. Even during the glittering years of 1758 and 1759 money was spared for preserving some measure of security to the comparatively remote and tranquil little settlement in the far south.

By 1760 the result of the war in North America was already virtually decided, but the outbreak of hostilities with the Cherokees at the back of South Carolina made Georgia anxious again about its defences. The Governor had already made some precautionary redispositioning of his forces against the Cherokee danger,[31] and in April 1760 the Assembly passed two Acts for strengthening the defensive works in the province.[32] These measures were not sufficient of themselves to assure the inhabitants they were safe in Georgia, and many families began to move into other provinces, especially when some of the Creek Indians proved unreliable allies and joined the French and Cherokees in attacking the English. It was in these circumstances that Ellis wrote to the Board of Trade in the summer and autumn of 1760 expressing surprise that the southern colonies were allowed to continue exposed for so long and that his remonstrances had had so little effect. For three years he had acted on his own initiative and been rewarded with some success in ensuring the protection of the colony and sustaining the goodwill of the Creeks: "but now people start as from a dream, finding themselves encompassed with, and threatened by, such formidable tribes of merciless barbarians, whose friendship appears so little to be depended upon. And their apprehensions naturally increase when they observe their government unable, either from its own resources or the assistance afforded it by the mother-country, effectually to protect them."[33]

Governor James Wright reiterated his predecessor's entreaties for more military backing from the mother-country. The Governor's early reports of Georgia's weakness and his request for swivel guns and a proper quantity of shot received a peremptory reply from the Board of Trade at the beginning of 1761. The Board admitted that the defence of the province seemed inadequate but could not agree that the case of Georgia was comparable to that of Nova Scotia as a frontier province exposed to hostile attack, because, so far as military affairs were concerned, Georgia was part of South Carolina, which shared with it the same natural situation, the same dangers, and the same interests. Hence the troops in South Carolina were for the defence of both provinces, which in all such matters had to be considered together, "and the wants and defects of the one balanced by the strength and opulence of the other."[34]

This reply did not deter Wright from asking again for military supplies later in the year, nor the Assembly from resolving to apply to the British Government for £10,000, that being the estimated amount of expenses incurred by Georgia for its own defence during the war.[35] But it is obvious that by this time the Government was not inclined to bother itself with what appeared to be trivialities when the result of the conflict in North America had

already been decided and when negotiations for peace were on
foot in Europe. There was nothing ungracious about the Government's attitude, for Georgia simply did not seem important after
1760, and to have supported the southern colonies militarily would
have been fighting the war at one remove so far as the Government was concerned.

The significance of Georgia in the conflict with France, however, consisted of more than mere attempt at establishing its own
defensive system and pacifying the Indians; it consisted also of
occasional concern in the general management of the war in North
America, and this can only be brought out in its proper perspective by a brief chronological review of the campaign there.

The Earl of Loudoun arrived in America in July 1756 to take
command of an army that Pitt had described as a "scroll of paper."
He sent the Forty-Fourth Regiment under Webb to strengthen
Fort Oswego, but before Webb reached it the fort was captured
in August by the French under the vigilant Marquis de Montcalm.[36] This threw the British temporarily on the defensive, and
an attack by the French and Indians on the back of the more
southerly colonies was expected. Such a diversion had been anticipated as early as the autumn of 1755 but had not then been
deemed a real danger.[37] The danger can hardly have been much
greater twelve months later, but Loudoun, nevertheless, instructed
the Governor of Georgia to put his frontiers in a good state of
defence, as he himself could do no more with the troops at his
command than resist attack.

Since no assistance could be expected from Loudoun, the Governor posted the troops at his disposal as best he could, and detachments were ordered to scout on the line south from Ebenezer
through the old fort of Argyll, where the main body of the rangers
was stationed, to the Altamaha.[38] This was as much as could then
be done, but it is doubtful whether it would have been adequate
if the anticipated attack had occurred. Loudoun was, in fact, near
the truth in predicting such an attack, for the Governor of Louisiana, Louis Billonart de Kerlerec, strove throughout the early
years of the conflict to organize an onslaught on Georgia and
South Carolina by southern Indians, the Chickasaws excepted, in
order not only to damage those provinces but also to relieve the
pressure on the French in Canada. Fortunately for the English,
however, the many difficulties involved, not the least being the
French Government's desire to economize in Louisiana, prevented
an attack in this early critical period of the war.[39]

It is evident that the attention of the British Government was not focused solely on Canada and the northern colonies at this time, for among the Duke of Newcastle's paper is a plan for the protection of Georgia and South Carolina. This points out that it may be assumed that the recent reinforcements sent to Louisiana presage an attack the next winter: "Therefore no time ought to be lost to secure our provinces against such a formidable force, destined for their destruction." Georgia has a very tiny fighting force and its small population is widely distributed: "So that this province may be overrun with as much ease by the force Louisiana can spare, as a troop might pass over Hounslow Heath at present." The protection of the southern colonies will cost nearly as much as would an invasion of Louisiana by the English, and so it would be good policy to attack now and make its conquest "morally certain" this winter. The number of men required would not be large, and the militia and Indians of South Carolina could be supplemented with men from North Carolina, Virginia, and Maryland.[40]

It was a commendable scheme, and in some ways even a realistic one, but it was not a practicable one in 1756, while 1757 was another year of gloom for Britain, with the abandonment of the contemplated attack on Louisbourg and the loss of Fort William Henry. But however extensive Britain's commitments, some precautions against a French inroad from the direction of the Mississippi were recognized as advisable. In February 1757 Loudoun was ordered to send a battalion of regulars to Virginia at once for the defence of the southern colonies. At the end of March a Highland battalion of Foot (about a thousand strong) under Lieutenant-Colonel Archibald Montgomery was ordered to be embarked at Cork for Charleston, where it was to act under Loudoun's orders and cooperate with Governor Lyttelton of South Carolina for colonial defence.[41]

At a meeting in Philadelphia begun on March 15 and continued by several adjournments to the 24th, Loudoun and the Governors of North Carolina, Virginia, Maryland, and Pennsylvania agreed that there ought to be two thousand men for the defence of South Carolina and Georgia in the event of aggression by the French or Indians, and of this number five hundred should be regulars and the remainder provided by South Carolina, North Carolina, Virginia, and Pennsylvania. These troops were to be placed under the command of Lieutenant-Colonel Henry Bouquet and transported as soon as possible at the expense of their respective provinces to

Charleston in South Carolina, where the cost of their provisions would be met by the Crown.[42]

In June, however, Loudoun complained to Pitt of the southern colonies' failure to raise the number of men they had promised, as a result of which Georgia remained weak and unable to resist attack. Bouquet had been ordered to give Georgia as much support as possible, but he was stationed too far away to do anything material, and the danger of sudden attack on Georgia was such that, in July, the Governor obtained the Council's approval to the distribution of some arms and ammunition to various officers of militia in the country.[43] Loudoun was aware of the colony's importance inasmuch as "its being in the enemy's hands would have very bad effect on the neighbouring provinces," and so ordered the Governor an advance of money to maintain the rangers there. This was justified, he wrote, because it seemed to him that Georgia was in danger of being captured by the French, and "it would be much less expense to the Government to support it than to retake it when lost."[44] Later a company of Virginians was detached to Savannah but withdrawn again before the end of the year, and no replacement was sent because the Georgia government was not prepared to shoulder the expense of troops stationed in the province.[45]

By 1758 the danger to Georgia seemed to have receded, and the initiative was passing to the English. Pitt's plan of campaign in America involved a comprehensive assault on the entire French position between Quebec and New Orleans, and was to follow three main directions. First, an attempt was to be made to recover the valley of the Ohio and sever French communications by reducing Fort Duquesne. Second, an expedition was to attack Canada from the south and penetrate as far as possible towards Montreal and Quebec. Third, a fleet was to cooperate with a land force in a renewal of the attack on Louisbourg. This last was most important. If Louisbourg was captured early enough in the year an immediate attack was to be made on Quebec by way of the St. Lawrence; but if the season was well advanced then attention was to be turned "upon the forts and places lying on the River Mobile as well as those on the Mississippi." And in any case, Brigadier-General John Forbes was to repair to one of the southern provinces in order to concert "any such offensive operations as may be judged by him most expedient for annoying the enemy, and most efficacious towards removing and repelling the dangers that threaten the frontiers of any of the southern colonies on the continent of America."[46]

Preparations for a campaign in the south were begun. In January Pitt gave instructions for General Amherst and Admiral Boscawen to be supplied with relevant information about the southern coasts of America, the forts on the Mobile and Mississippi, and the practicability of an attempt being made on them later in the year by troops sent from Halifax by sea.[47] But it was Pitt's policy to concentrate on one objective at a time, and the first preoccupation of 1758 was the campaign in Canada.

The paramount question was not whether Louisbourg would fall (that was not doubted by either side) but whether it would fall in time for the British to move against Quebec. When the fortress capitulated on July 26, Amherst and General Wolfe thought there was still time to strike at Quebec, but Boscawen hesitated, and the matter was decided for them by the arrival of the news of Montcalm's murderous repulse of Abercromby at Ticonderoga and the death of Lord Howe. The situation was not materially altered either by the seizure of Fort Frontenac in August by a supplementary force under Colonel Bradstreet, which cut off Canada from the French southwest, or by the enemy's abandonment of Fort Duquesne in November before the advance of Forbes's expedition, which ended the menace in western Pennsylvania.[48] Amherst and Wolfe realized that the scheme to move on Quebec was now impracticable, for it was necessary to send six battalions to join Abercromby as he retreated through the woods. This, with the despatch of three battalions to the St. Lawrence and two to the Bay of Fundy, they regarded as a better plan than the idea of attacking French settlements along the Mobile and Mississippi. Consequently, no operations could be undertaken that year against the enemy at the back of the southern colonies.[49]

At the beginning of 1759 Pitt's schemes for North America struck a new note. Hitherto the idea of a general onslaught on, and conquest of, the whole French empire in America had not been considered practical policy by English statesmen. Their central motive had not extended beyond the establishment of British domination there. Henceforward the conquest of all French possessions in Canada, Louisiana, and the West Indies became part of Pitt's determined policy. The importance of destroying French encroachments in the south and counteracting their influence with the Indians was recognized, and in February Pitt ordered Amherst

to consult with Admiral Saunders about an enterprise against the
French on the Mobile and the Mississippi towards the end of
the year.[50]

Prospects for success were good, for the French position was
very weak in 1759. Montcalm did not neglect the offensive element
necessary in a good defence, and he recommended raids on the
coasts of the southern colonies as a means of relieving pressure in
Canada. The French Government approved of this but could not
agree to it because of lack of money; nevertheless, a foothold was
to be kept in Canada even if it meant concentrating the forces
there into the narrowest limits.[51] Although an attack by the French
was out of the question, for they lacked both the money and the
troops, the Governor of Georgia nevertheless managed to persuade
his commander-in-chief that the colony's security required more
troops, and in October he was empowered to augment his forces.[52]
They were not required. Quebec, Ticonderoga, Fort Niagara, and
Guadeloupe all fell to the British, and the French hold on Canada
was nearly extinguished.

Notwithstanding these overwhelming victories, Pitt pressed energetically forward with preparations for the campaign of 1760.
The conquest of Canada would be "little more than a military
promenade,"[53] but the conquest of Louisiana might be a necessary
supplement to it. The possibilities were explored by Governor
Ellis in a letter to Pitt in April 1760. He suggested an expedition
against the enemy fort at Mobile, which, if captured, would lead
inevitably to the fall of other forts held by the French, and their
influence among the Indians at the back of Georgia would be
destroyed. "It may be objected," wrote Ellis, "that such a conquest
amongst the Spanish settlements would give umbrage to Spain,
which might happen, yet I am persuaded it would be our interest
to make it, even were we to yield it to the Spaniards afterwards,
who are less dangerous and in every view more eligible neighbours
than the French."[54] This opinion was supported by Governor
Arthur Dobbs of North Carolina when he heard that the French
had incited the Cherokees to attack Georgia and South Carolina. This, he told Pitt, was proof of the necessity to drive the
French out of Louisiana: "and in case the Spaniards should take
umbrage at our increase of power in their neighbourhood, and it
may be prudent at present not to have any brangles with them,
would it not be better to have that settlement entirely vacated by
both, or even given up to the Spaniards, than allow it to remain

in the hands of the French."[55] Although the war in Canada was
won before the end of 1760 there was a body of opinion in England, too, which believed that neither Virginia, the Carolinas, nor
Georgia would be safe while the French remained along the
Mississippi.[56]

These observers grossly over-stated the French danger to the
southern colonies, of course, but Pitt was not altogether unmind-
ful of the importance of the situation, and in October 1760 he
instructed Amherst to acquire information about French strength
in Louisiana, expressing the hope that some forces might be spared
for use there.[57] It must be remembered that a principle of British
policy at this time was to avoid any move that might antagonize
Spain, and since an attack on Louisiana would bring the English
near to the Gulf of Mexico, an eventuality to which the Spanish
Government was emphatically opposed, it is very probable that
the idea was never pressed with urgency. There was, moreover,
animosity in the Cabinet between Pitt and Newcastle and his
friends, the latter being fearful and jealous of their irascible col-
league.[58] Newcastle was also experiencing difficulties with the national finances, and it was doubtful whether the Cabinet would
consent to spend money on an unexciting and seemingly unessen-
tial campaign in the sunset regions of Georgia and South Carolina.

In fact, the danger to Georgia lay, if anywhere, with the Indians
only; the French menace was negligible. By 1760 France was in
a deplorable condition internally, her treasury bankrupt, her navy
destroyed, and she was quite unable to reinforce Louisiana. Hence,
when Governor Wright's entreaties for assistance were rejected in
1761 and 1762 the British Government was taking a realistic, if
not encouraging, line. It was true that the French at Forts Alabama and Mobile were believed to be attempting to provoke the
Creeks against the English in Georgia,[59] but that was hardly sufficiently injurious to warrant extra expense by a country that had
already spent enormous sums on a war that was now entering its
concluding phase. In 1762 the Government did intend for the
army that captured Havana to move on and attack New Orleans,
but the idea faded out.[60]

After Amherst's triumph at Montreal in September 1760 the
conflict behind the southern colonies diminished even further in
significance. The Government was watching affairs in Europe,
negotiations for peace were opened, and, most important of all,
divisions within the Ministry widened in 1760 and 1761. Prose-

cution of the war slackened as Pitt's influence waned, and in October 1761 he resigned. George III had come to the throne twelve months before, the Earl of Bute became the principal minister, and all promise that Georgia and the southern colonies would be relieved of the French menace by military or naval action disappeared; relief was to be finally accomplished in the peace treaty signed in 1763 after nearly four years of negotiation.

The arrangement of a peace had been broached as early as 1759. In that year Choiseul, the chief minister of Louis XV, induced Spain to mediate between France and Britain, and soon after the fall of Quebec the Spanish ambassador in London raised the subject to Pitt, who, however, insisted on Prussian participation in any negotiations, and by May 1760 the attempt at a bipartite settlement had failed. Nevertheless, the peace party in the Cabinet was growing stronger, and by 1761 included not only Newcastle but also Bedford, Hardwicke, and the military and naval advisers.[61] Speculation by English statesmen at this time on possible peace terms approached the North American question under three main headings: Canada, Louisiana, and the Newfoundland fishery. Louisiana, it was noted, had received less attention than Canada, "but ought nevertheless to be insisted on to make a part of the British dominions together with all the rivers that the French possessed or occupied in the Gulf of Mexico." And one of the reasons why the French should be dispossessed of Louisiana was that it enabled them to encroach on Georgia and South Carolina and keep the Indians along the borders in continual war with the inhabitants.[62] This was one of the principles of policy taken into the discussions which began when both countries exchanged plenipotentiaries in the summer of 1761, Stanley going to Paris and Bussy coming to London.

The French met the English views in many particulars, but they resolutely insisted on the retention of Cape Breton and a share in the Newfoundland fisheries, and drew an arbitrary line round Canada and the English colonies which was to serve as the basis of the limits of Louisiana.[63] This delineation of Louisiana was rejected by the British Government, which asserted that it would never admit the boundaries of Louisiana to extend to the confines of Virginia or of the other British possessions in the Ohio region.[64] The French Government, for its part, reaffirmed its fishing rights and demanded that the Indian tribes in the hinterland between Canada and Louisiana should be formed into a neutral barrier between the two nations.[65]

The negotiations continued in this vein during the winter of 1761-2. So far as Georgia was concerned the principal matter was that relating to Louisiana. The removal of the French from their threatening position along the Mississippi had been in the minds of the Georgia government throughout the war years, and since the scheme of a military expedition to eject them had never materialized it was natural to hope that the objective would be achieved in the peace settlement. The British Government was clearly determined that the French menace should be dispelled from the south by negotiation as it had been dispelled from Canada by conquest, but in 1762 another factor arose to complicate the issue. Spain was France's partner and was bound to take notice of territorial readjustments in an area where she had important interests, especially in the Gulf of Mexico;[66] the Florida region, too, was still of strategic significance, and in 1762 came into the peace discussions.

In May 1762 Choiseul insisted on the retention of Martinique and St. Lucia but offered to surrender the territory east of the Mississippi which, he pointed out, would not only give Britain a large territorial acquisition but would also place Louisiana and Florida in absolute dependence on the English colonies. Choiseul's offer, indeed, would have isolated Florida and given Britain a foothold on the Gulf of Mexico; this the Spanish Government would not concede, and countered by reviving its ancient claims both to Louisiana and to Georgia, and, fearful for the safety of Florida, suggested the erection of a neutral zone in the country between South Carolina and the Gulf.[67] This was the situation when the British commissioner, the Duke of Bedford, arrived in Paris in September to participate in the discussions.

Bedford had been instructed by the Government to take particular care over the definition of the Mississippi boundary,[68] but when he submitted proposals for the line of demarcation between the British colonies and Louisiana the Spanish negotiator protested that although his Government was prepared to relinquish its claims to Georgia and accept an equitable adjustment of the Florida frontier, it had a just title to Louisiana. The complexion of the whole affair was changed, however, by the fall of the Spanish stronghold of Havana, the news of which reached England at the end of September and "turned the heads of the wisest men"; it was generally affirmed in England that "this rich acquisition" must not be ceded without adequate material compensation.[69] "The nation in general," it was said, "will expect something very advantageous in the future treaty with Spain, in exchange for such a conquest; and it is well, if the old cry of Take and Hold is not revived on the occasion."[70]

Consequently, Britain stiffened her terms and stipulated that the price of the restoration of Cuba to Spain was the cession of Porto Rico or Florida.[71] Cuba was naturally more precious to Spain than was Florida, but she was reluctant to cede either, and to relieve her ally France offered Britain the land to the west as well as to the east of the Mississippi if Spain should be permitted to retain her possessions. Britain, preferring Florida, rejected the offer.[72] In thus standing firm for Florida the British Government was acting in the best interests of Georgia, for with the acquisition of the territory east of the Mississippi the French menace would be virtually destroyed in any case, and the dispossession of the Spaniards in Florida would remove whatever potential threat remained to Georgia's southern frontier.

The outcome proved more beneficial to Georgia than could have been anticipated. Neither France nor Spain regarded Louisiana as of any particular advantage, and when Britain refused it France handed it over to Spain with an alacrity matching the chagrin of the recipient, to whom its only value was that it would enable her to maintain a closer watch on English approaches to her treasure colonies.[73] On November 3, the same day as the preliminaries of peace were signed at Fontainebleau, the French king ceded to Spain that part of Louisiana west of the new British boundary. Spain accepted because she considered the loss of Florida less harmful than the acquisition by the English of the whole of Louisiana, which would enable them to smuggle into Mexico. This private transaction was not mentioned in the final treaty of peace signed on the evening of February 10, 1763.[74]

Georgia had never been prominent in the minds of the negotiators, but by virtue of the diplomatic exchanges over Louisiana, Florida, and the Mississippi the colony indirectly obtained substantial benefits in the definitive peace. By article 7 the limits of French possessions in North America were "fixed irrevocably by a line drawn along the middle of the River Mississippi from its source to the River Iberville, and from thence by a line drawn along the middle of this river and the Lakes Maurepas and Pontchartrain to the sea." France ceded Canada, Nova Scotia, Cape Breton, and all Louisiana east of the Mississippi except the island on which New Orleans was situated. By article 20 Spain ceded to Britain "Florida, with Fort St. Augustine and the Bay of Pensacola, as well as all that Spain possesses on the continent of North America to the east, or to the south-east, of the River Mississippi."

The treaty had a mixed reception in England. Many thought Britain had not taken sufficient advantage of her victories; Pitt said France had been treated too leniently and British interests sacrificed. Florida was considered a poor exchange for the conquest of Havana, Alderman Beckford comparing it to Bagshot Heath for barrenness,[75] while the Earl of Egremont, Secretary of State, admitted its "manifest inferiority."[76] But some concessions had to be made if peace was to be attained and the English ministers were more interested in other matters relating to Spain, such as renewal of commercial treaties and the maintenance of the right to cut logwood in the Gulf of Mexico.

In Georgia itself the people were relieved not only because the threat from the south had been dislodged but also because the menace in the west had been considerably lessened by the substitution of Spanish for French control, it being confidently predicted that the Spaniards would prove "more advantageous and less turbulent neighbours" than the French had been there.[77] All the colonies benefited from the peace, from the recession of the Spanish rival, the fall of French power in America, and from the resulting diminution of the Indian peril, and Georgia, as an exposed, immature, and weak frontier province benefited more than most.

In a sense, Georgia gained more from the peace treaty than its part in the war seemed to justify, for the colony had never been prominent. In the early years of the conflict, it is true, the need to protect the colony had not escaped the notice of the mother-country or the other provinces, and during the principal campaigns in Canada and elsewhere some provision was made for the security of the south. From almost the beginning of the war schemes had been entertained of relieving the colony at its back by attacking the enemy in Louisiana. Pitt seems to have kept the idea in mind and broached the subject every year. The French appreciated the advantage to be gained from inciting the Indians to make diversionary raids in the back-settlements, and on one or two occasions bodies of English troops were detached from the northern stations to defend Georgia. If the colony cannot be said to have ever occupied a prominent place in the counsels of the Government, it was not ignored, and by Pitt, in fact, appears at times to have received considerable attention. Therefore, although it is not difficult to understand why Georgia and the southern colonies have necessarily received only perfunctory treatment in accounts of the conflict,[78] it should be remembered that Georgia was the southern outpost of the English colonies in America throughout the Seven Years' War, and as such was not altogether unimportant strategically, a fact occasionally recognized by Pitt, the military commanders, and the colonial governors. The ever-expected attack did not materialize, but the menace was always present.

VIII

❧❧❧❧❧❧

The Indians

❧❧❧❧❧❧

A VITAL FACTOR for Georgia in the Anglo-French rivalry was the attitude of the Indians. It was always axiomatic that the French could not hope to launch a successful overland attack on the English colonies without the support of a large Indian force, and the result was bitter competition between the two European nations for Indian friendship as well as Indian trade. The Appalachian range was not an insurmountable barrier to the English colonists, and in the eighteenth century settlers and traders from Pennsylvania, Virginia, and the Carolinas were beginning to venture through the passes of the mountains, beyond which the way was clear to the Ohio, a movement which intensified the Anglo-French struggle for control of the southwest trade.

At the middle of the eighteenth century there were about twelve thousand male Indians in and around the southern colonies. Of these about 2,500 were Cherokees, living among the mountains and valleys of what became Tennessee and northern Alabama, who came into close contact with Georgia and South Carolina and were largely under British influence. Westward of them and nearer the Mississippi roamed the Chickasaws, who had been allies of the English since before the foundation of Louisiana. South of the Chickasaws were the Choctaws, a powerful tribe with some five thousand warriors and who, before 1756, were amenable to French influence. East of the Chickasaws and Choctaws was the Creek confederacy of many diverse tribes, whose territory stretched from the River Alabama on the west to the Ogeechee on the east and included the valleys of the Chattahoochee and the Flint and most of the Florida peninsula. The Creeks, Chickasaws, Choctaws, and Cherokees were the principal nations to which attention had to be paid in the south. The Catawbas, settled on the river of that name between the Carolinas, had only about three hundred fighting men but were valuable to the English in protecting South Carolina and the southern frontier. Finally, there were the wandering Shawnees, strategically situated on the headwaters of the River Coosa between the Cherokees and the Upper Creeks, who proved of some embarrassment to the English in the war with France.

Right from Georgia's inception it had been realized that sound policy demanded the reconciling of the Indians to English intrusion upon their lands, the gaining of their cooperation in commerce and the winning of their alliance against the French and Spaniards. Even before the beginnings of settlement, those concerned in the project had resolved that the Indians should "upon all occasions be treated with the strictest justice and utmost humanity."[1] Thus, attempts were made to restrict the interior traffic in rum, which the Indians often drank to stupefaction, causing trouble with the English traders and jeopardizing the establishment of the good relations so essential to an inchoate colony like Georgia, which could obviously not sustain a war on its frontiers. The Trustees always recognized the Indians as the original owners of the land and made no settlement without their consent, a policy which brought immediate and lasting success.

Soon after the landing of the first settlers, Oglethorpe negotiated with representatives of the neighbouring tribes of the Creek nation, and on May 21, 1733, a treaty was made. In return for a guarantee that compensation would always be paid for injuries done to them by merchants, the Creeks agreed to allow the inhabitants of Georgia to trade in their towns, goods being sold at rates fixed by mutual consent. In addition they ceded to the English all lands in the tidewater region which they themselves did not require, retaining only the islands of Ossabaw, Sapelo, and St. Catherines for bathing, hunting, and fishing, and a small tract lying above Yamacraw Bluff on the south bank of the river which was reserved as a place of encampment for whenever they wished to visit Savannah. They also agreed to have no more communication with the French or Spaniards and not to molest the settlers, and promised to observe the treaty "as long as the sun shall shine or the waters run into the rivers."[2] This treaty resulted in the pacification of all the tribes comprising the Lower Creek nation and enabled the new colony to extend itself up the Savannah and along the coast without hindrance; opposition in the early years was negligible, therefore, and one of the first settlers relates how in the woods he was always more fearful of rattlesnakes than of Indians.[3]

This good beginning was reinforced by the visit to England in 1734 of the aged Tomochichi and other chieftains of a small group of the Creek nation living at Yamacraw on the south bank of the Savannah, whose friendship for the English was deepened by the treatment accorded them throughout the visit. The King received them at Kensington and the Archbishop of Canterbury spoke with them at Lambeth Palace; they were taken to Eton, Windsor, Greenwich, and Hampton Court, lavished with gifts and mementos, and Tomochichi's portrait was painted and hung in the Trustees' office in London.[4] The Trustees promised to "endeavour to cement a strict alliance and friendship with you, your children shall be ours and ours shall be yours, and we are all under one God, Who will punish any who are guilty of breach of faith"; the mutual hope was expressed that the two peoples would always live peacefully together in Georgia.[5]

The climax of Anglo-Indian friendship in Georgia during Oglethorpe's residence was the ten-day conference held in August 1739 at Coweta, the principal town of the Lower Creeks, situated on the Chattahoochee. Accompanied by a few soldiers and servants Oglethorpe journeyed nearly three hundred miles through a trackless wilderness of morasses, thickets, and forests of pine to attend a great council of the tribes, with whom he feasted on fowls, beef, pork, venison, and many kinds of fruit, smoked the calumet of peace, and drank the sacred black medicine reserved for important people and special occasions.

Amid splendour and luxury Oglethorpe negotiated with sachems of the Creek, Cherokee, and Chickasaw nations, and on August 21 reached agreement on the regulation of trade, preservation of peace, and confirmation of the Trustees' title to the lands between the Savannah, the Ogeechee, and the St. Johns. The Creeks continued to hold the sea islands of Ossabaw, Sapelo, and St. Catherines, and the small strip of territory from Pipemakers Bluff to Savannah, while Oglethorpe promised that the English would neither appropriate any lands other than those ceded to the Trustees nor encroach on those reserved to the Indians.[6] The outcome of the conference was a triumph for Oglethorpe, a sick man at the time, in establishing a friendly understanding with the Indians when war with Spain was imminent and France, as always, was watching for an opportunity to embarrass her rivals in the New World.

It was not only with foreigners, however, that Indian troubles were encountered, for trade in the interior necessarily brought competing merchants from different colonies into contact and often into conflict also. Goods brought from Europe were received at Charleston and Savannah, sold to storekeepers in the interior towns, bought again by traders, conveyed on pack-horses into Indian country and there exchanged for skins and furs. In this way new territory was explored, for the traders had to travel many miles in advance of regular settlement, and the profits obtained provided capital for agricultural expansion. On all the frontiers southward from Pennsylvania the Indian trade became important, and differences over it arose between Virginia and South Carolina, and, later, between South Carolina and Georgia.

The origins of the differences between South Carolina and Georgia may be traced to the visit to England in 1734 of Tomochichi and the Indians of Yamacraw. Before returning to America, Tomochichi had asked for the Indian trade to be properly regulated because traders had demanded exorbitant prices for their goods and defrauded the Indians over weights and measures, thereby causing animosities and quarrels which frequently ended in bloodshed. The Trustees complied by preparing an Act expressly designed to maintain peace with the Indians. It was similar in form and content to one passed in South Carolina in 1731 which would, in fact, have been in force in the Georgia territory had it not been erected into a separate province; the Georgia Act differed only in that the Trustees excluded all traders not licensed by their authority from operating in the province. After June 24, 1735, any person without a license trading with the Indians in Georgia was to be fined £100 for each offence. Those merchants who did take out licences were to renew them annually and enter into a bond with the Trustees to the sum of £100 as a guarantee of good behaviour; they were to have their conduct supervised by commissioners, who were authorized to hear complaints from the Indians and arrange compensation for any injuries done to them. Supervision by commissioners was a sensible precaution because the Indians always demanded atonement or retribution for wrongs committed against them and were not particular about the identity of their victim if the true culprits could not be found.[7] This law was in no way remarkable, and its enactment was in line with the policies of the other colonies which had long ago recognized the need to regulate trade with the Indians.

On October 7, 1735, the Trustees wrote to the Duke of Newcastle asking him to inform the Lieutenant-Governor of South Carolina that the Act was ratified.[8] The request was a formal one and may have been due simply to the Trustees' sense of propriety, but it is also likely that they were already apprehensive of growing opposition from South Carolina and wanted the authority of the Secretary of State behind them. Of the hostility of the South Carolina traders there could be no doubt, especially against Patrick Mackay, who had been entrusted with the task of enforcing the Act and began a drastic reorganization of the whole of the Carolina trade in the Creek, Chickasaw, and Cherokee towns.[9] By the summer and autumn of 1735 the Indian trade was the main topic of conversation in Charleston, where it was rumoured that Oglethorpe was scheming to give Georgia a monopoly of it,[10] and feeling became so bad that some of the Carolina traders, notably Daniel Green, tried to incense the Indians against their Georgia rivals.[11]

It was an ironical situation, for Georgia was merely imitating the policy of South Carolina, which had previously sought to prevent Virginia participation in the trade with the Cherokees by requiring all licences to be issued in Charleston.[12] But when a similar measure was directed against themselves the Carolina traders liked it not at all and they protested vigorously in a petition from their General Assembly to the Government in London, complaining of the obstruction of their trade by commissioners employed by the Trustees. The Privy Council referred the petition in December 1736 to the Board of Trade, before whom the first formal hearings on the dispute opened on May 19, 1737. Having listened to the arguments of both sides, the Board sought opinions on the point of law from the attorney and solicitor-general, who asserted that the Trustees had no right to establish a monopoly over traffic with the Indians in Georgia, but that the requirement for merchants to take out a licence in the colony was a justifiable regulation of trade.

A decision was not reached until 1738 when the Government recommended each province to prepare legislation for settling the issue to their mutual benefit and satisfaction; for the continuance of the dispute, it was said, "may occasion the loss of those advantages which would otherwise arise by the said trade to the mutual benefit of both the said provinces, and may likewise be a means of interrupting and destroying that amity and good correspondence which ought to be maintained and cultivated with the said Indians." In the meantime the Trustees were to order their commissioners to grant licences without charge to all applicants from South Carolina who brought proper certificates from the Governor and Council, and who gave reasonable security for their good behaviour.[13]

This did not satisfactorily settle the dispute, however, and trouble between the traders of the two provinces continued. The Trustees were unhappy about the Government's decision, fearing that the obligation to licence all merchants who came with the recommendation of the Governor of South Carolina would lead to so many entering Georgia "as may entirely disgust the Indians." "This," wrote Lord Egmont, "is a very serious affair, and the very being of the Indian trade with respect to Carolina as well as Georgia depends on a proper adjustment of the differences between the two provinces."[14]

Not until December 1741, when Governor Glen of South Carolina dined with the Trustees in London, was an agreement reached designed to bring the controversy to an end. They decided that, since the heads of the Rivers Savannah and Altamaha were not properly known and it was impossible to determine definitely which Indian nations belonged to Georgia, South Carolina should have the licencing of half the Indian traders in Georgia in return for the remainder licenced in Georgia being allowed to trade with the Indians in South Carolina; traders were to give their securities in their respective provinces, and the punishment on those contravening the rules was to be inflicted in the province to which they belonged. William Stephens, then president of the Savannah county, was to be sent to Charleston to confer with the Assembly and make an agreement to be submitted for the Trustees' approval; thereupon South Carolina and the Trustees were to pass parallel Acts for settling the controversy finally to the satisfaction of all parties.[15]

The proposed Acts were never passed. The traders of neither province paid much attention to the commissioners of the other, and there were violations on both sides. Nevertheless, the trade was henceforward shared satisfactorily, if not always harmoniously, between the two colonies, with the bulk of the important Cherokee trade tending to pass to South Carolina, and Georgia having to be content mainly with the trade coming from the towns of the Upper Creeks.[16]

The need to regulate the fur trade continued throughout the colonial period, however, and under the royal government was accentuated by the problems associated with the trans-Appalachian country and Indian rights. Many business firms in the colonies and the mother-country were engaged in the fur trade by the 1750s, and their prosperity depended on protecting the Indian rights of occupation. Hitherto little attempt had been made by the Board of Trade to supervise the traders' activities directly, the superintendents of Indian affairs in the colonies concerning themselves primarily with political relations, but as the Seven Years' War began to draw to a close the Government realized that the dishonesty and lawlessness of the traders, which antagonized the Indians, would have to be stopped.[17]

In 1758 an Act was passed in Georgia to prevent private persons from trading with the Indians without licence or from illegally purchasing lands from them under penalty of a £1,000 fine.[18] This Act replaced the system of trade regulation that had been enacted during the Trusteeship, and it remained in force until the Revolution, but was not a success. The Indians trading with South Carolina often traversed the Georgia settlements on the way to the trading posts and sought their subsistence en route by plundering the plantations.[19] Since offenders against the Act could not be arrested or held to bail but only served with a process to answer any action or information brought against them, they could easily evade its penalties by moving out of the province as soon as the process was served and before the courts could hear their cases. Such evasion not only rendered the law nugatory but also put the province to some expense in constantly beginning ineffectual actions.

This state of affairs led to an amendment in December 1759 by which justices of the peace in a district or parish were empowered to issue a warrant against an offender and exact a surety of £100 for his appearance before the next general court.[20] Nevertheless, traders continued both to violate the law and to elude apprehension, and in February 1764 it was enacted that offenders who lacked the means to pay the prescribed fines were to suffer "corporal punishment by whipping not exceeding one hundred lashes and not less than fifty lashes," while in March 1765 the amount of surety a justice of the peace might exact was raised to £150;

however, it is evident that the law was incapable of strict and effectual enforcement.[21]

From the very beginning the principal centre of the traffic in Georgia had been in the fall line hills at Augusta, where an Irish trader, Kennedy O'Brien, had erected a well-furnished warehouse, and where by 1739 about six hundred people had already been employed in exchanging wool and iron for skins and furs.[22] The colony's trade with the Indians grew steadily until the outbreak of hostilities with France in 1755, a year in which 49,995 lbs. of deerskin were exported. The war brought about a diminution in the amounts exported, although much of the apparent decrease may have been due to the trade's passing through Charleston instead of Savannah and being credited to South Carolina,[23] but after 1762 the traffic increased sharply, exports rising to 273,460 lbs. in 1766 and reaching their zenith in 1768 with a figure of 306,510 lbs.[24] These exports were of great importance to British manufacturers, and when, in March 1768, Georgia imposed an export duty on raw hides the Government disallowed it on the ground that it would raise the price of "an article of importation in such general use and of such consequence to the manufacturers of this Kingdom."[25]

This Indian trade was achieved only after bitter competition with the French as they strengthened their position down the back of the English colonies. In 1734 the French were reported to have won the alliance of several of the Indian nations near the Mississippi, including the warlike Choctaws, and to be trying to alienate others against Britain.[26] In 1738 the French were thought to be aiming to destroy those tribes along the borders of South Carolina who were friendly towards the English, and by 1740 they were reported to be giving the Creeks and Chickasaws large presents of food, clothing, guns, and ammunition in an attempt to detach the Indians from English influence.[27] Some form of concerted action by the colonies was required if French tampering with the frontier Indians was to be stopped, and Oglethorpe and Lieutenant-Governor Clarke of New York made a proposal in 1741 to unite all of the colonies in the British interest as a means of defeating French designs and preventing further encroachments. Nothing came of the proposal.[28]

Both sides sought to obtain the alliance of the Indians by lavishing presents on them. From 1732 to 1738 the British Government had spent between £1,000 and £8,000 annually on the southern Indians, and in 1748 decided to send £3,000 worth of presents to Georgia and South Carolina. At the suggestion of the

Trustees the gifts were to be purchased in England where they would be cheaper and of a more dependable quality, and the first batch was sent out in 1749 and divided equally between the two provinces.[29] Another shipment was sent over in 1750, but from then until 1754 no money for gifts was forthcoming from the Government.[30] There is no obvious explanation of this. It may have been that the southern frontier seemed less important to the mother-country at a time when European diplomacy was in flux, or perhaps it was because the south tended to get overlooked during a period when French and English commissioners in Paris were wrangling over the boundaries of Nova Scotia. It is possible that the interruption was due to the fact that, with the termination of the Trustees' charter, it was deemed unwise to spend money on presents while the condition and future of Georgia were in some doubt. Whatever the real reason may have been, it was decided to recommence the practice when the first royal governor took office in 1754, and money for presents was voted in both the succeeding years.[31]

By this time it was feared that the French were carrying on a war of extermination against the Chickasaws at the back of Georgia and South Carolina and trying to win over the Upper Creeks, several sachems of whom were prevailed upon to go to Mobile where attempts were made to persuade them to put themselves under French protection against alleged English designs to steal their lands and make them slaves.[32] For some years the missionary at Augusta sent over by the Society for the Propagation of the Gospel had been concerned over the "unspeakable troubles" which the inhabitants were having with the neighbouring Indians, "merciless savages" he called them, who, acting with French connivance, were wont to threaten, scalp, or enslave persons in the English out-settlements.[33] In June 1754 Charles Pinckney, agent for South Carolina, appeared before the Board of Trade with a petition setting forth that "the dangers to Carolina and Georgia from the present army of French regulars and Indians at the backs of Virginia, and those which it is said are to join them from the Mississippi and the French settlements of Louisiana are very great, should they, as in all probability they will, when they have beat the English from their forts and settlements on the Ohio, march southerly into the Cherokee countries and make themselves masters there."[34]

The need to pay the most careful attention to Indian affairs had now become manifest, and in 1755 the Government recognized the necessity of maintaining an alliance with the Indians in view of the critical nature of Anglo-French relations generally. Governor Reynolds of Georgia was told that "preserving the friendship and alliance of the Indians ought at all times, but more especially at this conjuncture, to be a principal object of our attention."[35] It is clear that the mother-country was fearful not only for her colonies skirting the waterway of the St. Lawrence and the valley of the Ohio, but also for those which might become the target of a thrust from along the Lower Mississippi.

In 1756 the Government appointed two agents to superintend political relations with the Indians, Sir William Johnson for the northern and Edmund Atkin for the southern colonies, both of whom were expected to deal with all matters pertaining to the preservation of peaceful relations, such as cession of lands, trade disputes, inter-racial crimes, and the arrangement of congresses.[36] The work of the Indian agents was of special value to the southern colonies because throughout the struggle with France in the years after 1755 their main danger came from Indians in alliance with the French rather than from the French themselves. Indeed, Georgia's first major encounter in the French and Indian War was with the Upper Creeks, who resented the presence of English squatters on the River Ogeechee but who, after a little bloodshed, quickly re-established friendly relations.[37]

When Henry Ellis took over the governorship of Georgia towards the end of 1756 the relationship with the southern Indians was good, although they were apt to commit little disorders "such as killing of cattle and frightening the inhabitants." Ellis's only fear was that no presents would arrive from England, for gangs of Indians visited him every week expecting them: "We treat them in the best way we are able," he wrote, "furnishing them with provisions, some promises, a few presents and a great many fair words."[38]

Fortunately a large supply of presents arrived in May 1757. Presentation of the gifts enabled the Governor to confer with some members of the Creek nation and to seek to win their friendship by expatiating on the cruelties of the French, who "were creeping upon them like old age, which they could not see"; whereas the English bought any land they wanted and honestly paid the Indians for it, the French aimed to acquire territory by barbarously murdering the native inhabitants. English presents, said Ellis, were much better than those of the French which, "like the rum the Indians drink, however sweet now would make them terribly sick in the end"; when Englishmen talked "their tongue and heart were fast together," but "when the French hold out one hand to them in token of friendship, could they look into the other they would see a knife ready to cut their throats." He concluded by offering a reward of eight pounds of leather for every French scalp brought in, and sixteen pounds of leather for every prisoner.[39]

Ellis's tactics were greeted with success when he invited delegations from both the Upper and Lower Creeks to meet him in Savannah.[40] For a week the delegations were treated to military parades and salutes, bountifully feasted, and supplied with presents before assembling to conduct business in the Council Chamber. There, on November 3, 1757, they signed a treaty renewing their alliance with England. However, no attempt was made to induce them to take the offensive against the French, as this would have given umbrage to a strong party within the nation which was amenable to French influence. It was agreed that all existing grievances should be "forgiven and forgot as thoroughly as if they had never happened," and misdemeanours committed by individuals of either race should not, in future, be considered as acts of the whole nation to which the offenders belonged, but all disputes were to be adjusted amicably at meetings called for that purpose. At the wish of the Indians themselves, the islands of Ossabaw, Sapelo, and St. Catherines and the Indian reserve near Savannah were delivered "in trust to His Honour the present Governor" as the representative of the King of England. Finally, both sides agreed that "the friends of the one shall be eternally considered as the friends of the other, and the enemies of either as the enemies of both: and that the present treaty of peace and alliance shall remain firm and inviolable as long as the sun shall shine and the rivers run into the sea." It was a treaty of which Ellis was justly proud.[41]

In October 1758 Edmund Atkin, the superintendent for the southern Indians, began a trip into the Creek country with the aim of reaching a formal understanding with the Choctaws who inhabited the neighbourhood of Mobile and New Orleans and whose friendship the English had acquired by supplying their wants better than the French. Soon after arriving in the town of Cussita, Atkin was visited by messengers from the Choctaws and informed of their desire to be in friendship with the English and to be supplied with British goods like other Indian nations. Atkin demanded that deputies should be sent from those towns desirous of entering into a treaty, and on July 18, 1759, at the Upper Creek town of Waleyhatchie, in the presence of many Creeks, Chickasaws, and British traders, a treaty was signed whereby the Choctaws, in return for trade, agreed to make peace with the Chickasaws and commence hostilities against the French.[42]

Atkin, however, had no success with the Creeks. It is true that during his journey through the Creek towns he managed to conciliate many of the more hostile leaders and remove some of their fears by declaring, in public squares and private conferences alike, that the English wanted only to rectify differences and remain at peace with the Indians, and had no intention of acquiring land or building forts in Indian country. But his arguments were superficial, and eventually, indeed, he aroused against himself an antagonism, carefully fostered by French intrigue, that jeopardized the good work Ellis had been putting in with the Creeks. While addressing a meeting of their headmen in Tuckabatchie Square, Atkin had several strokes made at him by a tribesman with a hatchet. Though he survived the assault and nervously passed it off as the act of a madman, it was clear that he was disliked by some, at least, of the Creek nation. Moreover, he had aroused the enmity of several of the colonists, especially the traders, who had, he complained, "by propagating calumny and falsehoods, hatchetted my reputation in my absence worse than the savage did my body." He observed that he had been hazarding his life daily in the King's service, and bore on his body the honourable marks of his zeal, but had been obliged to do so with the full backing of only Governor Lyttelton of South Carolina.[43] Whether the suspicion of him was justified or not, Atkin had patently become more of a liability than an asset to the security of the southern colonies, and in 1760 Ellis told the Board of Trade that the superintendent was unfit for office.[44]

The outbreak of war between the English and the Cherokees in 1760 made Creek friendships vital to the safety of the southern provinces. If the Creeks and Cherokees allied, Georgia would be in very real danger, and Atkin and Ellis endeavoured to play off one tribe against the other. Incentives were offered to the Creeks to attack the Cherokees, Ellis promising them that for every enemy scalp they would receive "a trading gun, three pound of powder, six pound of shot, a blanket, a flap, a pair of Indian boots and a cag containing four gallons of trading rum."[45] Such inducements would be expensive, and the Governor advised the Board of Trade that further supplies of presents were essential if the goodwill of the Indians was to be preserved.[46] Ellis found it difficult to embroil the main body of the Creeks in a war with the Cherokees, for French and Cherokee influence among them was strong. Nevertheless, while continuing negotiation in public, Ellis attempted privately to employ straggling parties of Creeks, which visited him occasionally, as a means "to embroil their nation insensibly and as it were against its inclination," and he managed to prevail upon several gangs to go scalping.[47] Although relations with the Creeks remained precarious, the majority maintained a policy of neutrality and the danger gradually passed.[48]

The most serious menace came from the Cherokees, who had always been amicable towards the English and in 1757 volunteered to protect the frontier south of the Potomac.[49] During the early years of the Franco-British war they remained friendly, although the French successes of 1755 and 1756 shook their confidence in the English and the conduct of the rival Virginia and South Carolina traders annoyed them.[50] The danger of their allying with the French was recognized in the colonies, and in 1757 Governor Hardy of New York expressed his fear to Pitt that the French might inveigle the Cherokees into taking up the hatchet against the English, a contingency fraught with peril for the southern provinces.[51] It was not until the beginning of 1760, however, that the Cherokees began open hostilities against the English, and even then the outbreak was due in some degree to the indiscretions of Governor Lyttelton of South Carolina; diplomatic encouragement by the English might have induced some of the Cherokee towns to fight on their side, for the nation was at first far from united.[52]

The initial attacks were against South Carolina, but the danger to Georgia was obvious, especially as the company at Fort Augusta had been recalled by Lyttelton the previous autumn.[53] Ellis knew Georgia could not resist a total Cherokee assault, for his militia would have been outnumbered two to one, but it was possible to so manipulate the resources available as to render any onslaught hazardous and give the inhabitants a chance of saving themselves and their property. This was what Ellis proceeded to do. In the most exposed areas were erected log forts where people could shelter in emergencies; some part of the militia was kept on active duty throughout the crisis; the rangers, which had recently been augmented, were brought further back so that enemy braves could not easily approach without being discovered; the friendship of the Creeks and Chickasaws was confirmed; and finally assistance was sought both from the Board of Trade and from Amherst, commanding the British forces in Canada.[54]

South Carolina had already asked Amherst to send at least fifteen hundred regulars to the south, and Ellis supported the request. In April twelve hundred troops under Colonel Montgomery were despatched by Amherst with orders to strike a swift blow at the Cherokees and return quickly to the north. After ravaging the villages of the beautiful valley of the Keowee, consuming their magazines of corn, and slaying over sixty of the Cherokee population, some of them being burnt in their houses while their kinsfolk gazed at the flames from the tops of the adjacent hills, Montgomery re-embarked with his battalion of Highlanders for Halifax. He left behind four companies of regulars to protect the frontiers and South Carolina, which were in greater consternation than before the troops came.

Though the conflict was more inflamed,[55] Georgia remained quiet. Its most critical time was in May, when the French and Cherokees instigated the murder of several English traders in some Upper Creek towns.[56] The news of the attack led to the abandonment of the frontier, except for a few stockades at Augusta inhabited by merchants, but Ellis succeeded in lessening tension and regaining the goodwill of the majority of the Creeks by the adoption of a pacific attitude and offers of presents.[57]

Thus Georgia was comparatively little scathed by the Indian troubles of 1759 and 1760. The main reason was Ellis's realistic appraisal and sensible handling of the whole situation. Throughout his term of office he surveyed the problem of the Indians with an eye as clear as that of a missel thrush, playing on their emotions, appreciating their sentiments. His success owed nothing to the Government in the mother-country. Except for Montgomery's expedition against the Cherokees, the home Government contributed but little toward improving Georgia's security, either against the French or against the Indians, during the perilous years after 1755. The credit for the remarkably felicitous management of Indian affairs in Georgia was owing not so much to the Government's irregular supply of presents but rather to the diplomatic ingenuity of Governor Ellis.

It was on a plan of action originally proposed by Henry Ellis in March 1763 that Lord Egremont, then Secretary of State in England, ordered John Stuart, who had recently assumed the office of superintendent of the southern Indians, and the Governors of Georgia, Virginia, and the Carolinas to meet representatives of the most important southern tribes and remove their grievances. For this purpose a congress was convened at Augusta on November 5, 1763, with chiefs from the Catawbas, Creeks, Chickasaws, and Choctaws, a total of about seven hundred persons attending, and after rapid progress a treaty was signed on November 10. A complaint by the Creeks that settlers from Georgia encroached on their lands was resolved by a substantial cession, made by them in order to "prevent any mistakes, doubts or disputes for the future, and in consideration of the great marks of clemency and friendship extended to us by the said Creek Indians." Agreement was reached on the delimitation of Georgia's boundaries, and provision was made for the continuance of "a perfect and perpetual peace and sincere friendship" between the English and the Indians.[58] During the ensuing years this agreement was supplemented by understandings with the several tribes.

The treaty made at Augusta in 1763 was of great benefit to the future development and prosperity of Georgia. The accession of territory to the colony embodied in the treaty encouraged immigration of new settlers, who could come with confidence of there being ample tracts of land which they might easily acquire. The Indians, too, left Augusta apparently satisfied, and there was hope on both sides that friendly relations would henceforward be maintained. "We seem," wrote James Habersham, "to be in no more apprehension of danger from the savages than you are in London. They are very sensible of the advantages we possess over them by the settlement of the two Florida colonies, and behave very civil and I now begin to think the time is come when we shall no more be harassed and alarmed by them."[59] Unfortunately, however, individuals from both races continued to flout the law, to occasion disputes, and provoke disturbances, and in consequence Georgia continued to be discomposed by the problem of relations between white men and red.

IX

❧❧❧❧❧❧

The Old Colonial System

❧❧❧❧❧❧

THE MAIN INFLUENCE upon Britain's commercial policy in the eighteenth century was the concept of a self-sufficing empire, whereby the colonies produced raw materials for the use of the mother-country and consumed her manufactures in exchange. Georgia and the southern colonies fitted neatly into this concept. They had an economy in sharp contrast to that of their northern neighbours: they produced such valuable staples as tobacco, naval stores, rice, indigo, and cotton, and, having no local industries, they were obliged to obtain nearly all their manufactured goods from Britain. There was little to induce the inhabitants to engage in manufacturing on any significant scale when a livelihood could be more conveniently acquired by agriculture supported by Parliamentary bounties. In 1766 Georgia was reported to possess no manufactures of its own and to be supplied with everything "from and through Great Britain. Some few of the poorer and more industrious people make a trifling quantity of coarse homespun cloth for their own families, and knit a few cotton and yarn stockings for their own use," but there was nothing that might compete with the mother-country.[1] Consequently, Georgia and the southern colonies were rated in the United Kingdom more highly than the New England provinces, and it was to them, it was said, that it behoved the mother-country to direct her encouragement, "for by encouraging them she in fact encourages herself."[2]

The chief method of encouraging colonial production was a system of bounties paid for certain exports such as flax, hemp, silk, pitch, timber, tobacco, and indigo. In this way it was hoped to free the United Kingdom from dependence on foreign countries and also to keep the energies of the settlers absorbed in producing raw materials and diverted from manufacturing. In order to monopolize the raw materials thus produced the Government enumerated them so that they could be trans-shipped to England only and not sent directly elsewhere, a policy initiated by the Navigation Act of 1660 and extended to a long list of colonial goods by several enactments during the subsequent hundred years.

This, in brief, was the mercantilist system of the old colonial empire, but Georgia's economic development in the colonial period serves to illustrate the inability of governmental policy to direct its course. Georgia provides an excellent example for the thesis that colonial economic pursuits were determined not by English law or policy but rather by the natural resources of the land, the needs of the colonists themselves, and by the general conditions of world trade. As C. P. Nettels has pointed out: "When the origins of enterprise in America are considered, it appears that every important industry got its start by reason of the natural resources of an area, by virtue of the demand for a product, or because of such factors of trade as transportation or location."[3] The truth of this statement can be clearly seen in the development of colonial Georgia's production and trade.

In any analysis, however, two factors have to be borne constantly in mind. Firstly, the sparseness of Georgia's population meant that its trade in the colonial period remained small in relation to that of the other provinces. Of the mere 10,000 or so living in Georgia in 1760 about 3,600 were Negroes, a ratio of black to white inhabitants which conformed closely to that in Maryland and was comparable to that in Virginia and South Carolina.[4] The **white inhabitants** lacked homogeneity both in nationality and background, and many were of an undesirable character, "the sweepings of the streets of London and other populous places," as the Reverend James Macsparren discovered.[5] Secondly, any attempt to describe Georgia's trade is hampered not only by the scantiness of reliable statistics but also by variations in those that are available, which were not always computed on a uniform pattern. An additional source of confusion is that the various statistics do not always cover identical twelve-monthly periods; some run from December to December, others from January 5, and again others from October. Nor in the case of Georgia can it be certain that all the province's exports would appear in the list of port clearances, for a considerable part of its produce was exported through South Carolina and would consequently appear in

Charleston's clearance figures. This lack of uniformity in the compilation of figures is not necessarily a disadvantage; for, by a careful selection of averages and comparisons, by employing, wherever possible, estimates compiled from official sources or by semi-official investigations or by persons in a position to be well acquainted with the true conditions, and by avoiding figures quoted by pamphleteers which must in many instances have been little more than conjecture and probably garbled to comport with the bias of the authors, the trend and scale of Georgia's commercial development can be adequately educed. Therefore, although the statistics quoted are not put forward as exact, the general impression which they convey can be assumed to be an authentic one.

The Georgia Trustees envisaged the development of the new settlement in such a manner that it would fit snugly into the imperial system, exporting raw materials to the mother-country and importing manufactures in exchange. Thus when, in 1737, a silk and cotton dyer wrote from Rotterdam for permission to go over and practise his craft in the colony, he was rejected on the ground that manufacturing there would be detrimental to British interests: "what we mean to do," said the Trustees, "is to produce the material for the service of England, which is encouragement enough for our own people, but if we did anything more we should raise a great clamour in England against us."[6] Georgia's economy was intended to be founded on the intensive farming of tropical and semi-tropical crops, so that competition with the staples of the other southern colonies would be avoided and British manufactures not threatened. For this reason the Trustees looked mainly to such crops as indigo, cochineal, and especially silk and wine: "Several other things might be produced, and perhaps more immediately profitable to the planters, but it is apprehended that it is not any business of this colony, nor any benefit to the trade of England, to interfere with what other English plantations have produced."[7] Georgia was to develop in accordance with preconceived notions, on a pattern designed by well-meaning gentlemen in London.

The emphasis on silk is perhaps the most significant feature of the Trustees' economic policy. It represented, in effect, the long-cherished desire of Englishmen to free themselves from dependence on foreign markets for a commodity becoming more important in their standard of living; it was the continuation of a policy that had begun as long before as the reign of James I. The Trustees agreed to send over the necessary seeds and trees. They engaged some Piedmontese silk experts in whose ability to teach the trade to the people they placed great confidence. The Piedmontese were soon winding silk to perfection, but they eventually proved refractory, disagreed among themselves, and one of them "stole away the machines for winding, broke the coppers and spoiled all the eggs which he could not steal, and fled to South Carolina."[8] Grants of land were made on condition that mulberry trees were planted, and even when the Trustees ultimately allowed Negro labour and a provincial assembly they did so with careful provision for the encouragement of the silk industry.

Although economic conditions and the attitudes of the inhabitants were against the silk industry, and although the early optimism gradually sank, the Trustees were loath to be deflected from their original course. Even after ten years of uninspiring returns they were still persevering in the encouragement of silk culture, partly because success would endear the province to Parliament and the British public, and they reaffirmed their hope "that no opportunities are omitted of inciting the people to be industrious in propagating the mulberry trees and in raising of silk, because their progress in this . . . will be the surest means of reconciling the colony to the affection of the public and procuring future aid from Parliament."[9]

The hopes of the Trustees were shared by the Government, and despite disappointing results silk was encouraged throughout the colonial period. In February 1750 several samples of Georgia silk were laid before a committee of the House of Commons in order to testify to its excellent quality.[10] The Trustees requested that the encouragement they had given to silk culture should be continued after the lapse of their charter authority in 1752, and the Board of Trade recommended the appointment of a person with authority to draw bills on the Treasury to buy cocoons of raw silk from the growers, an appointment which the Government made in February 1753.[11] In 1755 a parcel of Georgia silk was described by some English traders as excellent in every respect, and the Board of Trade expressed the wish that it should be vigorously cultivated because it was essential to Britain's manufactures.[12]

In 1750 the Government had freed from duty raw silk imported from the American plantations,[13] and by 1761 it was spending £1,000 annually on the purchase of cocoons from the Georgia cultivators alone.[14] In 1764 George Grenville added raw silk to the list of enumerated articles that could be exported to England only, and after January 1, 1770, persons importing colonial raw silk into the port of London were paid a premium of twenty-five per cent ad valorem out of the customs by the receiver-general.[15]

The returns on this investment were disappointing, although the quality of the small amount of silk produced was said to be good. People could not be expected to engage in silk cultivation when more money could be earned at other labour, and it was clearly impossible to make the industry a commercial competitor to that of Italy, France, or the East, where labour was cheaper. Only 268 lbs. of raw silk were exported in 1756, and the zenith of silk production in Georgia was reached in 1766 when, owing to unusually favourable conditions, 1,084 lbs. of raw silk were made and exported. In that year, however, the Government reduced by half its bounty of three shillings per pound on cocoons, and thereafter production declined, and by 1770 output was down to 290 lbs.[16] The withdrawal of Parliament's annual appropriation in 1771, which by then had been reduced to £100, led to the virtual abandonment of silk culture, and the filature in Savannah discontinued operations.

Second only to silk in the minds of the Trustees had been the growing of vines, and their hopes were sustained by early reports of some successes.[17] These accounts, however, related only to isolated and occasional instances and did not represent a faithful picture of the general scene. Viticulture would no more succeed in Georgia than would silk culture; it resulted in the production of only a few gallons of wine before being abandoned. The settlers, confronted with the grim realities of founding a colony, with the exigencies of setting up a home and defending it, were not inclined to pay attention to fanciful designs based on hearsay and formulated in London. The progress of early Georgia was impeded primarily by the Trustees' inflexible preference for certain transplanted articles and their refusal to pay attention to the natural potentialities of the soil.

More suited to Georgia's natural capacities was the production of naval stores, for which the mother-country was in constant need and to which she was prepared to offer substantial assistance. It was Britain's policy to seek these stores in America in order to mitigate her dangerous dependence on Russia and the Scandinavian countries, with whom the balance of trade was always unfavourable. New England and North Carolina were the principal sources among the colonies, but it was hoped and expected that Georgia would become another, and almost as soon as the settlement had begun, inquiries were made as to the best methods of inducing the inhabitants "to apply their industry to the cultivation of naval stores of all kinds."[18] The Government had enumerated pitch, tar, turpentine, rosin, and hemp in 1705, and successive Acts of Parliament granted bounties on their production, until eventually they were being exported in rapidly increasing quantities from all the colonies, Georgia included.[19]

Hemp and flax were given bounties and freed from duty by the Government, but before 1750 there was little progress in the plantations toward making them commercial crops, and in 1740 the bounty on hemp, having failed to produce any effect, was allowed to expire. In 1763, however, some London merchants petitioned for revival of the bounties, and in 1764 the Board of Trade repeated its belief that, as to colonial hemp, it would be in Britain's interest "in every light, both political and commercial, to secure a supply of so important an article, which is not only a very valuable material of manufacture but is also essential to the commerce, the strength and security of this Kingdom, and for which we have hitherto remained in a dangerous state of dependence on foreign nations."[20] The Georgia Assembly encouraged both hemp and flax, and in 1767 provision was made for free distribution of seed to farmers and for publication of directions on cultivation. The following year bounties were granted, but neither hemp nor flax became important exports of any of the colonies which, in competing with the Baltic lands, had the disadvantage of higher costs of labour and of transport to Britain. Up to 1756, for example, the average price of Russian hemp was a little more than £21 a ton, including a freight charge of about £2, whereas American hemp cost as much as £29 a ton, including a freight charge of at least £4. The differences in freight charges arose in some degree from the fact that the ships used in the Baltic trade were more capacious, less expensive, and the method of packaging more economical.

The Board of Trade hoped that the circumstances operating in favour of Russian, as against American, hemp, would "under proper encouragement work out their own cure," while the difference in the prime cost of the material arising from the discrepancy in the prices of labour would be remedied by the application of the bounties.[21] Nevertheless, not much hemp was planted in Georgia, and the largest amount exported from the colony in any one year was in 1771 when 5,470 lbs. were shipped.[22]

Britain was obliged to import naval timber in the eighteenth century because of depletion in her own oak forests. She produced no trees suitable for masting, and the forests of western Europe provided only poor quality masts. She always regarded plantation lumber, however, as inferior in quality to that of her own or of the Baltic, especially as it was often insufficiently seasoned and liable to warp. But it seemed essential to attenuate the dangerous dependence on foreigners for naval stores, and in 1721 colonial lumber was admitted into England free of duty.[23] This statute was continued by others, but the quantity of lumber sent to the mother-country was never large until bounties on imported lumber of all kinds were granted in 1765, after which colonial exports grew, although Georgia's increase did not become noticeable until 1771.

A sample of Georgia timber in 1735 was judged by the experts in the King's yards in London to be excellent of its kind "but bad, very badly converted," and consequently of little use.[24] But the fact remained that if good quality lumber could be produced plentifully in the province it offered the prospect of a substantial and profitable trade, not only with the mother- country but also, after the removal of the prohibition on rum, with the West Indies, which had to import lumber and shingles for their dwellings, and staves, hoops, and other materials for their puncheons, hogsheads, and casks. By the end of 1741 Georgia was exporting some timber and boards, staves, hoops, and shingles,[25] but it was not until the close of the war with France that its exports in this field increased appreciably. In 1762 Georgia exported 417,449 feet of timber, 325,477 staves, and 685,265 shingles. The following year the figures for timber and shingles more than doubled, while those for staves increased by over two-thirds. By 1766 timber exports had doubled again, while shingles had increased by almost half, and staves by almost a quarter. In 1772 Georgia exported 2,163,582 feet of timber, 988,791 staves, and 3,525,930 shingles, representing an average increase of nearly five hundred per cent in ten years. Lumber was found to be more profitable than pitch, tar, and turpentine, which suffered in consequence, exports of them never reaching substantial amounts. After 1760 the exports of pitch, tar, and turpentine rose uncertainly to a peak figure of 1,311 barrels in 1766 and then receded to their former level by 1772, when the amount was only 702 barrels.[26]

A colonial staple of value to the mother-country and one comparatively easy to raise was tobacco. From 1660 onwards its production in England had been forbidden, so that the colonies enjoyed a protected market, but it remained among the enumerated commodities until the end of the colonial period, and, as English tobacco consumption levelled off, the market was glutted and the selling price fell. Moreover, the plantations never entirely monopolized the English market, but had to compete with tobacco coming from the East Indies, Holland, Ireland, Portugal, Spain, and Turkey.[27] Because the market was satiated the Trustees ignored the possibilities of tobacco in Georgia. Nevertheless, it had begun to flourish there before the War of Independence, and 57,116 lbs. were exported to the United Kingdom in 1773, although this was only a tiny fraction of the total American exports of tobacco that year, which came chiefly from Virginia, Maryland, and South Carolina.[28] Not until after the Revolutionary War, when a regular system of warehouses and inspection encouraged production, did tobacco become a principal export commodity and the market crop of pioneer settlers in the Georgia backcountry.[29]

Tobacco production in Georgia, however, was eventually to be largely displaced by cotton, which was introduced directly from the Bahamas and planted and grown experimentally during the 1730s.[30] In 1740 William Stephens tried it in the little five-acre plot he cultivated not far out of Savannah: "I thought cotton deserved a place not too scanty," he wrote; "at leastwise I would try whether it would turn to any account or not; for the West India cotton, which is perennial there, dies here every winter (as I have found) and the annual plant which will grow in this country produces plenty enough; and the cotton is at least equal to the other if not better."[31]

In 1741 a sample of Georgia cotton was taken to England, and the local fibre was used for clothing,[32] but its cultivation was not regarded as a commercial proposition by Britain at that time because Indian and Near Eastern cotton could be obtained cheaply from shippers in France, Ostend, and Smyrna. Furthermore, as its manufacture in England was not then far advanced the demand was not great; a better price could be obtained from indigo and rice, and as a result cotton cultivation in Georgia was neglected during the early period. No change of attitude came with the change to the royal government; John Earle planted black seed cotton as a crop on Skidaway Island in 1767, and the aged Patrick Mackay planted some on Sapelo, but production generally was very small indeed.[33] In 1768 the province sent only 300 lbs. of cotton to Britain, compared with 3,000 lbs. sent from South Carolina and 43,350 lbs. from Virginia; and in 1771 the amount declined to 235 lbs. compared with 2,000 lbs. exported from South Carolina.[34] Georgia's fields were never white with cotton bolls during the colonial period, but the forces of nature favoured the growth of cotton there, and by 1820, when Georgia was sixth on the list of the United States in the value of exports, it had become the staple produce.[35]

Rice was already a staple commodity in Georgia by the time of the Revolution. The Trustees had realized that rice had possibilities but had decided its production was unsuitable for white labour, whose health was likely to be impaired by the nature and conditions of the work. Nevertheless, the Salzburgers had attempted rice cultivation in 1739 and 1740 but lack of money had prevented the construction of a stamping-mill to make their rice merchantable.[36] The admittance of Negroes, however, and the security offered by the British occupation of Florida in 1763 assisted the growth of a rice industry, and crops were soon to be seen on both banks of the Savannah and along the Altamaha and Ogeechee. By 1765 James Habersham was able to produce seven hundred barrels of rice a year on his two plantations "without hurry and too much driving."[37]

Rice was a valuable article to the mother-country, who required it mainly for re-export to northern Europe. American rice had the reputation of being the best in the world, but its enumeration at the beginning of the eighteenth century,[38] with the heavy freight charges which increased its price by a third, had lost it the Portuguese market and resulted in the trade's passing to Italian rice-growers.[39] After 1730, however, South Carolina was allowed to export rice to any European port south of Cape Finisterre, and in 1735 the privilege was extended to Georgia.[40] But the best markets were in Holland, Germany, the Caribbean, and the Spanish Main, which remained under the restrictions. Agitation for permission for the two colonies to export rice to the Dutch, French, and Spanish islands began in the 1740s, but nothing was done until 1763 when they were allowed to export to any port south-

ward of them, the enumeration on markets north of Cape Finisterre remaining.[41]

Expanding the area of export did not appreciably quicken the
growth of Georgia's rice exports, which had been going on steadily
for several years. In 1755 exports of rice from Savannah totalled
2,299 barrels, about a fortieth of the total from Charleston. By
1762 exports from Savannah had multiplied nearly three and a
half times, more than doubled again by 1766, and in 1768 reached
the number of 17,783 barrels, a seventh of the Charleston figure
for that year.[42]

The mother-country had always looked to the forests of the New
World for the dyes obtained from braziletto, fustic, madder,
indigo, and cochineal; large quantities were imported from the
Spanish and Portuguese possessions and also, at one time, from
Jamaica. Indigo and dyewoods were enumerated, and the cultivation of indigo, in particular, had long been encouraged in the
colonies. Early in the eighteenth century indigo had been replaced
by sugar in the British West Indies, and Britain was obliged to
resort more to the French islands. In 1734 Parliament allowed the
free importation of indigo, and, after petitions from English
clothiers and dyers urging its encouragement, in 1748 enacted a
bounty of sixpence a pound on indigo from the American colonies, provided it was worth three-quarters as much per pound as
the best French produce.[43]

Thus indigo became an eligible commodity in the colonial economy, and it was said that its planters were able to double their
capital every three or four years.[44] It throve in South Carolina
after seeds were brought from Antigua in the early 1740s, but the
production of indigo in the southern provinces had the disadvantage that it could not be cut so often during the year as it could
in the West Indies, while the indigo of the French islands was of
much better quality, selling at four or five times the price of that
produced in South Carolina. The produce of the Spanish colonies
was of even higher quality, that of Guatemala being the best of
its kind in the world. On the other hand, Georgia and South
Carolina had the advantage over the West Indies in that their
indigo was grown by planters with surplus acres of high ground
and the land devoted to its cultivation had previously been of
little value, and was plentiful and cheap. Moreover, production
of indigo in Jamaica had languished into unimportance at this
time.[45]

Some indigo grown in Georgia in 1750 was reported to have sold at a better price than the French product.[46] The province's exports of indigo, nevertheless, were very small compared with those from South Carolina. They fluctuated in remarkable fashion, especially before 1763, but after the war with France there was a steady enough rise. The average annual export of indigo from Savannah in the nine years before 1763 was only 8,149 lbs. compared with 472,040 lbs. from Charleston. Thenceforward its export increased, and the annual average in the nine years after 1763 was nearly double that of the earlier period.[47]

Among the minor products of Georgia in the colonial period may be mentioned potash, which the Trustees had intended should relieve Britain of dependence on Russia; bricks were made near Savannah, and also a pottery that was common ware for most uses.[48] Fruit and vegetables were grown on a small scale, and the Georgia yam was already growing to perfection on some of the pine-barren lands, while between 1755 and 1772 the export of corn increased from 600 to 11,444 bushels.[49] In the early days there was a small herding industry which, with encouragement from the mild climate and good pasturage, soon proved to be remunerative, and flourished in the uplands. By 1755 some livestock and live-stock products were available for export; meat was normally barrelled for shipment to Europe and the West Indies, one thousand barrels being the average annual export of pork and beef in the years after 1763.[50]

Provisions generally had to be imported, for Georgia's own production of staple commodities was hardly more than experimental. Oatmeal and wheat were imported from the United Kingdom in small, but increasing, quantities.[51] By 1765 Georgia was importing rum, sugar, molasses, and coffee from the northern colonies and the West Indian islands.[52] In 1771 imports through Georgia's ports included 3,461 gallons of molasses, 26,978 gallons of rum, over 1,188 cwt. of sugar, and 10,530 bushels of salt.[53] Large quantities of manufactured goods were purchased from the mother-country, including British woollens, linen, shoes, metal implements, and domestic ware.[54] Even so, Georgia's expanding exports after 1763 prevented trade with the mother-country from becoming unduly one-sided, and between 1764 and 1772 the value of imports from Britain exceeded that of exports thereto by less than £8,000.[55]

In spite of the constricting influence of British statecraft it would be difficult to prove that the commercial system which the mother-country operated during the eighteenth century had a great adverse effect on Georgia's economic progress. The system brought the colony financial subsidies and encouragement of particular products; its exports were given a guaranteed, if limited, market, and some defence against Indians and foreigners was provided by the home Government. No nation in the world before the nineteenth century believed in allowing dependencies to develop their resources in a free manner. The main criticism of the policy towards Georgia is not that certain goods were enumerated or manufactures discouraged or commerce confined, but that too much emphasis was laid for too long on the cultivation of what the mother-country most required.

Economically, Georgia's development reflected all the commercial attributes of mercantilist theory and illustrated the mother-country's blind devotion to what was desirable and her consequent neglect of what was practicable or most suitable to the natural capacities of the overseas settlements. From this criticism neither the Trusteeship nor the royal government is exempt. The story of the growth of colonial Georgia's production and trade proved that natural resources and human needs were stronger factors than governmental directives in economic development. The limited influence of statecraft had been made apparent.

Epilogue

IT WOULD BE WRONG to regard Georgia as the last example of the principles governing a phase of British expansion that ended with the American Revolution. American independence may have been a watershed in British imperial history in many respects but it is misleading to treat it as the gravestone of one colonial system and the birth-pangs of another. The American war left Britain neither prostrate nor bankrupt; she remained firmly ensconced in both the East and the West Indies; she kept possession of Canada, Nova Scotia, and Gibraltar; and her settlement of New South Wales went along simultaneously with renewed activity in India, and with the acquisition of Cape Colony and the foundation of Sierra Leone in tropical Africa.

The motivation and mental outlook behind this expansion were not so different from the motivation and mental outlook behind the colonial expansion in North America as might have been expected, although the emphasis was altered a little. "Men's minds indeed conceive new thoughts and plan new projects," writes Vincent Harlow, "but out of ancient thinking and under the potent influence of long-established characteristics."[1] New circumstances certainly changed the emphasis in British policy, but the various strands of which it was composed substantially remained. Social considerations, commercial enterprise, and international rivalry all played their part in British policy throughout the eighteenth century.

The establishment of a purely penal settlement in New South Wales after 1788 was no more than a drastic culmination of a social policy which had a long history behind it, a phase of which only half a century before had sparked the foundation of Georgia. The principal social motive both in 1732 and in 1788 was clearly

133

one of convenience in enabling the mother-country to rid herself of persons she did not want. It was prison reform that had provided the final stimulus for Oglethorpe and his associates to establish a haven in America for unwanted paupers and debtors, and it was prison reform that raised the issue of despatching unwanted convicts to the Australian continent; in both cases, colonial settlement offered a solution to the social problem of accommodating undesirable persons without debasing and endangering the society which had condemned them.

After the recognition of American independence it was natural for British statesmen to start looking elsewhere for the naval stores and other commodities they had been encouraging in Georgia and the American colonies, for although many of the hopes of the American plantations had been dashed, Britain was slow to learn the lesson of her imperial mistakes—a fact that the history of colonial Georgia fully demonstrates. The balance of commercial power was swinging by the 1770s; Britain was looking for new markets and sources of supply for her factories and shipyards; the exploration of the Pacific in search of a southern continent that would fulfil these requirements was in the true spirit of British expansion. Harlow maintains that the American Revolutionary period increased economic strength and that the writings of Tucker, Price, and Adam Smith began to relax the force of the mercantilist regulations and transfer the emphasis from colonization to trade, leading on to the exploration of the trading potentiality of those areas of the globe which hitherto had been comparatively neglected. The cry that "we prefer trade to dominion" is significant, but the two activities are not easily dissociated. From the very beginning British maritime activity had nourished both trade and colonization, the one being the complement of the other, and it was only the dearth of good settlement areas after 1776 that made trading considerations appear more important than imperial considerations in British overseas development.

"In international relations," writes C. M. Andrews, "states were construed as in a condition of perpetual conflict with each other, each endeavouring to gain all it could at the expense of the rest. Whether the contest were for territory, or for markets, trade routes, staple products, negroes, gold, silver or other metals, or for such commercial advantages as would enrich one state at the expense of the others, the situation was the same: what one state gained another state lost."[2] He was referring to the seventeenth century, but the factor of international competition continued throughout the eighteenth century and later. It is reflected in the Government's approval of the establishment of Georgia as a barrier province, and in the secrecy surrounding Cook's instructions on his first voyage in 1768, one of the objectives of which was probably to anticipate French interest in a southern continent in the Pacific. Britain was losing her American colonies, France had lost Canada and India, and the long-standing rivalry between the two powers was finding new outlets for expression. Strategic interests and international competition were playing on the minds of British statesmen as they had done during the origination of the American colonies.

After the Napoleonic Wars the consideration of settlement colonies from the strategic and defensive point of view, as barriers against French and Spanish expansionist tendencies, lost its force. Britain demonstrated her naval supremacy at Trafalgar, and her nineteenth-century colonies grew during a period of assured British naval superiority. Moreover, international competition in the colonial field was virtually eliminated, for the French and Dutch empires were stagnating, the Spanish empire was subjected to wars of independence, and Germany and Italy were involved in their own respective problems of unification until 1870.

With circumstances changing in this way and with the experience of the American Revolution behind her, it would be reasonable to have expected considerable modifications in the conduct of Britain's colonial policy. The lesson of the American Revolution was not appreciated in London for a long time, however, and ministers and officials remained practically oblivious to the demonstrated fact that it was impossible to lay down a prescribed pattern for an empire whose peoples retain an unshakeable awareness of their rights as Englishmen. On many points British officials held less uncompromising views than they had held in colonial Georgia's time; but despite the disappearance of the old ideas of the eighteenth century mercantilist system, which had considered colonies not as ends in themselves but as a means for increasing the wealth of the mother-country, and notwithstanding the changed circumstances and the growth of a liberal school in England, the basic attitude remained unaltered.

The frequency with which old problems of colonial policy resurrect themselves in the nineteenth century is remarkable, and becomes more so when they invited at first answers similar to those the Americans had received. The fundamental reason seems to have been that certain features of the imperial relationship were always regarded as unalterable if the mother-country was to retain her supremacy and the colonies the subordination intrinsic to their character and origin. Fortunately, by the time these issues came to a head in the nineteenth century as they had done in the eighteenth, liberal and more statesmanlike views were gaining ground in England, and British statesmen were feeling their way towards a new concept of empire that was to hold it together in friendly association and increasing equality.

Notes

1. The text of the charter is in the *Colonial Records of the State of Georgia*, ed. A. D. Candler (26 vols., Atlanta, 1904-16), I, 11-26; hereafter cited as *Col.Rec.Ga.*
2. *Col.Rec.Ga.*, I, 65-6. *Political State of Great Britain*, XLIV (August, 1732), 149-50. The Seal had two faces, one for affixing to grants, orders and certificates and the other for authenticating legislation, deeds and commissions.
3. Martyn to Johnson, Jan. 24, 1732/3, Colonial Office Series 5, Vol. 666, p. 3, Public Record Office, London. *Gentleman's Magazine*, II (1732), 1029, 1079-80.
4. The best biography of Oglethorpe is that by A. A. Ettinger.
5. Coram had thought of accompanying the emigrants to Georgia, but was discouraged from doing so by Governor Belcher of Massachusetts, who told him the southern colonies had been "graves to the people of England": *The Belcher Papers* (Collections of the Massachusetts Historical Society, Sixth Series), VI, 112, 298.
6. C. C. Jones, *History of Georgia* (2 vols., Boston, 1883), I, 133.
7. *London Magazine*, VI (Jan. 1737), 50. *Gentleman's Magazine*, XXVI (Jan. 1756), 19.
8. *Political State of Great Britain*, XLVIII (Nov. 1734), 470. "An Impartial Inquiry into the State and Utility of the Province of Georgia" (London, 1741), *Collections of the Georgia Historical Society*, I, 174.
9. Bateman to Trustees, Sept. 3, 1734, C.O.5/636, fol. 21. *Col.Rec.Ga.*, IV, 208, 240.
10. Dobree to Trustees, Jan. 15 and 29, Feb. 6, 1734/5, C.O.5/636, foll. 108, 190, 270. Gordon to Trustees, May 7, 1735, C.O.5/637, fol. 9. Samuel Quincy to Edmund Quincy, Oct. 23, 1735, *Coll. of Mass. Hist. Soc.*, Second Series, II, 189.
11. C.O.5/656, foll. 150-2. Additional Manuscripts 33028, foll. 72-5, British Museum. Privy Council Registers, Series 2, Vol. 102, p. 233, Public Record Office.
12. Order in Council, May 28, 1752, C.O.5/644, A.3. P.C.2/103, p. 102.
13. A. Stokes, *A View of the Constitution of the British Colonies in North America and the West Indies . . .* (London, 1783), 139.
14. E. B. Greene and V. D. Harrington, *American Population before the Federal Census of 1790* (New York, 1932), 6, 126, 140-1, 175, 181. See also S. H. Sutherland, *Population Distribution in Colonial America* (New York, 1936), 260.

CHAPTER I

1. William Blackstone, *Commentaries on the Laws of England* (16th ed., London, 1825), 137-8.
2. 39 Eliz., c. 4.
3. *Journals of the House of Commons*, I, 596; hereafter cited as *Commons*

Journals. Records of the Virginia Company of London, ed. S. M. Kingsbury (1906), I, 489, 555; II, 526-8.

4. 4 Geo. I, cc. 11, 13, 14.

5. 6 Geo. I, c. 23.

6. *Letters on the English Nation by Batista Angeloni, a Jesuit who resided many years in London* (2 vols., London, 1756), I, 146-7.

7. 2 Geo. II, c. 20.

8. Oglethorpe to Berkeley, May 1731, *Correspondence of George Berkeley, afterwards Bishop of Cloyne, and Sir John Percival, afterwards Earl of Egmont*, ed. B. Rand (Cambridge, 1914), 266-7. Historical Manuscripts Commission, *Manuscripts of the Earl of Egmont: Diary of the First Earl of Egmont (Viscount Percival), 1730-1747*, ed. R. A. Roberts (3 vols., London, 1920-3), I, 45; hereafter cited as *Egmont Diary*.

9. "Letters of Thomas Coram," *Massachusetts Historical Society Proceedings*, LVI, 20. For strong argument in support of this view see V. W. Crane, *The Southern Frontier, 1670-1732* (Durham, N. C., 1928), 309-18.

10. Percival to Berkeley, Dec. 23, 1730, *Correspondence of George Berkeley . . . ,* 270.

11. *Egmont Diary*, I, 44-6, 99. Minutes of the Meetings of the Trustees for Instructing the Negroes in the Christian Religion and Establishing a Charitable Colony for the Better Maintenance of the Poor of this Kingdom, and other good purposes, according to d'Allone's Charity, March 21, 1729 to Dec. 3, 1735 (Archives of the Society for the Propagation of the Gospel, London), 1, 11.

12. B. Martyn, "Reasons for Establishing the Colony of Georgia" (London, 1733), *Coll. Ga. Hist. Soc.*, I, 204, 220.

13. *Political State of Great Britain*, XLIV (Aug. 1732), 151-2.

14. "A New and Accurate Account of the Provinces of South Carolina and Georgia" (London, 1733), *Coll. Ga. Hist. Soc.*, I, 56-8.

15. R. B. Morris, *Government and Labor in Early America* (New York, 1946), 23.

16. *Egmont Diary*, I, 274.

17. *Ibid.*, 372-5. *Commons Journals*, XXII, 146.

18. F. J. Hinkhouse, *Preliminaries of the American Revolution as seen in the English Press, 1763 to 1775* (New York, 1926) , 108.

19. E. E. Proper, *Colonial Immigration Laws* (New York, 1900), 81.

20. *Commons Journals*, XVI, 597. W. A. Knittle, *Early Eighteenth Century Palatine Emigration* (Philadelphia, 1937), 18.

21. C. P. Nettels, *Roots of American Civilization* (New York, 1938), 401.

22. *Some Account of the Designs of the Trustees for Establishing the Colony of Georgia in America* (London, 1732), 3. "A New and Accurate Account of the Provinces of South Carolina and Georgia," *Coll. Ga. Hist. Soc.*, I, 63-4.

23. V. T. Harlow, *Founding of the Second British Empire, 1763-93*, Vol. I (London, 1952), 171-2.

24. In giving a brief account of British policy on the southern frontier in this period it is necessary to acknowledge the debt owed to V. W. Crane's work on the subject.

25. *Journal of the Commissioners for Trade and Plantations, 1704-82* (14 vols., London, 1920-38), Aug. 16 and 23, 1720; hereafter cited as *Board of Trade Journal*.

26. Add. MSS. 35907, foll. 25-6. King MSS. 205, foll. 23-4, 37, British Museum.

27. *Collections of the South Carolina Historical Society* (5 vols., Charleston, 1857-97), I, 236. E. McCrady, *History of South Carolina under the Royal Government, 1719-76* (New York, 1899), 76-7.

28. Keene to Walpole, Nov. 3, 1727, Add. MSS. 32752, p. 316. Nicholson to Board of Trade, C.O. 5/360, fol. 22.

29. Crane, *Southern Frontier*, 234.

30. *Ibid.*, 292-4. C.O. 5/361, foll. 34, 78, 82, 95. C.O. 5/362, fol. 1. C.O. 5/400, pp. 283, 290, 326, 364. P.C. 2/91, p. 272.

31. *Egmont Diary*, I, 35.

32. K. E. Knorr, *British Colonial Theories, 1570-1850* (Toronto, 1944), 81-2.

33. *The Importance of the British Plantations in America to this Kingdom* (London, 1731), 62-3.

34. R. Montgomery, *A Discourse concerning the Designed Establishment of a New Colony to the South of Carolina in the most delightful country in the universe* (1717). *Board of Trade Journal*, Feb. 20, 1717/18.

35. *Ibid.*, June 9-11, July 23, 1724; June 15, 1725; March 25, 1729/30; June 13-16, 1732. A. Anderson, *Historical and Chronological Deduction of the Origin of Commerce* (4 vols., London, 1787-9), I, xlvii. *Historical Account of the Rise and Progress of the Colonies of South Carolina and Georgia* (2 vols., London, 1779), II, 26. Crane, *Southern Frontier*, 283-7.

36. Joshua Gee, *The Trade and Navigation of Great Britain Considered* (London, 1738), 23-5, 124.

37. E. L. Lord, *Industrial Experiments in the British Colonies of North America* (Baltimore, 1898), 1-3, 9-14, 17-41, 56.

38. C.O. 324/8, pp. 457-9.

39. 3 and 4 Anne, c. 10.

40. Gee, *Trade and Navigation of Great Britain Considered*, xv-xvi, 13, 15, 18, 31-2, 92-3, 131-7, 197, 208-11.

41. Admiralty 2/465, p. 460, P.R.O., London. *Egmont Diary*, I, 296.

42. C.O. 324/36, pp. 376-8. P.C. 2/92, pp. 23, 27, 49-50, 59.

CHAPTER II

1. *An Account of the European Settlements in America* (2 vols., London, 1777), II, 296.

2. C.O. 1/49, foll. 116, 117, 237. C.O. 324/4, p. 84. C.O. 391/4, pp. 52, 55-6, 64.

3. *Colonizing, or a plain investigation of that subject* (London, 1774), 9.

4. J. R. McCain, *Georgia as a Proprietary Province* (Boston, 1917), 63.

5. *Berkeley and Percival Correspondence*, 277.

6. A. E. McKinley, *Suffrage Franchise in the Thirteen English Colonies in America* (Philadelphia, 1905), 169-70.

7. *Col. Rec. Ga.*, II, 498-500.

8. McCain, *Georgia as a Proprietary Province*, 196-7.

9. C.O. 5/644, A.1 and 4. C.O. 5/672, pp. 1-2.

10. C.O. 5/644, A.14. P.C. 2/103, p. 395.

11. C.O. 5/672, pp. 34-40. C.O. 5/644, A.21. P.C. 2/104, pp. 78-80.

12. C.O. 5/644, A.27-30. P.C. 2/104, p. 216. *London Gazette* (No. 9397), Aug. 10-13, 1754.

13. C.O. 5/672, p. 104.

14. *Royal Instructions to British Colonial Governors, 1670-1776*, ed. L. W. Labaree (2 vols., New York, 1935), I, 95-6, 114. J. P. Corry, "Procedure in the Commons House of Assembly," *Georgia Historical Quarterly*, XIII (June, 1929), 110-27. McKinley, *op. cit.*, 170-1. E. K. Ware, *Constitutional History of Georgia* (New York, 1947), 15.

15. L. W. Labaree, *Royal Government in America* (New Haven, 1930), 188.

16. C.O. 5/644, A.72. P.C. 2/104, p. 509.

17. C.O. 5/672, p. 360. C.O. 5/644, A.71. P.C. 2/104. pp. 507, 510.

18. *Ibid.* C.O. 5/672, pp. 369-72.

19. Instructions to Sir Nicholas Lawes, Art. 96, C.O. 5/189, pp. 344 *et seq.*

20. P. S. Flippin, "The Royal Government in Georgia, 1752-76," *Georgia Historical Quarterly*, VIII, 96-8, 114, 255. A. B. Saye, *New Viewpoints in Georgia History* (Athens, Ga., 1943), 119-20.

21. Reynolds to Board of Trade, Sept. 22, 1755, C.O. 5/645, B.3. Reynolds to Hardwicke, July 28, 1758, Add. MSS. 35909, fol. 298.

22. Board of Trade to H.M.. July 29, 1756, C.O. 5/653.

23. Halifax to Hardwicke, July 20, 1756, Add. MSS. 35909, fol. 239. Fox to Board of Trade, Aug. 3, 1756, C.O. 5/645, B.23. Reynolds to Hardwicke, May 19, 1757, Add. MSS. 35909, fol. 273. Reynolds to Board of Trade, Oct. 14, 1757, C.O. 5/646, C.1.

24. See H. Hale Bellot, "Council and Cabinet in the Mainland Colonies," *Transactions of the Royal Historical Society*, Fifth Series, V (1955), 161-76.

25. This view of Henry Ellis is based on the work of William W. Abbot.

26. See Labaree, *Royal Government in America*, 224-5.

27. Flippin, "Royal Government in Georgia," *Georgia Historical Quarterly*, VIII, 280.

28. O. M. Dickerson, *American Colonial Government, 1696-1763* (Cleveland,

1912), 227. E. B. Greene, *Provincial Governor in the English Colonies in North America* (Cambridge, Mass., 1898), 237 *et seq.*

29. Board of Trade to Ellis, April 21, 1758, C.O. 5/673, p. 28. A similar Act passed in South Carolina in 1696 had been disallowed in 1734: *Acts of the Privy Council of England, Colonial Series*, ed. W. L. Grant and J. Munro (6 vols., Hereford, 1908-12), III, no. 285. *Board of Trade Journal*, Jan. 9 and 10, Feb. 6, 1734.

30. P.C. 2/108, pp. 415-6.

31. J. H. Smith, *Appeals to the Privy Council from the American Plantations* (New York, 1950), 638-40.

32. *Col. Rec. Ga.*, VII, 42-7. Flippin, "Royal Government in Georgia," *Ga. Hist. Quart.*, X, 255-8.

33. *Col. Rec. Ga.*, XVIII, 372-88. Jones, *History of Georgia*, I, 466.

34. Anthony Stokes, *View of the Constitution of the British Colonies in North America*, 135. *Col. Rec. Ga.*, VII, 45-6, 88. Flippin, "Royal Government in Georgia," *Ga. Hist. Quart.*, X, 269. For an example see the examination of John Bishop, mariner, concerning acts of piracy committed by him upon subjects of the King of Spain, Dec. 24, 1764, C.O. 5/658, p. 195.

35. Stokes, *op. cit.*, 121. Labaree, *Royal Government in America*, 406-7. A. B. Keith, *Constitutional History of the First British Empire* (Oxford, 1930), 265.

36. H. D. Hazeltine, "Appeals from Colonial Courts to the King in Council, with special reference to Rhode Island," *Annual Report of the American Historical Association* (1894), 301-2. E. Channing, *History of the United States* (5 vols., New York, 1905-25), II, 241 n.

37. Keith, *Constitutional History*, 306-7.

38. C.O. 324/17, pp. 133 *et seq.*

CHAPTER III

1. Martyn, "Reasons for Establishing the Colony of Georgia," *Coll. Ga. Hist. Soc.*, I, 222-3.

2. *Egmont Diary*, I, 292.

3. Dorme to Verelst, Nov. 12, 1735, C.O. 5/638, fol. 89.

4. Martyn to Mayor of Liverpool, March 1, 1732/3, C.O. 5/666, p. 12. Martyn to Oglethorpe, March 31, 1733, *ibid.*, p. 14. Stanley to Martyn, March 23, 1734/5, C.O. 5/636, fol. 172.

5. Martyn to Bishop of Bath, C.O. 5/667, p. 12.

6. Martyn to Abercorn and Penn, May 9 and 24, 1733, C.O. 5/666, pp. 22 and 23.

7. Martyn to Oglethorpe, Jan. 24, 1732/3, C.O. 5/666, p. 7.

8. *Egmont Diary*, I, 272-3, 367.

9. 6 Geo. II, c. 25, par. 7.

10. *Political State of Great Britain*, XLVI, (Sept. 1733), 241.

11. Martyn to Harrington, May 19, 1736, C.O. 5/666, p. 223.

12. Verelst to Oglethorpe, Aug. 25, 1738, C.O. 5/667, p. 199.

13. *Commons Journals*, XXII, 260-1. *Egmont Diary*, II, 23, 38, 41-5, 53.

14. Add. MSS. 33039, fol. 72. *London Magazine*, XXVI (Dec. 1757), 590.

H. B. Fant, "Financing the Colonization of Georgia," *Ga. Hist. Quart.*, XX (March 1936), 29.

15. Trustees to Walpole, June 22, 1737, C.O. 5/667, p. 45. Add. MSS. 35909, fol. 74. *Egmont Diary*, II. 414-5.

16. *Ibid.*, 419, 421, 437, 457, 463.

17. *Egmont Diary*, III, 104, 113.

18. *Egmont Diary*, III, 103, 107-8, 112.

19. *Egmont Diary*, III, 108-9, 113.

20. *Commons Journals*, XXIII, 609, 623-4. *Egmont Diary*, III, 177-8, 180-1, 185.

21. *Egmont Diary*, III, 82, 84, 105, 118, 139, 176, 200, 205, 264.

22. P.C. 2/97, p. 119. *Col. Rec. Ga.*, I, 396.

23. *Commons Journals*, XXIV, 192.

24. *Ibid.*, 268, 285, 288. *Egmont Diary*, III, 265. *Col. Rec. Ga.*, V, 641. E. Lonn, *Colonial Agents of the Southern Colonies* (Chapel Hill, 1945), 46-9.

25. *Egmont Diary*, II, 155-6, 239, 286; III, 113.

26. *Ibid.*, II, 236, 269; III, 265.

27. R. S. Dunn, "Trustees of Georgia and the House of Commons, 1732-52," *William and Mary Quarterly*, XI (Oct. 1954), 552-4.

28. *Ibid.*, 560-1. *Egmont Diary*, III, 9-17, 25-8, 32-3.
29. W. E. Heath, "Early Colonial Money System of Georgia," *Ga. Hist. Quart.*, XIX (June 1935), 147. Jones, *History of Georgia*, I, 429-30. *Col. Rec. Ga.*, II, 56, 113-4. *Egmont Diary*, II, 189.
30. *Col. Rec. Ga.*, XXV, 354-5.
31. *Col. Rec. Ga.*, II, 523.
32. Board of Trade to Reynolds, May 5, 1756, C.O. 5/672, pp. 374-86.
33. Ellis to Board of Trade, April 24, 1759, C.O. 5/646, c. 63.
34. C.O. 5/682, fol. 18-24. *Col. Rec. Ga.*, XIII, 29-45; XVI, 32-3, 35; XVIII, 48-63.
35. *Board of Trade Journal*, Oct. 8, 1756; March 21, 1758. C.O. 5/682, foll. 130-1. *Col. Rec. Ga.*, XIII, 204, 210, 217; XVI, 224, 229.
36. Board of Trade to Ellis, April 21, 1758, C.O. 5/673, pp. 4-37. The Act of Queen Anne's reign was 6 Anne, c. 57. The Parliamentary resolution of 1740 is to be found in the *Commons Journals*, XXIII, 527-8. The Act of 1751 (not 1750 as the Board of Trade says in its letter to Ellis) was 24 Geo. II, c. 53.

37. E. B. Russell, *Review of American Colonial Legislation by the King in Council* (New York, 1915), 214-5.
38. C.O. 5/682, foll. 210-12. *Col. Rec. Ga.*, XIII, 335, 337; XVI, 318, 325, 329.
39. C.O. 5/682, foll. 289-98. P.C. 2/108, pp. 393, 414, 422.
40. Board of Trade to H.M., June 23, 1761, C.O. 5/674, pp. 192-7.
41. 4 Geo. III, c. 34.
42. *Royal Instructions to British Colonial Governors*, I, 189-90.
43. Add. MSS. 33029, fol. 122. Salaries of the Governor and civil officers came to £1,020; bounties on silk to £1,000.
44. Reynolds to Board of Trade, Jan. 5, 1756, C.O. 5/645, B. 10.
45. *Annual Register*, I (1758), 129; III (1760), 187.
46. Keith, *Constitutional History of the First British Empire*, 188.
47. *Acts of the Privy Council, Colonial Series*, II, 427-33.
48. This theory is inferred by Dickerson, *American Colonial Government*, 194-5.
49. *Commons Journals*, XXVI, 96.

CHAPTER IV

1. Samuel Quincy to Edmund Quincy, Oct. 23, 1735, *Coll. Mass. Hist. Soc.*, Second Series, II, 189.
2. Dotree to Trustees, C.O. 5/639, fol. 178.
3. Tracy to Verelst, Aug. 25, 1739, C.O. 5/640, fol. 360.
4. Stephens to Trustees, Dec. 20, 1737, C.O. 5/640, foll. 26-8. *Col. Rec. Ga.*, IV, 11, 29.
5. *An Account of the European Settlements in America* (2 vols., London, 1777), II, 266-7.
6. *Col. Rec. Ga.*, IV, 122.
7. Martyn to Oglethorpe, March 31, 1733, C.O. 5/666, p. 14. *Col. Rec. Ga.*, II, 14, 23-4.
8. "Impartial Inquiry into the State and Utility of the Province," *Coll. Ga. Hist. Soc.*, I, 165. B. Martyn, *Account Showing the Progress of the Colony of Georgia* (London, 1741), 6-7.
9. Dickerson, *American Colonial Government*, 251.

10. P.C. 2/91, pp. 556-7, 574-5. *Board of Trade Journal*, Dec. 17, 1731. *Digest of the Laws of the State of Georgia down to 1800* (Philadelphia, 1801), app. VI.
11. Belcher to Oglethorpe, May 25, 1734, *Belcher Papers*, II, 69-70. See also letter to Thomas Coram dated Oct. 7, 1733, *ibid.*, I, 392.
12. "Letters of Thomas Coram," *Mass. Hist. Soc. Proceedings*, LVI, 48.
13. *Egmont Diary*, II, 103; 106-7. *Col. Rec. Ga.*, II, 48.
14. *Egmont Diary*, II, 473-4.
15. *Ibid.*, III, 31, 34, 78-9, 81. *Col. Rec. Ga.*, I, 345-6.
16. *Ibid.*, II, 271, 300-1.
17. *Ibid.*, 336.
18. *Egmont Diary*, III, 157. *Col. Rec. Ga.*, II, 338, 340.
19. *Egmont Diary*, III, 199. *Col. Rec. Ga.*, II, 357-60, 394-5.
20. *Col. Rec. Ga.*, I, 398-9, 405.
21. *Ibid.*, II, 500. R. B. Morris, *Studies in the History of American Law*,

with special reference to the Seventeenth and Eighteenth Centuries (New York, 1930), 88.

22. *Col. Rec. Ga.,* III, 412.
23. B. W. Bond, *Quit-Rent System in the American Colonies* (New Haven, 1919), 45-50, 62-4, 92-3, 97-8, 108, 126-7, 350, 456.
24. *Royal Instructions to British Colonial Governors,* II, 516-7.
25. *Col. Rec. Ga.,* XIII, 687; XVI, 428.
26. Bond, *op. cit.,* 350-3.
27. *Royal Instructions to British Colonial Governors,* II, 516-7, 565-7.
28. Reynolds to Board of Trade, Jan. 25, 1755, C.O. 5/644, A.57.
29. *Col. Rec. Ga.,* XIII, 22; XVI, 11-22.
30. C.O. 5/672, pp. 335, 341-2, 350-6. C.O. 5/644, A.63, 68. P.C. 2/104, pp. 471, 485, 499.
31. *Col. Rec. Ga.,* IV, 192, 208, 238, 333; XXV, 508. Morris, *Government and Labor in Early America,* 393, 460.
32. W. B. Stevens, *History of Georgia* (2 vols., New York and Philadelphia, 1847 and 1859), I, 291-2.
33. *Col. Rec. Ga.,* XXVI, 20-1.
34. *Ibid.,* II, 206.
35. *Ibid.,* 361. Egmont Diary, III, 203.
36. *Col. Rec. Ga.,* I, 415.
37. Text in *Col. Rec. Ga.,* I, 49-54. P.C. 2/93, pp. 71, 79, 118, 141.
38. McCrady, *History of South Carolina under the Royal Government,* 232.
39. *Documents illustrative of the History of the Slave Trade to America,* ed. E. Donnan (4 vols., Washington, 1930-5), IV, 131-2. *American Historical Review,* I (Oct. 1895), 88-9.
40. Martyn to Eveleigh, May 1, 1735, C.O. 5/666, p. 112. Martyn, *Account showing the Progress of the Colony of Georgia,* 8-9.
41. Eveleigh to Martyn, Sept. 10, 1735, C.O. 5/637, p. 224.
42. Eveleigh to Martyn, Jan. 17, 1734/5, C.O. 5/636, fol. 133.
43. H. McCall, *History of Georgia* (2 vols., Savannah, 1811-6), I 206.

44. *Commons Journals,* XXIV, 288.
45. *Col. Rec. Ga.,* I, 400-1.
46. Martyn to Stephens, May 10, 1743, C.O. 5/668, p. 124.
47. Martyn to Stephens, July 18, 1746, C.O. 5/668, p. 225.
48. *Col. Rec. Ga.,* I, 495.
49. *Ibid.,* 506-7.
50. *Col. Rec. Ga.,* I, 530-2. Martyn to Stephens, May 19 and July 7, 1749, C.O. 5/668, pp. 328 and 334.
51. *Col. Rec. Ga.,* I, 56-62. McCain, *Georgia as a Proprietary Province,* 186-7, states incorrectly that there is no evidence that the Act was ever considered by either the Privy Council or the Board of Trade. In fact, the Act was referred by the Privy Council on Nov. 15, 1750, to the Board of Trade, which recommended royal approval in Aug. 1751; P.C. 2/102, p. 90. *Board of Trade Journal,* Nov. 20, 1750; March 5, 1750/1; June 18, July 18, and Aug. 2, 1751.
52. Text in *Col. Rec. Ga.,* I, 44-9. P.C. 2/93, pp. 71, 79, 118, 141.
53. Martyn to Savannah bailiffs, Oct. 28, 1734, C.O. 5/666, p. 75.
54. *American Historical Review,* I, 88-90.
55. Jenys to Trustees, Sept. 6, 1734, C.O. 5/636, fol. 25. MacKay to Trustees, Nov. 20, 1734, *ibid.,* fol. 72. Christie to Trustees, May 28, 1735, *ibid.,* fol. 302. Oglethorpe to Trustees, C.O. 5/639, fol. 14.
56. *Col. Rec. Ga.,* IV, 122.
57. *Col. Rec. Ga.,* I, 54-6, 398-400, 411-2; V, 583.
58. Martyn to Oglethorpe, Aug. 10, 1742, C.O. 5/668, pp. 100-1. *Commons Journals,* XXIV, 288.
59. P.C. 2/97, pp. 296-7, 303-4. *Board of Trade Journal,* Aug. 6, 20, 28, 29, 1742; March 4, 1743; April 19, 1744.
60. P.C. 1/49, bundles 33 and 36. Martyn to Hill, May 9, 1744, C.O. 5/668, p. 169. *Col. Rec. Ga.,* I, 407, 453-4.

CHAPTER V

1. John Tate Lanning, *The Diplomatic History of Georgia: A Study of the Epoch of Jenkins' Ear* (Chapel Hill, 1936).
2. The text of the patent is in *Documentos Inéditos del Archivo de Indias,* XXII (1874), 26-32, and translated by James Alexander Robertson in the *Florida Historical Quarterly,* XIV (July 1935), 9-14.
3. Antonio de Herera, *Historia General de los hechos de los Castellanos en*

las Islas i tierra firme del Mar oceano (1601), translated by Florence P. Spofford and edited by T. Frederick Davis in the *Florida Hist. Quart.*, XIV, 16-23. J. G. Shea, "Ancient Florida," *Narrative and Critical History of America*, ed. Justin Winsor (New York, 1884-89), II, 232-6.

4. Herbert Eugene Bolton and Mary Ross, *The Debatable Land . . .* (Berkeley, 1925), pp. 1-3. John Tate Lanning, *The Spanish Missions of Georgia* (Chapel Hill, 1935), pp. 33-67.

5. Lanning, *Spanish Missions*, pp. 111-35. Verne E. Chatelain, *The Defenses of Spanish Florida, 1565 to 1763* (Washington 1941), 14-5. George R. Fairbanks, *The History and Antiquities of the City of St. Augustine . . .* (New York, 1858), 17-9.

6. Henry Harrisse, *Jean et Sébastien Cabot . . .* (Paris, 1882), 97-9, 103-5. George R. Fairbanks, *History of Florida . . .* (Philadelphia, 1871), 13-4. Shea, "Ancient Florida," *op. cit.*, 231. The passage from Peter Martyr is translated in Richard Hakluyt, *The Principal Navigations, Voyages, Traffiques & Discoveries of the English Nation . . .* (Glasgow, 1903-5), VII, 152.

7. Lanning, *Diplomatic History of Georgia*, 131.

8. *European Treaties bearing on the History of the United States and its Dependencies*, ed. Francis Gardiner Davenport and Charles Oscar Paullin (Washington, 1917-37), IV, 46-9.

9. Instructions to Keene, Stert, and Goddard, Aug. 19, 1730, Add. MSS. 33006, foll. 298-303. Lanning, *Diplomatic History of Georgia*, 132.

10. Amos A. Ettinger, *James Edward Oglethorpe, Imperial Idealist* (Oxford, 1936), 174.

11. *Egmont Diary*, II, 282.

12. Oglethorpe to the governor of St. Augustine, Apr. 10, 1736, C.O. 5/654, fol. 45.

13. Oglethorpe to Dempsey, Apr. 10, 1736, *ibid.*, foll. 50-51.

14. Oglethorpe to Newcastle, Apr. 17, 1736, *ibid.*, foll. 60-61.

15. Newcastle to Oglethorpe, July 2, 1736, *ibid.*, fol. 64. *Egmont Diary*, II, 289.

16. Geraldino to Newcastle, Sept. 21/Oct. 2, 1736, State Papers 100/58, Public Record Office. *Egmont Diary*, II, 300-301. *Col. Rec. Ga.*, I, 260.

17. *Board of Trade Journal*, Sept. 29, Oct. 13, 14, 20, and 21, 1736.

18. Trustees to George II, Oct. 20, 1736, C.O. 5/654, fol. 78. Martyn to Newcastle, Feb. 9, 1736/7, *ibid.*, 5/667, p. 10. *Col. Rec. Ga.*, I, 262.

19. Newcastle to Geraldino, Nov. 25, 1736, S.P. 100/58.

20. Bolton and Ross, *The Debatable Land*, 73.

21. C.O. 5/654, foll. 66-8. Add. MSS. 32794, foll. 255-60. John Harris, *Navigantium atque Itinerantium Bibliotheca, or a complete collection of voyages and travels* (London, 1744-8), II, 331-2.

22. *Egmont Diary*, II, 410; III, 141. John Tate Lanning, "The Legend that Governor Moral Sanchez was Hanged," *Ga. Hist. Quart.*, XXXVIII (Dec. 1954), 349-55.

23. Harold W. V. Temperley, "The Causes of the War of Jenkins' Ear, 1739," Royal Historical Society, *Transactions*, 3rd Ser., III (1909), 200-1.

24. Add. MSS. 32794, foll. 242, 306-7, *ibid.*, 32795, fol. 1.

25. Keene to Newcastle, Apr. 22, 1737, *ibid.*, 32794, foll. 337-40.

26. *Egmont Diary*, II, 398. Lanning, *Diplomatic History of Georgia*, 69, 97-8.

27. Newcastle to Keene, Mar. 24, 1736/7, S.P. 94/129.

28. Newcastle to Keene, May 5, 1737, *ibid.*

29. Newcastle to Keene, June 23, 1737, *ibid.*

30. Geraldino to Newcastle, July 28/Aug. 8, 1737, S.P. 100/59. *Egmont Diary*, II, 426-7.

31. *The Daily Post*, No. 5600 (Aug. 23, 1737).

32. *Egmont Diary*, II, 429-30.

33. Stevens, *A History of Georgia*, I, 148-9.

34. Newcastle to Keene, Sept. 12, 1737, S.P. 94/129. William Coxe, *Memoirs of the Life and Administration of Sir Robert Walpole, Earl of Orford* (London, 1798), I, 561.

35. Newcastle to Geraldino, Sept. 2, 1737, S.P. 100/59.

36. Newcastle to Keene, Sept. 12, 1737, *ibid.*, 94/129. Keene to Newcastle, Oct. 14, 1737, Add. MSS. 32796, fol. 11.

37. Newcastle to Keene, Sept. 12, 1737, S.P. 94/129.

38. Keene to Newcastle, Oct. 14, 1737, S.P. 94/128. Keene to Newcastle, Oct. 21, 1737, Add. MSS. 32796, fol. 26.

39. Ettinger, *Oglethorpe*, 202.

40. Richard Pares, *War and Trade in the West Indies, 1739-1763* (Oxford, 1936), 29.

41. Newcastle to Keene, Nov. 4, 1737, Add. MSS. 32796, foll. 119-20.

42. *Arredondo's Historical Proof of Spain's Title to Georgia . . .* , ed. Herbert E. Bolton (Berkeley, 1925), 113.

43. *Ibid.*, 213-4.

44. Keene to Newcastle, Mar. 17, 1738, S.P. 94/130.

45. Geraldino to Newcastle, Mar. 27/ Apr. 7, 1738, *ibid.*, 100/59.

46. Newcastle to Hardwicke, Sept. 25, 1738, Add. MSS. 35406, fol. 19.

47. Newcastle to Geraldino, Apr. 11, 1738, S.P. 100/59.

48. Geraldino's memorial to the king, May 29/June 9, 1738, *ibid.*

49. Newcastle to Keene, June 1, 1738, *ibid.*, 94/132. Keene to British consuls, June 28, 1738, Add. MSS. 32798, fol. 151. Pares, *War and Trade in the West Indies*, 49.

50. Minutes of the Lords of Council, June 13, 1738, Chatham Papers, XCII, Public Record Office. Minutes of the Council, June 14, 1738, S.P. 94/132.

51. Account of meeting of Walpole, Stert, and Geraldino, June 16, 1738, Chatham Papers, XCII. Newcastle to Geraldino, June 21, 1738, S.P. 100/59 and 94/132.

52. From Geraldino, Aug. 7, 1738, S.P. 100/59.

53. Newcastle to Keene, Aug. 21, 1738, Chatham Papers, XCII.

54. Keene to Walpole, Aug. 2, 1738, Coxe, *Walpole*, III, 510.

55. Keene and Castres to Newcastle, Oct. 13, 1738, S.P. 94/131.

56. Keene to Newcastle, Oct. 2/13, 1738, Chatham Papers, XCII.

57. Temperley, "Causes of the War of Jenkins' Ear," *loc. cit.*, 217-8, 223-4.

58. Basil Williams, "The Foreign Policy of England under Walpole," *English Historical Review*, XV (1900), 273.

59. *Egmont Diary*, III, 18, 24.

60. Coxe, *Walpole*, I, 563.

61. *The Parliamentary History of England . . .* , ed. W. Cobbett and J. Wright (London, 1806-20), X, cols. 1068-77.

62. *Ibid.*, cols. 1113-4.

63. *Ibid.*, cols. 1171-84, 1211-23.

64. *Ibid.*, cols. 1114, 1223, 1283, 1304.

65. *Ibid.*, col. 1272.

66. *Ibid.*, cols. 1280-3.

67. However unwarranted this fear may have been in the light of later events, it must be remembered that French military support of Spain seemed very possible to English statesmen in 1739, and that it was ultimately this alliance which humiliated Britain in 1782. See Paul Vaucher, *Robert Walpole et la politique de Fleury, 1731-1742* (Paris, 1924), 289-93.

68. *Parliamentary History*, X, col. 1065.

69. *Ibid.*, cols. 1204-5.

70. *Egmont Diary*, III, 31-2.

71. Coxe, *Walpole*, III, 519-20.

72. [John Perceval, 2nd Earl of Egmont], *Faction Detected by the Evidence of Facts* (Dublin, 1743), 28-9.

73. *Observations on the Present Convention with Spain* (London, 1739), 29-34.

74. Newcastle to Oglethorpe, Mar. 18, 1738/9, C.O. 5/654, fol. 203.

75. Some observations relative to the boundaries of Florida and Georgia, Add. MSS. 35893, fol. 71.

76. Cf. Vaucher, *Walpole*, 283.

77. *Egmont Diary*, III, 35, 44-5.

78. Jean Olivia McLachlan, *Trade and Peace with Old Spain, 1667-1750* (Cambridge, 1940), 120.

79. Keene to Newcastle, June 9, 1739, S.P. 94/133.

80. Keene to Newcastle, June 29, 1739, *ibid.*

81. *Political State of Great Britain*, LVIII (1739), 215-6, 553.

82. Keene to Newcastle, Apr. 24 and May 18, 1739, S.P. 94/133.

83. Lanning, *Diplomatic History of Georgia*, 172, 188.

84. Oglethorpe to Verelst, June 15, 1739, letter 2881, Cholmondeley (Houghton) MSS., Sir Robert Walpole's

Archive, University Library, Cambridge. C.O. 5/667, p. 278. *Egmont Diary*, III, 80.

85. Oglethorpe to Newcastle, Feb. 28, 1738/9, C.O. 5/654, fol. 197. South Carolina Historical Society, *Collections*, II (Charleston, 1858), 270. *The Report of the Committee of both Houses of Assembly of . . . South Carolina [on] . . . the late expedition against St. Augustine . . .* (London, 1743), 10.

86. Oglethorpe to Newcastle, Oct. 8, 1739, C.O. 5/654, fol. 223. Newcastle to Oglethorpe, Oct. 9, 1739, *ibid.*, fol. 225.

CHAPTER VI

1. *Col. Rec. Ga.*, IV, 427-8.
2. Rockingham Papers, M. 25, pp. 81-93, Wentworth Woodhouse Muniments in the Sheffield City Library. These documents are cited by courtesy of Earl Fitzwilliam and his trustees of the Wentworth-Woodhouse Estates Co.
3. Martyn to Harrington, Nov. 23, 1733, C.O. 5/666, p. 45.
4. P.C. 2/93, p. 216. C.O. 5/667, p. 2. C.O. 5/638, fol. 326. *Board of Trade Journal*, Aug. 20, Sept. 19, 1735; May 19, Nov. 25 and 30, 1736.
5. *Egmont Diary*, II, 311.
6. Martyn to Oglethorpe, April 1, 1736, C.O. 5/666, p. 206.
7. James Vernon to Stone, Nov. 16, 1735, C.O. 5/654, fol. 28.
8. *Egmont Diary*, II, 339-40.
9. War Office Papers, Series 25, Vol. 19, pp. 55-6, P.R.O., London. *Ibid.*, 25/133, p. 45. *Egmont Diary*, II, 368, 412, 417.
10. *Col. Rec. Ga.*, II, 213. J. W. Fortescue, *History of the British Army* (13 vols., London, 1899-1930), II, 43.
11. Admiralty 2/55, p. 165.
12. H. W. Richmond, *The Navy in the War of 1739-48* (3 vols., Cambridge, 1920), I, 7. Stevens, *History of Georgia*, I, 152. Jones, *History of Georgia*, I, 259.
13. Instructions to Oglethorpe, May 8, 1738, C.O. 5/654, fol. 133.
14. Oglethorpe to Heathcote, Nov. 20, 1738, C.O. 5/640, fol. 225.
15. Admiralty 2/55, p. 231. Richmond, *op. cit.*, III, 269, 272-3.
16. Admiralty 2/55, p. 186.
17. Richmond, *op. cit.*, I, 5-6, 10.
18. Oglethorpe to Archer, Sept. 19, 1738, C.O. 5/640, fol. 184.
19. Admiralty 2/55, p. 445.
20. Instructions to Vernon, July 16, 1739, Add. MSS. 32692, foll. 128-32.
21. Newcastle to Oglethorpe and Instructions to Oglethorpe, Oct. 9, 1739, C.O. 5/654, foll. 225 and 229.
22. Wager to Vernon, Oct. 7, 1739, *Original Letters to an Honest Sailor* (London, 1744), 5.
23. Oglethorpe to Walpole, April 2, 1740, Cholmondeley MSS., letter 2948. Oglethorpe to Trustees, April 2, 1740, C.O. 5/640, fol. 461. *Journal of the South Carolina Commons House of Assembly, 1739-41* (S. C. Historical Commission), 16-305 *passim*. *Egmont Diary*, III, 136. McCrady, *History of S. C. under the Royal Government*, 191-5.
24. Richmond, *op. cit.*, III, 269.
25. *Egmont Diary*, III, 144-5, 146, 148-9.
26. *Col. Rec. Ga.*, IV, 507-8; XXII, pt. ii, 288-9.
27. Oglethorpe to Walpole, Jan. 23, 1739/40, Cholmondeley MSS., letter 2941. *Col. Rec. Ga.*, XXII, pt. ii, 314-5. *London Magazine*, IX (April 1740), 197.
28. Account of Oglethorpe's proceedings in Florida, May 1740, Cholmondeley MSS., Vol. 87, no. 2a. *Col. Rec. Ga.*, IV, 583-4.
29. W. L. Clowes, *The Royal Navy. A history from the earliest times to the present* (7 vols., London, 1897-1903), III, 269.
30. The principal sources for the siege are "Letters of Montiano at the Siege of St. Augustine," *Coll. Ga. Hist. Soc.*, VII, pt. i, esp. pp. 54-62. Account by a Georgia ranger of Oglethorpe's proceedings, 1740-2, Stowe MSS. 792, British Museum. Account of Oglethorpe's proceedings against St. Augustine received from him by Colonel Cecil, his cousin, and brought over by Capt. Hugh Mackay who left the general at Frederica, Aug. 31, 1740, Cholmon-

deley MSS., Vol. 87, no. 4. G. Cadogan, *The Spanish Hireling Detected* (London, 1743). E. Kimber, *A Relation or Journal of a late expedition to the gates of St. Augustine on Florida, by a gentleman volunteer in the said expedition* (London, 1744). *Report of the Committee of both Houses of Assembly of South Carolina on the expedition against St. Augustine* (London, 1743). And a good, balanced narrative in the *London Magazine*, XXVII (Jan. 1758), 21-4.

31. Oglethorpe to Walpole, Jan. 25, 1739/40, Cholmondeley MSS., letter 2942.

32. Admiralty 2/56, pp. 443-4.

33. W.O. 4/36, p. 394.

34. Oglethorpe to Walpole, April 28 and May 12, 1741, Cholmondeley MSS., letters 3093 and 3095. Oglethorpe to Newcastle, May 12, 1741, C.O. 5/654, fol. 338.

35. Oglethorpe's proposals on war in Georgia, Oct. 5, 1741, C.O. 5/654, fol. 363 (the handwriting is that of Verelst). See also Proposals relating to the war in Georgia by Oglethorpe, April 28, 1741, Cholmondeley MSS. letter 3095, enclosure. Bladen to Newcastle, Nov. 19, 1741, C.O. 5/5, fol. 170.

36. *List of the Vernon-Wager MSS. in the Library of Congress*, ed. W. C. Ford (Washington, 1904), 98-9. Courand to Oglethorpe, Oct. 19, 1741, C.O. 5/654, fol. 365.

37. C.O. 5/654, foll. 369, 380. Bladen to Newcastle, Nov. 19, 1741, C.O. 5/5, foll. 172-4.

38. *Egmont Diary*, III, 232.

39. Oglethorpe to Walpole, Dec. 7, 1741, C.O. 5/655, no. 10.

40. Oglethorpe to Newcastle and Wilmington, June 7, 1742, C.O. 5/655, nos. 15 and 19.

41. The principal sources for the Spanish invasion are Oglethorpe to Newcastle, July 30, 1742, C.O. 5/655, no. 26. Account of the invasion drawn out by Lieut. Patrick Sutherland, Cholmondeley MSS. no. 6 and C.O. 5/655 nos. 44-7. Account by a Georgia ranger of Oglethorpe's proceedings, 1740-2, Stowe MSS. 792. *The Spanish Official Account of the Attack on the Colony of Georgia,*

Coll. Ga. Hist. Soc., VII, pt. iii, 68-96. *London Magazine*, XI (Sept. and Oct., 1742), 461, 515. *Gentlemen's Magazine*, XII (Sept. 1742), 494, 693-6. *Col. Rec. Ga.*, XXIII, 377-8, 382. See also M. D. Cate, "Fort Frederica and the Battle of Bloody Marsh," *Ga. Hist. Quart.*, XXVII (June 1743), 130-50.

42. Oglethorpe to Stone, Feb. 16, 1743, C.O. 5/655, no. 94.

43. Oglethorpe to Newcastle, Jan. 22 and Feb. 14, 1743, C.O. 5/655, nos. 65 and 93. Dunbar to Newcastle, June 13, 1743, *ibid.*, no. 123.

44. Stone to Oglethorpe, June 9, 1743, *ibid.*, no. 122.

45. Oglethorpe to Newcastle, April 15, 1744, Add. MSS, 32702, fol. 347. Oglethorpe to Newcastle, Aug. 24, 1744, C.O. 5/655, no. 149. At the same time as Oglethorpe was losing his patience, Spanish vessels were reported to be menacing the coasts of South Carolina: Glen to Admiralty, Sept. 22, 1744, Admiralty 1/3817.

46. Treaty of Worms, Sept. 13, 1743.

47. This neglect of the Georgia frontier question after 1743 was reciprocated on the part of Spain: J. T. Lanning, "Descriptive catalogue of some legajos on Georgia in the Spanish archives," *Ga. Hist. Quart.*, XIII (Dec. 1929), 418.

48. Considerations on the security of British commerce and colonies in America, Sept. 24, 1743, C.O. 5/43, foll. 17-23.

49. Account of the extra services in Georgia, Add. MSS. 35893, fol. 90. *Commons Journals*, XXIV, 615.

50. Fox to Newcastle, May 18, 1747, W.O. 4/43, p. 250. C.O. 5/655, no. 173.

51. Chesterfield to Trevor, Aug. 13, 1745, *Trevor MSS.*, H.M.C. Fourteenth Report, Part IX, 127-8.

52. Trevor to Pelham, July 30 and Aug. 3, 1745, *ibid.*, 122-5.

53. Newcastle to Hardwicke, Aug. 11, 1746, Add. MSS. 36120, fol. 211. Add. MSS. 33009, fol. 49.

54. This is most obvious in S.P. 100/9 and 100/59, and in the correspondence between Keene and Newcastle in Add. MSS. 32807. According to J. T. Lanning in the *Ga. Hist. Quart.*, XIII, 412, there is the same

paucity of material in Spanish archives.

55. Martyn to Chetwynd, with enclosure, April 7, 1748, C.O. 5/656, foll. 60-106.

56. The text of the treaty is in *London Magazine*, XVII (Nov. 1748) 503-12, and in *European Treaties bearing on the History of the United States*, IV, 73-5 (in French).

CHAPTER VII

1. Eveleigh to Martyn, Oct. 30, 1734, C.O. 5/636, fol. 46.
2. *Col. Rec. Ga.*, III, 413-5. *Coll. of S. C. Hist. Soc.*, II, 263.
3. Oglethorpe to Newcastle, April 15, 1744, Add. MSS. 32702, fol. 347.
4. *Gentleman's Magazine*, XXVI (Jan. 1756), 19-20.
5. M. Postlethwayt, *Great Britain's Commercial Interest Explained and Improved* (2d ed., 2 vols., London, 1759), I, 477-8.
6. Reynolds to Board of Trade, May 1, 1755, C.O. 5/644, A.66. C. C. Jones, *Dead Towns of Georgia* (Savannah, 1878), 124-7.
7. Fox to Oglethorpe, Nov. 24 and Dec. 27, 1748, W.O. 4/45, pp. 262 and 347. Fox to Pitt, Dec. 29, 1748, and to Heron, Jan. 13, 1748/9, *ibid.*, pp. 360 and 405.
8. *Col. Rec. Ga.*, XIII, 46-7; XVI, 30.
9. P.C. 2/104, pp. 368, 369. Reynolds to Board of Trade, Dec. 5, 1754, C.O. 5/644, A.48. *Board of Trade Journal*, March 19, 1755.
10. Board of Trade to Reynolds, Aug. 6, 1755, C.O. 5/672, pp. 357-9.
11. C.O. 5/682, foll. 2-16.
12. C.O. 5/693, fol. 139.
13. Wright to Board of Trade, Dec. 23, 1760, C.O. 5/648, p. 117.
14. For examples see W.O. 34/34, foll. 172-215, 238-48, 256.
15. Reynolds to Board of Trade, Jan. 5, 1756, C.O. 5/645, B.10. Reynolds to Loudoun, July 23, 1756, W.O. 34/34, foll. 173-5. Ellis to Board of Trade, Oct. 5, 1756, C.O. 5/645, B.24.
16. P.C. 2/105, pp. 320-1. Board of Trade to His Majesty, Oct. 9, 1756, C.O. 5/672, pp. 437-40. *Board of Trade Journal*, Oct. 8, 1756.
17. P.C. 2/105, pp. 339-40. King in Council, Nov. 19, 1756, C.O. 5/645, B.38, 39.
18. Ellis to Board of Trade, May 25, 1757, C.O. 5/646, C.4.
19. *Col. Rec. Ga.*, XIII, 149.
20. C.O. 5/646, C.9.

21. Ellis to Pitt, Aug. 1, 1757, *Correspondence of William Pitt with Colonial Governors*, ed. G. S. Kimball (2 vols., New York, 1906), I, 90. Board of Trade to Admiralty, Nov. 22, 1758, C.O. 5/673, pp. 180-1.
22. Ellis to Board of Trade, July 20, 1758, C.O. 5/646, C.45.
23. *Col. Rec. Ga.*, XIII, 187-8.
24. For an account of naval strategy in the war see Pares, *War and Trade in the West Indies*, ch. 7.
25. Ellis to Board of Trade, Jan. 1, 1758, C.O. 5/646, C.31.
26. Ellis to Pitt, Oct. 31, 1758, *Correspondence of William Pitt*, I, 376.
27. Ellis to Board of Trade, May 20, 1758, C.O. 5/657, fol. 180.
28. Ellis to Board of Trade, Oct. 25, 1758, *ibid.*, fol. 199.
29. Board of Trade to Pitt, Feb. 8, 1759, C.O. 5/673, pp. 220-1. Pitt to Amherst, March 15, 1759, *Correspondence of Pitt*, II, 67.
30. C. in C. to Ellis, June 1, 1759, W.O. 34/34, fol. 244.
31. *Col. Rec. Ga.*, VIII, 160, 250-1, 324.
32. C.O. 5/682, foll. 265-8, 275-7.
33. Ellis to Board of Trade, June 17 and Oct. 20, 1760, C.O. 5/648, nos. 36 and 40.
34. Board of Trade to Wright, Feb. 27, 1761, C.O. 5/674, pp. 13-6.
35. Board of Trade to Egremont, Jan. 21, 1762, C.O. 5/658, p. 5. *Col. Rec. Ga.*, XIII, 681-2.
36. L. H. Gipson, *British Empire before the American Revolution* (9 vols., Caldwell, Idaho, 1936-56), VI, 192-203. R. Waddington, *La guerre de sept ans* (5 vols., Paris, 1899), I, 230-3.
37. Sketch for next year's campaign in North America, Sept. 6, 1755, *Military Affairs in North America*, ed. S. Pargellis (New York, 1936), 136.
38. *Col. Rec. Ga.*, VII, 407-9, 451.
39. J. R. Alden, *John Stuart and the Southern Colonial Frontier* (Ann Arbor, 1944), 50-2.
40. Add. MSS. 33029, foll. 257-70.

41. Pitt to Loudoun, Montgomery and Lyttelton, March 31, 1757, W.O. 34/71, pp. 297, 299, and 301.

42. W.O. 34/36, p. 227. *Minutes of the Provincial Council of Pennsylvania,* VII (1756-8), 470-1.

43. *Col. Rec. Ga.,* VII, 600.

44. Loudoun to Pitt, June 17, 1757, *Correspondence of Pitt,* I, 74. Loudoun to Ellis, June 19, 1757, W.O. 34/34, foll. 239-40.

45. *Col. Rec. Ga.,* VII, 691-2.

46. C.O. 5/213, pp. 129-43, 221-39. Pitt to Abercromby, Dec. 30, 1757, *Correspondence of William Pitt,* I, 143-51. J. S. Corbett, *England in the Seven Years War* (2 vols., London, 1907), I, 305-7.

47. Pitt to Lyttelton, Jan. 27, 1758, *Correspondence of Pitt,* I, 120-1.

48. Corbett, *England in the Seven Years War,* I, 320-1, 329-30. Waddington, *La guerre de sept ans,* II, 358-60, 387-9, 403-8. Gipson, *British Empire before the American Revolution,* VII, 239-45, 283-4.

49. Lyttelton to Pitt, Nov. 4, 1758, *Correspondence of Pitt,* I, 387-8. Corbett, *op. cit.,* I, 331.

50. Pitt to Amherst, Feb. 10, 1759, *Correspondence of Pitt,* II, 37.

51. Waddington, *La guerre de sept ans,* III, 252-8.

52. C. in C. to Ellis, Oct. 25, 1759, W.O. 34/34, fol. 246.

53. Corbett, *England in the Seven Years War,* II, 105-6.

54. Ellis to Pitt, April 16. 1760, *Correspondence of Pitt,* II, 277-9.

55. Dobbs to Pitt, June 14, 1760, *ibid.,* 300-1.

56. *Gentleman's Magazine,* XXX (Nov. 1760), 533; XXXI (Jan. 1761), 15.

57. Pitt to Amherst, Oct. 24, 1760, *Correspondence of Pitt,* II, 346-7.

58. Horace Walpole, *Memoirs of the last ten years of the Reign of George the Second,* ed. Lord Holland (3 vols., London, 1847), III, 181. Waddington, *La guerre de sept ans,* IV, 393-6.

59. Wright to Board of Trade, Sept. 15, 1761, C.O. 5/658, p. 9.

60. Alden, *John Stuart,* 66n.

61. Z. E. Rashed, *The Peace of Paris, 1763* (Liverpool, 1951), 45-54. Corbett, *England in the Seven Years War,* II, 73-7, 171-3.

62. Speculations on peace terms between Britain and France in America, April 13, 1761, Add. MSS. 33030, fol. 1. Notes on British and French possessions in America with a view to the terms of peace, April 19, 1761, Add. MSS. 35913, fol. 73.

63. Notte de Bussy, Aug. 18, 1761, Chatham Papers, LXXXV: "Pour fixer les limites de la Louisiane du côte des colonies anglaises et du Canada, on tirera une ligne qui s'étendra depuis Rio Perdido entre la Baye de la Mobile et celle de Pensacola, en passant par le Fort Toulouse chez des Alimabous, et qui se prolongeant par la pointe occidentale du Lac Erie, enfermera la rivière des Miamis, et par l'extremité orientale du Lac Huron, ira aboutir à la hauteur des terres du côté de la Baye d'Hudson vers le Lac des Abitibis, d'où la ligne sera continuée de l'Est à l'Ouest jusques et compris le Lac Superieur."

64. Paper of points to be delivered by Stanley to Choiseul, July 25, 1761, Chatham Papers, LXXXV. Papers on Anglo-French negotiations, Add. MSS. 35421, foll. 18, 34, 82.

65. French reply to Britain sent by Choiseul to Stanley, Aug. 5, 1761, Chatham Papers, LXXXV.

66. Bedford to Egremont, Sept. 19, 1762, *Correspondence of John, Fourth Duke of Bedford,* ed. Lord John Russell (3 vols., London, 1842-6), III, 102.

67. A. S. Aiton, "The Diplomacy of the Louisiana Cession," *American Historical Review,* XXXVI (July 1931), 714-6. W. R. Shepherd, "The Cession of Louisiana to Spain," *Political Science Quarterly,* XIX (Sept. 1904), 442-4. Rashed, *Peace of Paris,* 147-8, 153, 160.

68. *Ibid.,* 165-6, 168.

69. Lord Bute to Bedford, Oct. 14 and 24, 1762, *Correspondence of Bedford,* III, 136-7. For the importance of Havana see the *Annual Register,* V (1762), 36, and Kate Hotblack, "The Peace of Paris, 1763," *Transactions of the Royal Historical Society,* Third Series, II (1908), 245-8. Cuba commanded the Gulf of Mexico, and Havana, which had long been considered the symbol of Span-

ish sovereignty in the west, commanded the Florida channel through which had to pass the Spanish treasure ships bound for Europe from Central and South America.

70. Viscount Royston to Dr. Birch, Sept. 30, 1762, *Memoirs of the Marquis of Rockingham and his Contemporaries,* ed. George Thomas, Earl of Albemarle (2 vols., 1852), I, 124.

71. Rigby to Bedford, Sept. 30, 1762, *Correspondence of Bedford,* III, 133. Egremont to Bedford, Oct. 26, 1762, *ibid.,* 139.

72. Shepherd, *op. cit.,* 448.

73. *Ibid.,* 439. Cf. Aiton, *op. cit.,* 719.

74. Text in *European Treaties bearing on the History of the United States,* IV, 92-8, and in Corbett, *England in the Seven Years War,* II, 377-90. For analyses of the treaty see *Correspondence of Bedford,* III, 196-8, and Hotblack, *op. cit.,* 257-8.

75. H. Walpole, *Memoirs of the Reign of King George the Third,* ed. G. F. Russell Barker (4 vols., London, 1894), I, 174, 179-82.

76. Egremont to Bedford, Oct. 26, 1762, *Correspondence of Bedford,* III, 139.

77. "Letters of the Hon. James Habersham, 1756-75," *Coll. Ga. Hist. Soc.,* VI, 18.

78. E.g., Waddington, *La guerre de sept ans,* in five volumes totalling 2,867 pages mentions Georgia only once (I, 245), and that only in a list of what individual colonies could contribute towards the campaign of 1757. Corbett, *England in the Seven Years War,* in two volumes totalling 883 pages does not mention Georgia at all. In Gipson, *British Empire before the American Revolution,* Vols. VI-VIII, the colony receives just over four pages of the 1200 or so devoted to the war period.

CHAPTER VIII

1. Oglethorpe to Berkeley, May 1731, *Correspondence of Berkeley and Percival,* 278.

2. G. White, *Historical Collections of Georgia* (New York, 1855), 121. It was customary for Indians to surrender their land easily at this time, for they attached much less importance to it than did the white men: see S. G. Drake, "Early History of Georgia, and Sir Alexander Cuming's embassy to the Cherokees," *New England Historical and Genealogical Register,* XXVI (July 1872), 260.

3. *Memoirs and Anecdotes of Philip Thicknesse* (2 vols., London, 1788), I, 49.

4. *Egmont Diary,* II, 112-32. *Gentleman's Magazine,* IV (1734), 329, 449-50, 571. *London Magazine,* III (1734), 605; IV (1735), 162.

5. *Col. Rec. Ga.,* I, 177-8. C. C. Jones, *Historical Sketch of Tomochichi, Mico of the Yamacraws* (Albany, 1868) *passim.* T. R. Reese, "An Indian Visit to Eighteenth Century England," *History Today,* IV (May 1954), 334-7.

6. Stowe MSS. 792, British Museum. Oglethorpe to Verelst, Sept. 5, 1739, C.O. 5/640, fol. 362. *Col. Rec. Ga.,* XXII, pt. ii, 208, 214-5. *Egmont Diary,* III, 121. *London Magazine,* XXVI (Dec. 1757), 591. White, *Historical Collections of Georgia,* 121. McCall, *History of Georgia,* I, 141.

7. *Col. Rec. Ga.,* I, 31-44, 184-5. J. Harris, *Navigantium atque Itinerantium Bibliotheca* (2 vols., London, 1744-8), II, 328. F. Moore, "Voyage to Georgia begun in the year 1735" (London, 1744), *Coll. Ga. Hist. Soc.,* I, 96.

8. C.O. 5/654, fol. 18.

9. Broughton to Trustees, Oct. 9, 1735, C.O. 5/638, foll. 1-13. Popple to Martyn, Dec. 10, 1735, *ibid.,* fol. 104. *Col. Rec. Ga.,* I, 241-2; XXI, 3-5. R. L. Meriwether. *Expansion of South Carolina, 1729-65* (Kingsport, 1940).

10. Eveleigh to Oglethorpe, July 7, 1735, C.O. 5/637, fol. 168. This is confirmed by a letter from South Carolina dated June 30, 1736, in the Jefferies MSS. XIII, fol. 148, Reference Library, Bristol.

11. Oglethorpe to Trustees, May 10, 1736, C.O. 5/654, foll. 58-9. *Col. Rec. Ga.,* XXI, 161.

12. W. R. Smith, *South Carolina as a Royal Province, 1719-76* (New York, 1903), 216-9.

13. Popple to Martyn, Dec. 14, 1736, C.O. 5/638, fol. 372. Royal instructions to Trustees, July 25, 1738, C.O. 5/668, p. 49. P.C. 2/94, pp. 21, 32, 593. *Board of Trade Journal,* May 19, June 21, Sept. 14, 1737. *Royal Instructions to British Colonial Governors,* II, 475-6. J. P. Corry, *Indian Affairs in Georgia, 1732-56* (Philadelphia, 1936), 54-61.

14. *Egmont Diary,* II, 494, 498, 500-1.

15. *Col. Rec. Ga.,* V, 546-8.

16. Corry, *Indian Affairs in Georgia,* 63-6. Meriwether, *Expansion of South Carolina,* 223.

17. C. W. Alvord, *Mississippi Valley in British Politics* (2 vols., Cleveland, 1917), I, 106, 215-6; II, 24.

18. *Col. Rec. Ga.,* XVIII, 247-9.

19. *Ibid.,* XVI, 294.

20. *Ibid.,* XVIII, 359-61.

21. *Ibid.,* 594, 703-5.

22. *A State of the Province of Georgia attested upon oath* (London, 1742), 6-7. *Col. Rec. Ga.,* I, 353; II, 292; XXII, pt. ii, 108-9. *Gentleman's Magazine,* XXVI (Jan. 1756), 19.

23. Governor Wright said that nearly all deerskins shipped from South Carolina were from Georgia: Flippin, "Royal Government in Georgia," *Ga. Hist. Quart.,* IX, 225.

24. Aggregate of Georgia exports by the Savannah customs-comptroller, reprinted in B. Romans, *Concise Natural History of East and West Florida* (New York, 1775), 104. These figures do not always conform to those given by Governor Wright in his report to the Board of Trade in 1766, King MSS. 205, foll. 310-11, but they do conform with J. Campbell, *Political Survey of Britain* (2 vols., London, 1774), II, 655n., and average closely with those in D. Macpherson, *Annals of Commerce, Manufactures, Fisheries and Navigation* (4 vols., London, 1805), III, 453, which runs from October to October.

25. P.C. 2/115, pp. 252-3.

26. *Col. Rec. Ga.,* III, 413-5. *Coll. of S. C. Hist. Soc.,* II, 263.

27. President of S. C. to Board of Trade, May 25, 1738, C.O. 5/283, pp. 69-70. *Col. Rec. Ga.,* IV, 134, 398-9, 471, 563, 585.

28. Martyn to Stone, July 26, 1742, C.O. 5/655, no. 21. Oglethorpe to Clarke, July 12, 1741, *Documents relative to the Colonial History of the State of New York,* ed. E. B. O'Callaghan (15 vols., Albany, 1853-87), VI, 211.

29. Martyn to Potter, May 25, 1748, C.O. 5/668, p. 281. Bedford to C.O. Georgia, May 28, 1748, C.O. 324/37, foll. 225-6. S.P. 41/19, p. 4. Alden, *John Stuart,* 14-5, incorrectly states that the Government decision was made in 1747.

30. Martyn to Board of Trade, June 3, 1754, C.O. 5/644, A.24.

31. P.C. 2/104, pp. 172, 201. Board of Trade to H.M., June 27, 1754, C.O. 5/672, p. 57. Martyn to Board of Trade, Jan. 28, 1755, C.O. 5/644, A.45. Treasury to Board of Trade, Oct. 15, 1756, C.O. 5/645, B.26. W. R. Jacobs, *Diplomacy and Indian Gifts* (Berkeley, Calif., 1950), 38-9, maintains there was a delay of three years after the request for presents in 1754 before they arrived in Georgia. This is untrue, for Governor Reynolds wrote to the Board of Trade on Oct. 8, 1755, that presents had arrived: C.O. 5/645, B.4.

32. *Col. Rec. Ga.,* VI, 448-9; VII, 33-4. C.O. 5/693, foll. 41, 50, 54-5.

33. S.P.G. Journals of Proceedings, XII, 121; XIII, 44. *Col. Rec. Ga.,* 306.

34. P. M. Hamer, "Anglo-French Rivalry in the Cherokee Country 1754-7," *North Carolina Historical Review,* II (July 1925), 305. *Board of Trade Journal,* June 27, 1754.

35. Board of Trade to Reynolds, March 26, 1755, C.O. 5/672, p. 329.

36. Flippin "Royal Government in Georgia," *Ga. Hist. Quart.,* XIII (June 1929), 140-1.

37. C.O. 5/694, foll. 26-7. Reynolds to Board of Trade, Sept. 29, 1756, C.O. 5/645, B.33. Alden, *John Stuart,* 89-90.

38. Ellis to Board of Trade, May 5, 1757, C.O. 5/646, C.3.

39. C.O. 5/694, fol. 102.

40. C.O. 5/696, fol. 20.

41. C.O. 5/694, fol. 26. Ellis to Loudoun, Dec. 1, 1757, W.O. 34/34, fol. 189. Ellis to Pitt, Dec. 10, 1757, *Correspondence of Pitt,* I, 129-31.

42. Atkin to Pitt, March 27, 1760, *Correspondence of Pitt,* II, 269-70. Alden, *John Stuart,* 97-8, incorrectly gives the date of the treaty as July 10.

43. Atkin to Pitt, March 27, 1760, *Correspondence of Pitt*, II, 270-2.
44. Alden, *John Stuart*, 98-100. Atkin was not in fact succeeded until 1762 when John Stuart took up the appointment.
45. *Col. Rec. Ga.*, VIII, 248.
46. Ellis to Board of Trade, Feb. 15, 1760, C.O. 5/657, fol. 205.
47. Ellis to Pitt, April 16, 1760, *Correspondence of Pitt*, II, 277.
48. For English relations with the Creeks in Georgia between 1757 and 1762 see W.O. 34/34, foll. 189-92, 216, 219-25, 251, and also Meriwether, *Expansion of South Carolina*, 221-5.
49. The Cherokees sent parties of warriors to assist the English expedition under Forbes against Fort Duquesne.
50. Alden, *John Stuart*, 50.
51. Hardy to Pitt, Feb. 26, 1757, *Correspondence of Pitt*, I, 12-3.
52. McCrady, *History of South Carolina under the Royal Government*, 331-5, gives an account of negotiations between Lyttelton and the Cherokees.

See also W. J. Rivers, "The Carolinas," *Narrative and Critical History of America*, ed. J. Winsor, V (1887), 333, and C. J. Milling, *Red Carolinians* (Chapel Hill, 1940), 296.
53. *Col. Rec. Ga.*, VIII, 191-2.
54. Ellis to Pitt, Feb. 16 and March 5, 1760, *Correspondence of Pitt*, II, 254 and 259. Ellis to Board of Trade, April 16, 1760, C.O. 5/649, E.1. Board of Trade to Ellis, April 25, 1760, C.O. 5/657, foll. 202-6.
55. McCrady, *History of South Carolina*, 346-7. Milling, *Red Carolinians*, 302. Meriwether, *Expansion of South Carolina*, 228-32, 237.
56. Ellis to Board of Trade, June 17, 1760, C.O. 5/649, E.3.
57. Alden, *John Stuart*, 109-10.
58. *State Records of North Carolina* (26 vols., Goldsboro, 1886), XI, 176-85. Meriwether, *Expansion of South Carolina*, 245. Alden, *John Stuart*, 176-85.
59. "Letters of James Habersham," *Coll. Ga. Hist. Soc.*, VI, 27.

CHAPTER IX

1. Wright to Board of Trade, Nov. 18, 1766, King MSS. 206, p. 7.
2. *American Husbandry, by an American* (2 vols., London, 1775), II, 233-4.
3. C. P. Nettels, "British Mercantilism and the Economic Development of the Thirteen Colonies," *Journal of Economic History*, XII (1952), 108.
4. E. B. Greene and V. D. Harrington, *American Population before the Federal Census of 1790* (New York, 1932), 6, 126, 140-1, 175, 181.
5. *America Dissected, being a full and true account of all the American colonies in sundry letters from a clergyman there* (Dublin, 1753), 8.
6. *Egmont Diary*, II, 405.
7. *A State of the Province of Georgia attested upon oath*, 11.
8. Moore, "Voyage to Georgia," *Coll. Ga. Hist. Soc.*, I, 99. Martyn to Oglethorpe, April 4, 1733, C.O. 5/666, p. 16. C.O. 5/670, pp. 46-50. *Egmont Diary*, I, 297-8, 305, 309.
9. Martyn to Stephens, April 24, 1741, and May 10, 1743, C.O. 5/668, pp. 10 and 121. Verelst to Stephens, Aug. 10, 1742, *ibid.*, p. 102. Verelst to

Oglethorpe, March 29, 1740, C.O. 5/667, p. 310.
10. *Commons Journals*, XXV, 996-7.
11. Martyn to Robinson, March 8, 1752, C.O. 5/669, p. 128. Board of Trade to P.C., July 9, 1752, C.O. 5/657, fol. 106. Board of Trade representation to Crown, Dec. 20, 1752, C.O. 5/672, p. 10. C.O. 5/644, A.8 and 9. P.C. 2/103, pp. 267, 303-4.
12. Board of Trade to Reynolds, March 26, 1755, C.O. 5/672, p. 332. Certificate of several manufacturers and traders, March 29, 1755, C.O. 5/644, A.52. *Gentleman's Magazine*, XXV (April 1755), 185. *London Magazine*, XXIV (April 1755), 186.
13. 23 Geo. II, c. 20.
14. "Letters of James Habersham," *Coll. Ga. Hist. Soc.*, VI, 9. Macpherson, *Annals of Commerce*, III, 346, 360.
15. 9 Geo. III, c. 38. O. M. Dickerson, *The Navigation Acts and the American Revolution* (Philadelphia, 1951), 12-3.
16. Aggregate of Georgia exports by the Savannah customs-comptroller, in Romans, *Concise Natural History of East and West Florida*, 104. See also

King MSS. 210, fol. 44. *Ibid.*, 213, p. 45. *Historical Account of the Rise and Progress of S. C. and Georgia*, II, 209.

17. For examples see Martyn to Oglethorpe, March 31, 1733, C.O. 5/666, p. 13. Trustees to Hawkins, Nov. 4, 1737, C.O. 5/667, p. 85. "Impartial Inquiry into the State and Utility of Georgia," *Coll. Ga. Hist. Soc.*, I, 164.

18. Eveleigh to Martyn, Oct. 30, 1734, C.O. 5/636, fol. 45.

19. G. L. Beer, *Commercial Policy of England towards the American Colonies* (New York, 1893), 101-2. C. M. Andrews, *Colonial Period of American History* (4 vols., New Haven, 1934-8), Vol. IV, "England's Commercial and Colonial Policy," 102-3, 339, 391.

20. Board of Trade report on whale fishery, fur trade and hemp bounty, Feb. 9, 1764, Add. MSS. 38337, fol. 164. P.C. 2/110, pp. 288-90.

21. P.C. 2/110, pp. 290-1.

22. Aggregate of Georgia exports, in Romans, *Concise Natural History*, 104. L. C. Gray, *History of Agriculture in the Southern United States to 1860* (Washington, 1933), 182.

23. 8 Geo. I, c. 12.

24. Jasper to Oglethorpe, Sept. 11, 1735, C.O. 5/638, fol. 26.

25. *Col. Rec. Ga.*, XXIII, 151.

26. Aggregate of Georgia exports, in Romans, *op. cit.* See also W. J. Ashley, *Surveys Historic and Economic* (London, 1900), 329.

27. Andrews, *Colonial Period of American History*, IV, 88-9.

28. J. B. Holroyd (Lord Sheffield), *Observations on the Commerce of the American States* (London, 1784), table 1. This gives Britain's total imports of tobacco in 1773 as 100,472,007 lbs.

29. Gray, *History of Agriculture*, 223, 605.

30. *A Documentary History of American Industrial Society* (Cleveland, 1910), I, 268. E. J. Donnell, *Chronological and Statistical History of Cotton* (New York, 1872), 21.

31. *Col. Rec. Ga.*, IV, 535, 541.

32. V. S. Clarke, *History of Manufactures in the United States, 1607-1860* (Washington, 1916), 85.

33. "Correspondence on the beginning of cotton cultivation in Georgia," *Ga. Hist. Quart.*, I (March 1917), 40.

34. Add. MSS. 15485, p. 4. Customs report of imports and exports of American ports, 1771-2, possessed by the Massachusetts Historical Society at Boston and transcribed in Sutherland, *Population Distribution in Colonial America*, 299.

35. H. C. Carey and I. Lea, *The Geography, History and Statistics of America and the West Indies* (London, 1823), 231.

36. *Col. Rec. Ga.*, XXII, pt. ii, 420, 465.

37. "Letters of James Habersham," *Coll. Ga. Hist. Soc.*, VI, 39.

38. 3 and 4 Anne, c. 5.

39. A. M. Schlesinger, *Colonial Merchants and the American Revolution 1763-76* (New York, 1918), 33-4. Beer, *Commercial Policy of England*, 53.

40. 3 Geo. II, c. 28. 8 Geo. II, c. 19.

41. 4 Geo. III, c. 27. Andrews, *Colonial Period of American History*, IV, 96-7.

42. Aggregate of Georgia exports, in Romans, *op. cit.* Cf. King MSS. 213, p. 44, which gives higher but only approximate figures. The statistics for Charleston are taken from List of Exports from Charleston, 1747-66, King MSS. 206, fol. 29. Add. MSS. 15485 contains the figures for 1768-9. McCrady, *History of South Carolina*, 389-91.

43. 7 Geo. II, c. 18. 21 Geo. II, c. 30.

44. Schlesinger, *Colonial Merchants and the American Revolution*, 34.

45. Gray, *History of Agriculture*, 293-4. Pares, *War and Trade in the West Indies*, 101, 417.

46. *Board of Trade Journal*, June 27, 1751.

47. Aggregate of Georgia exports, in Romans, *op. cit.* The figures for Charleston are from King MSS. 206, fol. 29. According to Holroyd, *Observations on the Commerce of the American States*, table 1, Britain imported 1,521,476 lbs. of indigo in 1773, of which 57,116 came from Georgia.

48. *Col. Rec. Ga.*, IV, 253; IV, Suppl., 25; XXII, pt. i, 168, 221; XXII, pt. ii, 53,277,291. Moore, "Voyage to Georgia," *Coll. Ga. Hist. Soc.*, I, 106. *Description of Georgia by a gentleman who has resided there* (London, 1741), 4.

49. W. Range, "The Agricultural Revolution in Royal Georgia," *Agricultural History*, XXI (Oct. 1947), 253.

50. *Ibid.*, Romans, *Concise Natural History*, 91-2.

51. Account of corn exported from England, 1746-63, Add. MSS. 38387, foll. 33-51.

52. King MSS. 205, p. 632.

53. Customs report of imports and exports of American ports, in Sutherland, *Population Distribution*, 277-95.

54. King MSS. 205, fol. 309.

55. Tables showing value of exports and imports of each American colony, 1739-73, Rockingham Papers, R.61, ix, in the Sheffield City Library.

EPILOGUE

1. V. T. Harlow, *Founding of the Second British Empire*, Vol. I (London, 1952), 2.

2. Andrews, *Colonial Period of American History*, IV, 8.

Bibliography

PRIMARY SOURCES

MANUSCRIPTS

PUBLIC RECORD OFFICE, LONDON.

Colonial Office Papers

The volumes listed C.O.5/636-712 constitute the most valuable body of source material available for the study of colonial Georgia. Some of it has been printed in the *Colonial Records of the State of Georgia* (*q.v.*), but a substantial number of the documents can only be found in the original. C.O.5/360-2 and C.O.5/400 show British policy on the southern frontier before 1732 as outlined in chapter one.

C.O.5/636-48, Original correspondence to the Board of Trade from the Trustees, Oglethorpe, the governors, and others (1734-64).

C.O.5/653, Drafts of letters.

C.O.5/654-6, Letters from Oglethorpe and the Trustees to the Secretary of State (Aug. 13, 1735-Aug. 28, 1754).

C.O.5/657, Miscellaneous papers (1733-83) largely supplemental to the preceding three volumes.

C.O.5/658, Letters from Governor James Wright.

C.O.5/666-9, Out-letters from the Trustees (1732-52).

C.O.5/670-1, Trustees' entry books of land grants, petitions, etc., (1732-52).

C.O.5/672-4, Letters from the Board of Trade (1752-81).

C.O.5/675, Abstracts of grants of land (1760-8).

C.O.5/681-2, Acts (1732-50 and 1755-60).

C.O.5/686-8, Journal of the Trustees.

C.O.5/689-91, Minutes of the Council of the Trustees.

C.O.5/692, Minutes of the Council in Georgia (1741-53).

C.O.5/693-700, Minutes of the Council and Assembly in Georgia (1753-68).

C.O.5/709-10, Shipping returns (1752-67).
C.O.5/360-2, Board of Trade papers on South Carolina (1725-33).
C.O.5/400, Commissions and instructions to South Carolina (1720-30).

Other volumes containing some material relating to Georgia include the following:

C.O.5/5, Secretary of State despatches and miscellaneous correspondence on colonial affairs (1733-48).
C.O.5/43, Secretary of State miscellaneous papers.
C.O.5/213, Secretary of State despatches to governors and commanders in North America.
C.O.5/283, Verelst's observations on Britain's right to territory in America.
C.O.323/32, Abstracts of letters from governors to the Board of Trade (1756-8) in which pp. 37-90 are from Georgia.
C.O.324/37, Entry book of grants and warrants (1736-49).
C.O.388/40, Board of Trade commercial correspondence (1739-42).

State Papers

The Foreign Series is necessary for the diplomacy of the period, and is especially important for the controversy with Spain leading up to the War of Jenkins' Ear.

The drafts of letters between Benjamin Keene in Spain and the Secretary of State in England are contained in S.P. 94/128-133, which cover the years from July 1737 to August 1739. Papers concerning the Spanish minister in England are in S.P. 100/58-59, which cover the years 1733-80.

Privy Council Records

Important for all aspects of Government policy. They have been calendared.
P.C. 2/90-115, Privy Council registers (1727-71).
P.C. 1/48-51, Unbound papers (1732-65).
P.C. 1/5, Bundle 28 contains an account of the proceedings on the declaration of war against Spain (July-Nov., 1739).

Admiralty Records·

Of only occasional interest, Georgia very seldom receiving specific attention, but the following volumes may be mentioned:
Adm. 1/3817-9, Letters from colonial governors (1728-70).
Adm. 2/55-6, Orders and instructions (1736-40).

War Office Papers

Surprisingly little that bears directly on Georgia. Such as there is is normally reproduced among the Colonial Office papers. The following volumes are the most helpful:

W.O. 4/36, Out-letters of the Secretary at War (June 1740-Aug. 1741).
W.O. 4/43, Out-letters of the Secretary at War (Dec. 1746-Aug. 1747).
W.O. 4/45, Out-letters of the Secretary at War (May 1748-Feb. 1749).
W.O. 25/19-20, Commission books (1737-43).
W.O. 25/133, Notification books (1735-40).

Amherst Papers

Contain some scattered information relative to Georgia during the war with France. The most valuable are:
W.O. 34/34, Correspondence between the Governors of Maryland and Georgia and the Commander in Chief (1756-63).
W.O. 34/35, Letters from the Governors of the Carolinas to the Commander in Chief (1756-63).
W.O. 34/71, Letters from Secretaries of State and Government departments to the Commander in Chief in North America (Aug. 1753-July 1757).

Chatham Papers

Useful for military and diplomatic affairs, especially volumes LXXXV and XCII, catalogued under the prefix 30/8.

BRITISH MUSEUM.

Newcastle Papers

Invaluable for Government policy in general and useful also as a supplement to the State Papers for diplomatic affairs. The following volumes deserve special mention:
Add.MSS. 32692-4, Home correspondence (1739-40).
Add.MSS. 32794-32801, Diplomatic correspondence (1737-9).
Add.MSS. 32992, General correspondence (undated).
Add.MSS. 33006-9, Diplomatic correspondence (1728-48).
Add.MSS. 33028-30, Papers relating to America and the West Indies (1701-1802).

Hardwicke Papers

Contain much official correspondence which supplements that in the Newcastle Papers.

Add.MSS. 35406, Political correspondence (1723-40).
Add.MSS. 35421, Political correspondence (June 1761-July 1762).
Add.MSS. 35893, Miscellaneous collection of military papers (1713-59).
Add.MSS. 35907-13, Reports and papers relating to America (1710-65).

Liverpool Papers

Of some use for commercial information.

Add.MSS. 38331-9, Official papers of the first Earl of Liverpool
   (1744-66).
Add.MSS. 38387, Papers relating to colonial trade (1763-5).

King MSS.

Of considerable use for trade and production and of general interest
for the condition of all the colonies.

205, Reports on the state of the American colonies.
206, State of manufactures, mode of granting land, and fees of officers in
   America.
210, Volume One of De Brahm's survey of America.
213, Journal of an officer in the West Indies (1764-5).

Other Papers

Add.MSS. 14034, Collection of Board of Trade papers on the colonies.
Add.MSS. 15484, Description of North American ports (c. 1770).
Add.MSS. 15485, Account of shipping, imports, exports, their value and
   character of articles carried (1768-9).
Add.MSS. 22680, Miscellaneous papers relating to America (1739-72).
Add.MSS. 27857, (Francis Place papers), Notes on North America.
Add.MSS. 29973, A short description of South Carolina by G. M. John-
   ston (1763).

SOCIETY FOR THE PROPAGATION OF THE GOSPEL.

The archives of the S.P.G. provide confirmatory data concerning the
philanthropic origins of Georgia. The following volumes are of special
value:
Journals of Proceedings of the Society, Vols. V-XVI.
'B' MSS., Letters and reports of missionaries, Vols. V, IX, XII-XVIII.
The Minutes of the Meetings of the Trustees for Instructing the
Negroes in the Christian Religion and Establishing a Charitable
Colony for the Better Maintenance of the Poor of this Kingdom, and
other good purposes, according to d'Allone's charity (March 21, 1729-
Dec. 3, 1735).

PRINTED SOURCES

BRITISH OFFICIAL DOCUMENTS.

The calendars of the Privy Council registers and the State Papers are
convenient for reference and checking, and L. F. Stock's compilation of

Parliamentary debates respecting North America is an invaluable guide.

Acts of the Privy Council of England, Colonial States, ed. W. L. Grant and J. Munro (6 vols., Hereford, 1908-12). Volumes III (1720-45), IV (1745-66) and VI (The unbound papers).

Calendar of State Papers, Colonial Series, America and the West Indies, 1574-1736 (London, 1860-1953).

Calendar of Treasury Books and Papers, 1729-45, ed. W. A. Shaw (5 vols., London, 1897-1903).

Journal of the Commissioners for Trade and Plantation, 1704-82 (14 vols., London, 1920-38).

Journals of the House of Commons.

Journals of the House of Lords.

Parliamentary History of England (36 vols., London, 1806-20).

Proceedings and Debates of the British Parliaments respecting North America, up to 1754, ed. L. F. Stock (5 vols., Washington, 1924-41).

Royal Instructions to British Colonial Governors, 1670-1776, ed. L. W. Labaree (2 vols., New York, 1935).

COLONIAL AND STATE DOCUMENTS.

The published colonial records of Georgia comprise the most comprehensive body of printed material bearing specifically on Georgia. They are chiefly transcriptions from the Colonial Office series in the Public Record Office. The colonial records of some of the other colonies contain some information relating to Georgia, especially those of South Carolina and New York.

Colonial Records of the State of Georgia, ed. A. D. Candler (26 vols., Atlanta, 1904-16).

Volume I, Charter and laws; Journal of the Trustees (1732-52).

II, Minutes of the Common Council (1732-52).

III, General account of all monies and effects (1732-51).

IV, and Supplement, Journal of William Stephens (1737-41).

V, Journal of the Earl of Egmont (June 1738-May 1744).

VI, Proceedings of the President and Assistants (1741-54).

VII-IX, Proceedings and minutes of the Governor and Council (1754-66).

XIII-XIV, Journal of the Commons House of Assembly (1755-68).

XVI-XVII, Journal of the Upper House of Assembly (1755-74).

XVIII, Statutes enacted by the royal legislature (1754-68).

XXI-XXVI, Correspondence of the Trustees, Oglethorpe, and others (1735-52).

Acts passed by the General Assembly of the Colony of Georgia, 1755-74 (Wormsloe, 1881).

Documents illustrative of the History of the Slave Trade to America,
    ed. E. Donnan (4 vols., Washington, 1930-5). Volume IV, 587-635,
    deals with Georgia.
A Digest of the Laws of the State of Georgia down to 1800, Watkins,
    (Philadelphia, 1801).
Documents relative to the Colonial History of the State of New York,
    ed. E. B. O'Callaghan (15 vols., Albany, 1853-87).
Journal of the South Carolina Commons House of Assembly, 1736-42
    (3 vols., S. C. Historical Commission, 1951-3).

PRIVATE CORRESPONDENCE.

There are several collections bearing in some measure on the subject.
The Berkeley and Percival correspondence and Coram's letters are useful for the origins of Georgia, and Habersham's for local conditions at
the end of the period. Montiano's give the Spanish viewpoint at the
siege of St. Augustine. Pitt's are valuable for the strategy of the French
and Indian War.
Bedford. *Correspondence of John, Fourth Duke of Bedford, selected
    from the originals at Woburn Abbey,* ed. Lord John Russell (3
    vols., London, 1842-6) .
Belcher. "The Belcher Papers," *Collections of the Massachusetts His-
    torical Society,* Sixth Series, Vols. VI and VII.
Berkeley. *The Correspondence of George Berkeley, afterwards Bishop
    of Cloyne, and Sir John Percival, afterwards Earl of Egmont,* ed.
    B. Rand (Cambridge, 1914).
Coram. "Letters of Thomas Coram," *Massachusetts Historical Society
    Proceedings,* LVI, 15-56.
Habersham. "Letters of Hon. James Habersham, 1756-75," *Collections
    of the Georgia Historical Society, VI.*
Keene. *Private correspondence of Sir Benjamin Keene,* ed. R. Lodge
    (Cambridge, 1933).
Montiano. "Letters of Montiano at the Siege of St. Augustine," *Collec-
    tions of the Georgia Historical Society, VII,* pt. i.
Percival. See Berkeley, above.
Pitt. *Correspondence of William Pitt with Colonial Governors,* ed.
    G. S. Kimball (2 vols., New York, 1906).

DIARIES, JOURNALS, MEMOIRS, TRAVELS.

Of tremendous importance is the diary of Lord Egmont. One of the
instigators of the Georgia project and the first president of the Trustees, Egmont was conversant with public affairs from early manhood
and intimately acquainted with leading public figures, including
Walpole. In his diary he kept a detailed record of all affairs concern-

ing Georgia and made comprehensive reports of many Parliamentary debates. Inevitably, therefore, his diary has been used extensively as a prolific source of usually reliable information about Georgia's position in the counsels of the Government. Unfortunately, it tends to peter out after 1741. A good source for affairs within Georgia in the late 1730s is Wesley's journal, which naturally has a religious bent but also contains portraits of life and people in the colony. Particular mention must be made of Stephens's journal, which is a minute, often trivial account of internal affairs in Georgia and a mine of information about the activities of malcontents.

Of the memoirs those by Coxe and Walpole are useful in a general sense, while those of Thicknesse are very entertaining, although only the opening pages deal with Georgia.

Travellers' accounts can often be misleading, especially when they only touch on a place as did Bartram, Burnaby, and Macsparren on Georgia. The best, fullest, and most reliable account is that by Francis Moore of his voyage to Georgia in the late 1730s.

Bartram, J., "Diary of a Journey through the Carolinas, Georgia and Florida, 1765-6," *American Philosophical Society Transactions,* XXXIII (Philadelphia, 1942), 1-120.

Burnaby, Andrew, *Travels through the Middle Settlements in North America in the years 1759 and 1760, with observations upon the state of the colonies* (London, 1775).

Coxe, William, *Memoirs of the Life and Administration of Sir Robert Walpole, Earl of Orford. With original correspondence* (3 vols., London, 1798).

Egmont. *The Diary of Lord John Percival, First Earl of Egmont, 1730-47* (3 vols., Historical Manuscripts Commission, 1920-3).

Macsparren. *America Dissected, being a full and true account of all the American colonies in sundry letters from a clergyman there* (Dublin, 1753) .

Moore, Francis, "A voyage to Georgia begun in the year 1735" (London, 1744), *Collections of the Georgia Historical Society,* I, 79-152.

Stephens. "Journal of William Stephens, 1737-41," in *Colonial Records of Georgia,* IV and Supplement. *The Journal of William Stephens, 1741-5,* ed. E. M. Coulter (2 vols., Athens, Ga., 1958-9, Wormsloe Foundation Publications Nos. 2 and 3.

Thicknesse. *Memoirs and Anecdotes of Philip Thicknesse, late Lieutenant Governor of Land Guard Fort, and unfortunately father to George Touchet, Baron Audley,* (2 vols., London, 1788).

Walpole, Horace, *Memoirs of the last ten years of the Reign of George the Second,* ed. Lord Holland (3 vols., London, 1847).

————————, *Memoirs of the Reign of King George the Third,* ed. G. F. Russell Barker (4 vols., London, 1894).

Contemporary works directly concerning Georgia.

Some Account of the Designs of the Trustees for Establishing the Colony of Georgia in America (London, 1732).

Martyn, Benjamin, "Reasons for Establishing the Colony of Georgia with regard to the trade of Great Britain, the increase of our people and the employment and support it will afford to great numbers of our own poor as well as foreign persecuted Protestants" (London, 1733), *Collections of the Georgia Historical Society*, I, 203-38.

"A New and Accurate Account of the Provinces of South Carolina and Georgia" (London, 1733), *Collections of the Georgia Historical Society*, I, 42-78.

A Brief Account of the Establishment of the Colony of Georgia under General James Oglethorpe (1733).

A New Voyage to Georgia by a young gentleman, giving an account of his travels in South Carolina (2nd edn., London, 1737).

Martyn, B., *An Account showing the progress of the Colony of Georgia in America from its first establishment* (London, 1741).

"An Impartial Inquiry into the State and Utility of the Province of Georgia" (London, 1741), *Collections of the Georgia Historical Society*, I, 153-202.

A Description of Georgia by a gentleman who has resided there upwards of seven years and was one of the first settlers (London, 1741).

Tailfer, Patrick, and Others, *A True and Historical Narrative of the Colony of Georgia in America from the first settlement thereof until the present period; . . .* (Charleston, S. C., 1741), ed. C. L. Ver Steeg (Athens, 1960), Wormsloe Foundation Publications No. 4.

A State of the Province of Georgia attested upon oath in the court of Savannah, Nov. 10, 1740 (London, 1742).

A Brief Account of the Causes that have retarded the Progress of the Colony of Georgia in America, attested upon oath, being a proper contrast to A State of the Province of Georgia attested upon oath and other misrepresentations on the same subject (London, 1743).

Harris, John, *Navigantium atque Itinerantium Bibliotheca, or a complete collection of voyages and travels* (2 vols., London, 1744-8). Vol. II, 323-47 deals with "The history of the rise, progress and present state of the colony of Georgia."

An Historical Account of the Rise and Progress of the Colonies of South Carolina and Georgia (2 vols., London, 1779).

A True Account of the Colonies of Nova Scotia and Georgia (Newcastle, c. 1780).

Tracts and other Papers relating principally to the origin, settlement and progress of the colonies in North America from the discovery of the country to the year 1776, comp. P. Force (4 vols., Washington, 1836-46).

OTHER CONTEMPORARY WORKS.

Several works throw light on the public attitude towards colonies, and also furnish useful information about the commercial aspects. The following are among the more helpful:

Gee, Joshua, *The Trade and Navigation of Great Britain Considered* (London, 1738). First published in 1729.

The Importance of the British Plantations in America to this Kingdom with the state of their trade and methods for improving it, as also a description of the several colonies there (London, 1731).

The National Merchant, or discourses on commerce and colonies (London, 1736).

Postlethwayt, Malachy, *Great Britain's Commercial Interest Explained and Improved* (2nd edn., 2 vols., London, 1759).

Romans, Bernard, *A Concise Natural History of East and West Florida* (New York, 1775).

Stokes, Anthony, *A View of the Constitution of the British Colonies in North America and the West Indies at the time the civil war broke out on the continent of America* (London, 1783).

Holroyd, J. B. (Lord Sheffield), *Observations on the Commerce of the American States* (London, 1784).

PERIODICALS.

Of the following the first three contain scattered letters and accounts referring to Georgia as well as useful reports on Parliamentary debates, while the last three have a little of interest:

The Gentleman's Magazine.

The London Magazine.

The Political State of Great Britain.

The Annual Register.

The Grub Street Journal.

The Historical Register.

WORKS CONTAINING SOME PRIMARY MATERIAL.

An account of the Designs of the Associates of the late Dr. Bray (London, 1769).

Anderson, Adam, *An Historical and Chronological Deduction of the Origin of Commerce,* revised edition by W. Combe (4 vols., London, 1787-9).

A Documentary History of American Industrial Society, ed. U. B. Phillips (Cleveland, 1910).

European Treaties bearing on the History of the United States and its Dependencies, ed. F. G. Davenport and C. O. Paullin (4 vols., Washington, 1917-37).

List of the Vernon-Wager Manuscripts in the Library of Congress, ed. W. C. Ford (Washington, 1904).

Macpherson, David, *Annals of Commerce, Manufactures, Fisheries and Navigation* (4 vols., London, 1805).

Military Affairs in North America, ed. S. Pargellis (New York, 1936).

White, George, *Historical Collections of Georgia, containing the most interesting facts, traditions, biographical sketches, anecdotes, etc. relating to its history and antiquities, from its first settlement to the present time* (3rd edn., New York, 1855).

Statistics of the State of Georgia, including an account of its natural, civil and ecclesiastical history (Savannah, Ga., 1849).

SECONDARY AUTHORITIES

COMPREHENSIVE WORKS.

Alvord, Clarence W., *The Mississippi Valley in British Politics. A study of the trade, land speculation and experiments in imperialism culminating in the American Revolution* (2 vols., Cleveland, 1917).

Andrews, Charles M., *Colonial Period of American History* (4 vols., New Haven, 1934-8).

Beer, George L., *The Commercial Policy of England toward the American Colonies* (New York, 1893).

——————, *British Colonial Policy, 1754-65* (New York, 1907).

Bond, Beverly W., *The Quit-Rent System in the American Colonies* (New Haven, Conn., 1919).

Channing, Edward, *A History of the United States* (5 vols., New York, 1905-25).

Clark, Victor S., *History of Manufactures in the United States, 1607-1860* (Washington, 1916).

Corbett, Julian S., *England in the Seven Years War. A study in combined strategy* (2 vols., London, 1907).

De Bow, J. D. B., *The Industrial Resources, etc. of the Southern and Western States* (3 vols., New Orleans, 1852-3).

Dickerson, Oliver M., *American Colonial Government, 1696-1763. A study of the British Board of Trade in its relation to the American colonies, political, industrial, administrative* (Cleveland, 1912).

——————, *The Navigation Acts and the American Revolution* (Philadelphia, 1951).

Donnell, E. J., *Chronological and Statistical History of Cotton* (New York, 1872).

Doyle, John A., *The English in America* (5 vols., London, 1882-1907).

Gipson, Lawrence H., *British Empire before the American Revolution* (9 vols., Caldwell, 1936-56).

Gray, Lewis C., *History of Agriculture in the Southern United States to 1860* (Washington, 1933).

Greene, Evarts B., and Virginia D. Harrington, *American Population before the Federal Census of 1790* (New York, 1932).

Jacobs, Wilbur R., *Diplomacy and Indian Gifts. Anglo-French rivalry along the Ohio and north-west frontiers, 1748-63* (Berkeley, Calif., 1950).

Jernegan, Marcus W., *Labouring and Dependent Classes in Colonial America, 1607-1783* (Chicago, 1931).

Johnson, Emory R., *et al., History of Domestic and Foreign Commerce of the United States* (2 vols., Washington, 1915).

Keith, A. Berriedale, *Constitutional History of the First British Empire* (Oxford, 1930).

Knorr, Klaus E., *British Colonial Theories, 1570-1850* (Toronto, 1944).

Labaree, Leonard W., *Royal Government in America. A study of the British colonial system before 1783* (New Haven, Conn., 1930).

Lonn, Ella, *The Colonial Agents of the Southern Colonies* (Chapel Hill, N. C., 1945).

McCrady, Edward, *The History of South Carolina under the Royal Government, 1719-76* (New York, 1899).

McKinley, Albert E., *The Suffrage Franchise in the thirteen English Colonies in America* (Philadelphia, 1905).

Morris, Richard B., *Studies in the History of American Law, with special reference to the seventeenth and eighteenth centuries* (New York, 1930).

————————, *Government and Labor in Early America* (New York, 1946).

Osgood, Herbert L., *The American Colonies in the Eighteenth Century* (4 vols., New York, 1924).

Pares, Richard, *War and Trade in the West Indies, 1739-63* (Oxford, 1936).

Richmond, Herbert W., *The Navy in the War of 1739-48* (3 vols., Cambridge, 1920).

Russell, Elmer B., *The Review of American Colonial Legislation by the King in Council* (New York, 1915).

Schlesinger, Arthur M., *The Colonial Merchants and the American Revolution, 1763-76* (New York, 1918).

Smith, Joseph H., *Appeals to the Privy Council from the American Plantations.*

Sutherland, Stella H., *Population Distribution in Colonial America* (New York, 1936).

Waddington, Richard, *La Guerre de Sept Ans* (5 vols., Paris, 1899).

HISTORIES OF GEORGIA.

There are several books on the history of Georgia, but the following are the best:

Coulter, E. Merton, *A Short History of Georgia* (Chapel Hill, N. C., 1933).

Johnson, Amanda, *Georgia as Colony and State* (Atlanta, Ga., 1938).

Jones, Charles C., *The History of Georgia* (2 vols., Boston, 1883).

McCall, Hugh, *The History of Georgia, containing brief sketches of the most remarkable events up to the present day* (2 vols., Savannah, Ga., 1811-16).

Stevens, William B., *A History of Georgia from its first discovery by Europeans to the adoption of the present constitution in 1798* (2 vols., New York and Philadelphia, 1847-59).

BIOGRAPHIES.

Oglethorpe is the most important subject and the best book on him is by Ettinger, although that by Church deals more fully with affairs in Georgia.

Bruce, Henry, *Life of General Oglethorpe* (New York, 1890).

Church, Leslie F., *Oglethorpe. A study of philanthropy in England and Georgia* (London, 1932).

Ettinger, Amos A., *James Edward Oglethorpe, Imperial Idealist* (Oxford, 1936).

Harris, Thaddeus M., *Biographical Memorials of James Oglethorpe in America* (Boston, 1841).

Wright, Robert, *A Memoir of General James Oglethorpe, one of the earliest reformers of prison discipline in England and the founder of Georgia in America* (London, 1867).

Moore, H., *Life of Rev. John Wesley, in which is included the life of his brother Charles Wesley* (London, 1824).

Tyerman, Luke, *The Life of the Rev. George Whitefield* (2 vols., London, 1876-7).

SPECIALIZED WORKS RELATING TO GEORGIA.

Abbot, William W., *The Royal Governors of Georgia, 1754-75* (Chapel Hill, N. C., 1959).

Alden, John R., *John Stuart and the Southern Colonial Frontier. A study of Indian relations, war, trade and land problems in the southern wilderness, 1754-75* (Ann Arbor, Mich., 1944).

Bolton, Herbert E. and Mary Ross, *The Debatable Land. A sketch of the Anglo-Spanish contest for the Georgia country* (Berkeley, Calif., 1925).

Chatelain, Verne E., *The Defenses of Spanish Florida, 1565-1763.* (Washington, 1941).

Coleman, Kenneth, *The American Revolution in Georgia, 1763-89.* (Athens, Ga., 1958).

Corry, John P., *Indian Affairs in Georgia, 1732-56* (Philadelphia, 1936).

Crane, Verner W., *The Southern Frontier, 1670-1732* (Durham, N. C., 1928).

Jones, Charles C., *The Dead Towns of Georgia* (Savannah, Ga., 1878).

Lanning, John T., *The Spanish Missions of Georgia* (Chapel Hill, N. C., 1935).
‒‒‒‒‒‒‒‒‒‒‒‒‒‒‒‒‒, *The Diplomatic History of Georgia. A study of the epoch of Jenkins Ear* (Chapel Hill, N. C., 1936).
McCain, James R., *Georgia as a Proprietary Province. The execution of a trust* (Boston, 1917).
Meriwether, Robert L., *Expansion of South Carolina, 1729-65* (Kingsport, Tenn., 1940).
Saye, Albert B., *New Viewpoints in Georgia History* (Athens, Ga., 1943).
Strickland, Reba C., *Religion and the State in Georgia in the Eighteenth Century* (New York, 1939).
Ware, Ethel K., *A Constitutional History of Georgia* (New York, 1947).

ARTICLES.

Aldridge, Alfred O., "George Whitefield's Georgia Controversies," *Journal of Southern History,* IX (Aug. 1943), 357-80.
Caldwell, Norman W., "The Southern Frontier during King George's War," *ibid.,* VII (Feb., 1941), 37-54.
Cate, Margaret D., "Fort Frederica and the Battle of Bloody Marsh," *Georgia Historical Quarterly,* XXVII (June, 1943), 111-74.
Corry, John P., "Procedure in the Commons House of Assembly," *ibid.,* XVI (June, 1932), 136-45.
Dunn, Richard S., "The Trustees of Georgia and the House of Commons 1732-52," *William and Mary Quarterly,* XI (Oct. 1954), 551-65.
Fant, H. B., "The Indian Trade Policy of the Trustees," *Georgia Historical Quarterly,* XV (Sept. 1931), 207-22.
‒‒‒‒‒‒‒‒‒‒‒‒‒‒‒‒‒, "The Labor Policy of the Trustees," *ibid.,* XVI (March, 1932), 1-16.
‒‒‒‒‒‒‒‒‒‒‒‒‒‒‒‒‒, "Financing the Colonization of Georgia," *ibid.,* XX (March, 1936), 1-29.
Flippin, Percy S., "The Royal Government in Georgia, 1752-76," *ibid.,* VIII-XIII (1924-9), *passim.*
Hamer, M. B., *"Edmund Gray and his Settlement at New Hanover,"* *ibid.,* XIII (March, 1929), 1-12.
Heath, William E., "The Early Colonial Money System of Georgia," *ibid.,* XIX (June, 1935), 145-60.
Holland, James W., "The Beginning of Public Agricultural Experimentation in America: the Trustees' garden in Georgia," *Agricultural History,* XII (July, 1938), 271-98.
Jones, Charles C., "The English Colonization of Georgia," *Narrative and Critical History of America,* ed. J. Winsor (8 vols., New York, 1884-9), Vol. V (1887), 357-406.

Lanning, John T., "The American Colonies in the Preliminaries of the War of Jenkins' Ear," *Georgia Historical Quarterly* XI (June, 1927), 129-55.

————————, "A Descriptive Catalogue of some Legajos on Georgia in the Spanish Archives," *ibid.*, XIII (Dec. 1929), 410-21.

McKinstrey, Mary T., "Silk Culture in Colonial Georgia," *ibid.*, XIV (Sept. 1930), 225-35.

Pennington, Edgar L., "Anglican Influences in the Establishment of Georgia," *ibid.*, XVI (Dec. 1932), 292-97.

Range, Willard, "The Agricultural Revolution in Royal Georgia," *Agricultural History*, XXI (Oct. 1947), 250-5.

Spalding, Thomas, "Sketch of the Life of Gen. James Oglethorpe," *Collections of the Georgia Historical Society*, I (1840), 239-95.

Stevens, William B., "Sketch of the Life of James Habersham," *Georgia Historical Quarterly*, III (Dec. 1919), 151-68.

Strickland, Reba C., "The Mercantile System as Applied to Georgia," *ibid.*, XXII (June, 1938).

Index